AF572688

The Institute of Strategic and International Studies, a non-profit limited company established under Malaysia's Companies Act of 1965, is dedicated to objective and independent policy research in five central areas of concern: defence, security and foreign affairs; national and international economic affairs; policies for nation-building; energy and natural resources; and science, technology and industry.

First published in 1989 by ISIS Malaysia.
P O Box 12424
50778 Kuala Lumpur, Malaysia
Tel 03-2939366
Telex MA31679
Fax 603-2939430

Distributed by Kegan Paul International
P O Box 256
London WC1B 3SW, England
Tel 01-580-5511
Telex 261771 KEGANP G
Fax 01-436-0899

International Edition.

ISBN 0 7103 0383 1 (soft cover)
ISBN 0 7103 0372 6 (hard cover)

Printed by Art Printing Works Sdn Bhd.
Designed by Genrevela Associates.

A CIP catalogue record for this book is available from the British Library.
Library of Congress Catalogue in Publication Data Applied for.

Contents

Preface

THE Asia-Pacific Roundtable, which has its genesis in a Manila meeting of Asia-Pacific scholars in September 1985, was instituted to provide a forum for exchange of views on issues of peace and security, and for the exploration of proposals and measures to build confidence and reduce conflict in the Pacific. Since its institution (the First Asia-Pacific Roundtable was held in Kuala Lumpur on January 10-11, 1987), the 'peace process' in the Pacific has steadily gained momentum. Relations among the major powers continue to improve and hitherto 'intractable' regional conflicts are moving towards settlement or a more stable situation. There is a general 'yearning' in the region for a more stable international environment.

The reasons for this quest are many and some of them are discussed in the papers contained in this volume. For certain, the strategic environment in the Pacific is complex and there are a great many domestic and international factors that can quite easily obstruct the peace process but it behooves all concerned to nudge the process forward. Because the Asia-Pacific Roundtable draws interest and participation from all sectors and all countries in the region, it can in a modest way contribute to the building of a more stable environment in the Pacific.

The Second Asia-Pacific Roundtable, organised and hosted by ISIS Malaysia, was held in Kuala Lumpur from July 1-4, 1988. A total of 101 participants from Brunei, Indonesia, Malaysia, the Philippines, Singapore, Thailand, Laos, Vietnam, the South Pacific Forum, Australia, New Zealand, the People's Republic of China, the Democratic People's Republic of Korea, the Republic of Korea, the Mongolian People's Republic, Canada, Japan, the Soviet Union and the United States attended the meeting. The roundtable focussed on the following:

- Prospects for big power rapprochement in the Pacific;
- Dynamics of the arms build-up and prospects for arms control in the Pacific;
- Relevance of the European experiences for the Asia-Pacific region;
- Confidence building and conflict reduction in Northeast Asia;
- Confidence building and conflict reduction in Southeast Asia;
- The Cambodian conflict; and
- Confidence building and conflict reduction in the South Pacific.

This volume comprises the seven papers presented at the Second Asia-Pacific Roundtable. No paper was presented for the session on confidence building and conflict reduction in Southeast Asia. The papers presented at the First Asia-Pacific Roundtable have been published in an ISIS volume entitled *In Search of Peace*. It is the sincere hope of ISIS Malaysia that these two volumes, by drawing attention to the key issues and more generally the 'peace process', can be of value to readers interested in peace and stability in the Asia-Pacific region. ISIS is also planning to hold the Third Asia-Pacific Roundtable in Kuala Lumpur from June 16-19, 1989.

We would like to express our appreciation to the authors for kindly allowing ISIS to publish their papers. Our gratitude also goes to all those who have assisted in the publication of this volume.

MUTHIAH ALAGAPPA
Senior Fellow, ISIS Malaysia

Keynote address

DATO' ABU HASSAN OMAR
Minister for Foreign Affairs, Malaysia

IT is an honour and a privilege for me to address this distinguished group of eminent scholars and officials. On behalf of the government and the people of Malaysia may I wish you all a warm welcome and a pleasant and productive stay in the country. We are deeply honoured to be able to host the conference in Kuala Lumpur and to offer our hospitability to you.

We are here to discuss a very pertinent issue central to world peace and development. The theme of this conference, 'Confidence Building and Conflict Reduction in the Pacific' represents a major preoccupation confronting most governments today and which poses serious challenges for the future. You will of course address these concerns in the midst of unpredictable changes in the political environment. You have to somehow anticipate and manage such changes. For developing countries where systems including political systems are evolving, the task is enormous.

When we talk about conflict reduction and confidence building, we cannot ignore a central consideration in the issue, which is security. I would like to cite the Asean (Association of Southeast Asian Nations) example as a model to reflect the theme of our discussions. In Asean's case, there is a consensus that, collectively, our security could best be served through increased co-operation amongst its members. Having defused whatever tensions and irritants that exist between them, Asean states are then able to work towards removing big power rivalry in the region.

Asean provides the much needed structure for mutual understanding, confidence, trust and goodwill among the six member states. This structure has enabled

Asean states to resolve differences between them. Even more important, it minimises the possibility of conflict between them. I need not go into detail on this. Let me say that if there was no Asean, misunderstandings would have been difficult to resolve. These then might have developed into serious disputes between the Asean countries which, needless to say, could affect the peace and stability in the region.

In our search for conflict reduction and confidence building in this part of the world, Asean countries introduced the concept of ZOPFAN (Zone of Peace, Freedom and Neutrality). In the 1971 Kuala Lumpur Declaration, Asean declared its commitment to secure the recognition of and respect for Southeast Asia as a Zone of Peace, Freedom and Neutrality.

The occupation of Kampuchea in 1978 and increased superpower rivalry in the region have to some extent hindered our efforts, but have definitely not dampened our commitment to make ZOPFAN a reality. On the contrary Asean has become more resolute in pursuing this goal and with a sense of urgency.

One important step for advancing the early realization of ZOPFAN is the establishment of a Southeast Asia Nuclear-Weapons-Free Zone (SEANWFZ) comprising all Southeast Asian states. The establishment of a Southeast Asia Nuclear-Weapons-Free Zone will serve as an effective measure for reducing tension and promoting peace and security in the region. Asean would intensify its efforts towards the early establishment of the Southeast Asia Nuclear-Weapons-Free Zone including the consideration of all aspects relating to its establishment and of an appropriate instrument to establish the zone. Establishment of the nuclear-weapons-free zone would constitute a milestone in our efforts towards the realization of ZOPFAN.

Though there is an accord on Afghanistan, Asia is still far from being free of conflicts. There remains in Southeast Asia the longstanding problem of the Vietnamese occupation of Kampuchea. The occupation of Kampuchea by Vietnam has been a source of tension in the Southeast Asian region and the focus of regional and international concern. Although we are not a party directly involved in the conflict, Malaysia is interested and concerned about the peace and stability in Southeast Asia. Malaysia believes that this problem requires a comprehensive political solution which takes into account the interests of the Kampuchean people, the region and the world at large. In this regard, Malaysia and Asean will persist in their diplomatic efforts to restore Kampuchean independence, sovereignty and territorial integrity. In an endeavour to find a settlement, Malaysia and the other Asean countries would continue to support the Coalition Government of Democratic Kampuchea (CGDK) and the pivotal role of Prince Norodom Sihanouk in finding a comprehensive political settlement to the problem.

Malaysia welcomes the latest initiative to convene an Informal Meeting in Jakarta among the Khmer factions, Vietnam and other concerned parties. I am gratified to know that Vietnam and other parties to the conflict have indicated their willingness to attend the Jakarta Informal Meeting in late July 1988. This latest development indicated that the conflicting parties have eventually recognised the benefits of a negotiated settlement rather than sticking to the present stalemate.

Though it is too early to predict the outcome of the meeting, we anticipate some basic agreement would be reached to pave the way for more substantive negotiations towards a comprehensive settlement of the problem.

While the Kampuchean problem may remain with us for some time yet, a new situation of great concern is developing in the South China Sea. The Spratly Islands have become a new area of conflict; armed skirmishes had occurred recently. There will be further skirmishes in the future if restraint and good sense do not prevail between the disputing parties. The islets and atolls are contested in part or in whole by five parties, all of whom have established their presence in the area. Therefore, whether we like it or not, we all have to put our minds together so that together we would be able to work out a satisfactory and acceptable mechanism to regularise activities in the area. Our good sense tells us that the first thing we must do is talk. The mere act of talking in itself will help reduce the tension. Once tension is reduced, we would be able to look into suitable mechanisms to ensure peace and stability in the area.

The success of the Moscow Summit recently is an essential step towards promoting peace and stability in this world. Malaysia welcomes the efforts of the United States and the Soviet Union in seeking improved relations. We expect the outcome of the summit to have a favourable influence on the international climate in general and on the situation in the Asia-Pacific region. Malaysia is also hopeful that both superpowers will now approach the talks on the Strategic Arms Reduction Treaty (START) with renewed vigour. Such a treaty could reverse the trend towards a dangerous militarisation of Asia and the Pacific Basin. Malaysia also welcomes the statement made by the American and Soviet leaders in which they reaffirmed their intention to continue discussion at all levels aimed at helping parties to regional conflicts to find a peaceful solution. The warming up of relations between Moscow and Beijing is also another positive development towards international peace and stability.

Political stability could not be attained without economic security; hence we need economic development. In the case of Asean, after years of impressive economic growth, we now find ourselves in a slightly disadvantaged situation. Commodity prices which propelled growth in the past are now given to volatile fluctuations, affecting the economy. To lessen the impact of such price fluctuations in the economy, Asean countries have sought to improve their non-commodity export performance only to run into a plethora of protectionist sentiments, tariffs and non-tariff barriers in the European Economic Community (EEC), Japan and the United States. Deprived of the means to earn sufficient revenue from trade and burdened with debt servicing, Asean countries have had to seriously cut back on development expenditure, the very thing that is needed to enhance national resilience and confidence building.

Over the last few years, we have witnessed an intensification of trade tensions in the Pacific which threaten to undermine one of the most economically buoyant and strategically important regions in the world. Since Pacific trade is dominated by the US and Japan, their actions and policies have profound impact on the economic health of the other Pacific nations. The ever-increasing US current accounts deficit with Japan has given rise to strong protectionist sentiments in the US. Since Congressional legislation is rarely country-specific, the countries which can least afford to absorb the impact of trade restrictions are the most affected.

These economic difficulties have now reached the point where they constitute a threat to confidence building and regional security. We can no longer adopt the view that trade is trade and foreign policy is foreign policy. Economics is politics. Trade is security. It is therefore incumbent on those of us concerned with regional security to help ensure that the marketplace upon which our future will be decided remains free from protectionist barriers. Both the United States and Japan, as leaders of the free enterprise system in the Pacific, must take the lead in revitalising confidence and ensuring that it does not languish for lack of political will. Japan's contribution to regional security must therefore necessarily be in enhancing the national and economic resilience of the countries in the region. With its vast economic strength and technological innovativeness, it is uniquely poised to foster a continuation of high economic growth in the region. Untied economic assistance, open markets and an imaginative transfer of technology will do more for regional security than an increase in Japan's defence spending.

Finally, I wish to touch briefly on the Antarctica. Malaysia's position is very clear with regard to the system of management existing in the continent. The present two-tier system of consultative and non-consultative parties, and the outright reluctance of the Antarctica Treaty System (ATS) to be more transparent by allowing the United Nations System's participation in the management of the continent could lead to tensions. The recent conclusion of an Antarctic Mineral regime further aggravates the situation. The Antarctic Treaty Parties again chose to disregard the relevant 42nd United Nations General Assembly resolutions which, *inter alia*, call for a moratorium on the mineral regime negotiation. The continued denial of the evolution of a truly democratic and universal regime in Antarctica will not lead to the development of genuine and lasting peace in the continent.

Let me conclude my remarks by leaving these thoughts with you. As officials and scholars from your respective countries, I am sure you will look at all the issues squarely and with integrity. I am confident that this conference will make its contribution towards our objective to reduce conflicts and promote confidence building in the Asia-Pacific region.

The prospects for big power rapprochement in the Pacific

JAMES A BOUTILIER
Head, Department of History and Political Economy, Royal Roads Military College, Canada

Introduction

DURING the Soviet-American summit conference in Moscow in May 1988, Mikhail Gorbachev, General Secretary of the Communist Party of the Soviet Union (CPSU), observed that the world was at a turning point in its history. While it is easy to overstate the forces of change, all the evidence suggest that Gorbachev was right; that the global community is being re-ordered in a significant fashion, particularly in the Asia-Pacific region. The main engine of that re-ordering is economics. The main characteristic is political and military contraction. And the main outcome appears to be a greater degree of international stability, at least in the short term.

What we are witnessing are events of very considerable moment. While this paper is primarily a short to mid-term forecast, if we were to take the long-term view we would probably be obliged to conclude that the United States has peaked as a world power. Its economy is in difficulty, its relative decline is widely acknowledged and its imperial ends exceed its means.[1] China, though still profoundly backward, is by way of comparison in the ascendant. United, independent and potentially powerful, it has taken up a pivotal position between the United States and the Soviet Union.[2] The latter power has embarked on a programme of economic restructuring vital to its survival and to that of the Communist Party itself. Both Russia and China have begun to retreat from orthodox Marxist-Leninism, to abandon the expansionist dynamic inherent in that ideology and to adopt new, flexible and pragmatic foreign policies.[3] Inextricably interconnected with these shifts has been a reduction in superpower military might. That reduction in turn reflects and effects a desire for and a perception of greater stability in the Asia-Pacific region. There are, however, still problem areas in the region. The relationships within and between the two Koreas remain volatile.[4] Experiments in democracy in the Philippines and South Korea are fragile and unpredictable. The Vietnam-Kampuchea conflict has yet to be resolved satisfactorily and there are growing concerns throughout East Asia about the possibility of a more aggressive and militarily powerful Japan.[5] These issues notwithstanding, the mood of the region is guardedly optimistic. There seems more and more reason to hope for a rapprochement between many of the major players in the Asia-Pacific game. The object of this paper is to explore the relationships between the players and suggest the grounds for that hope.

Background

Ten years ago the Asia-Pacific region was a more dangerous, less promising, place.[6] The Sino-Japanese Treaty of Peace and Friendship (1978) and the establishment of full diplomatic relations between Washington and Beijing fuelled Soviet fears that a *de facto* Sino-Japanese-American alliance had been constructed to encircle the Soviet Union along its eastern flank.[7] Soviet East Asian policy has sought, since the early 1970s, to exploit the power vacuum created by the Anglo-American withdrawal from Asia and to prevent such encirclement. The Soviets had relied heavily on military solutions to their foreign policy problems in keeping with Dibb's thesis of the incomplete superpower.[8] They allied themselves to Vietnam in 1978, projected their naval power southward to Cam Ranh Bay (in pursuit of Gorshkovian tenets) and invaded Afghanistan in 1979. These moves, coupled with a huge increase in conventional and nuclear weaponry along the Sino-Soviet border and at naval bases on the Pacific coast, had the effect of encouraging rather than discouraging a greater dialogue between Washinton and Beijing. At the same time the Vietnamese invasion of Kampuchea alarmed the Asean (Association of Southeast Asian Nations) states[9] and China, while the Russian build-up in general and the stationing of Soviet troops on the Northern Islands in particular alarmed the Japanese.

Soviet policy in the Asia-Pacific region during the period 1978 to 1986 can best be described as a 'multifold failure'.[10] Russian emphasis on military solutions generated widespread suspicion and hostility in the region and accelerated the decline of the Soviet economy. When Gorbachev was elected General Secretary in March 1985 he was confronted with a hostile array of Asian-Pacific states, a moribund economy and an aggressive United States that had translated Lehman's Forward Strategy from the Atlantic to the Pacific and was building up its naval power to destroy Russian war-making potential close to home.[11]

Gorbachev had two choices, neither of them particularly palatable. He could continue Brezhnev's heavy-handed and counter-productive foreign policy or he could orchestrate a series of tactical accommodations with the Chinese, the Americans and the Japanese, and run the risk of being toppled by Russian hardliners. At stake was Russia's continued superpower pretensions and the Communist Party's monopoly of power. If the fundamental systemic shortcomings of the Soviet economy were not addressed and addressed quickly, the burden of defence might bankrupt the state and the CPSU might well be preempted by the sort of anti-party forces taking shape in Eastern Europe. Thus Gorbachev found himself cast in much the same role as Louis XVI in 1789 when the only solution to France's economic problems was for the political elite to commit suicide by divesting itself of power. Louis XVI faltered and the job was done for him. Gorbachev seized the initiative and advertised his reforming zeal in a broad policy statement at Vladivostok on July 28, 1986.[12]

The Vladivostok speech

The Vladivostok speech has probably been more valuable in terms of its tone than its substance. It helped create an image of a Soviet leader willing to be reasonable and conciliatory.[13] Having attempted to legitimise his proposals by underscoring the Asia-Pacific character of the Soviet Union, Gorbachev highlighted the need to develop the industrial and mineral potential of Siberia and the Far Eastern province. Then, turning to arms control and confidence building proposals, he observed that it was necessary to make 'an urgent radical break with many conventional approaches to foreign policy'.[14] The proposals he outlined were intended to address the basic asymmetry in power between the Soviet Union and the United States. The former is a land power with only one major out-of-country military installation (Cam Ranh Bay). The latter is a maritime power heavily reliant on wide-ranging carrier battle groups and a network of Asia-Pacific bases.

Unlike Brezhnev's nebulous recommendations regarding a collective Asian security system, Gorbachev's proposals focussed on the elimination of nuclear weapons, military alliances with forward bases, the utilisation of nuclear-armed vessels, and the limitation of competition in the sphere of anti-submarine weapons. Thus while the Vladivostok speech constituted a more coherent and comprehensive formulation of existing Soviet foreign policy initiatives, it did not break with the past in terms of the consistent Russian ambition to undermine US strategy and maritime power.[15]

What the speech did do, however, was to suggest an improved diplomatic climate for renewed Sino-Soviet negotiations. China was the principal beneficiary of the Vladivostok declaration since the apparent Soviet willingness to discuss troop withdrawals from Afghanistan and Mongolia, to amend the riverine frontier on the Amur, to pursue Sino-Soviet economic co-operation, and to encourage a resolution of Sino-Vietnamese tensions clearly played to the audience in Beijing.[16] It is this speech which marks symbolically, and in many ways practically, the initiation of a new climate in the Asia-Pacific region which is the focus of this paper.

Upper Volta with rockets

Probably the most important single element in the complex calculus of Asia-Pacific peace and stability is the fate of the Soviet economy. In a word, the economy is a mess.

By virtue of spending 15 per cent of their GNP on defence the Russians can match the Americans missile for missile but in almost every other respect Russia is a Third World country.[17] Gorbachev has no other choice but to reduce defence expenditure, stem the flow of aid to parasitic economies like Cuba and Vietnam, divert income to light industries and consumer goods (thereby restoring some of communism's non-existent credibility), and begin the wholesale development of Siberia and the Far East where much of the Soviet Union's resource wealth lies.

His 'attempted revolution' involves huge risks. For the past 20 years the Soviet Union has enjoyed a no-growth economy.[18] The Stalinist economic model, with its emphasis on heavy industry, initiative-sapping central planning, and political and cultural repression, has been manifestly unable to cope with the complexities of modern economies. Instead, obsessed with gigantomania and production figures, it has stagnated. Inertia, shoddiness and mismanagement are the order of the day.

Initially, Gorbachev sought to exhort Soviet workers to work harder and more efficiently. It soon became apparent, however, that mere exhortation was not sufficient. What was needed was some sense of change, of participation. Hence *glasnost*, an invitation to make constructive criticism of the bureaucratic workings of the system without challenging the system itself.[19] Paralleling *glasnost* is *perestroika*, the concept of restructuring the economy. *Perestroika* is not an invitation to establish capitalism. Rather it is an attempt to make the existing system more efficient by introducing greater degrees of local decision-making and incentive.

So far so good. But *perestroika* depends first and foremost on political will. It is not at all clear whether that will exists. For the moment restructuring has produced the very uncertainty and disorder — without tangible results — that plays into the hands of Gorbachev's critics. More troubling still is the fact that at the grassroots level the average Russian seems particularly resistant to change. If Gorbachev moves too fast he is certain to alarm his opponents. If he moves too slowly he will lose whatever popular support he enjoys. And so far *perestroika* is only in its initial phase. The Russians want to gain greater access to world markets but that will involve exposing the Soviet economy to the sort of aggressive competition for which it is entirely unprepared.[20] The Soviets lack hard currency, their agricultural system is in a shambles and their pricing system is totally distorted. The fundamental question is, would the Soviet economy ever be able to survive in the face of foreign competition? Of equal if not greater concern is the effect of economic reform on the political environment. Freer economics seems destined to stimulate the demand for freer politics.[21] The communist world, far from being in the vanguard, finds itself taking up the rear. The gap between what the political system has promised and what it has delivered has become ever greater. If the political system is to survive it must deliver. But the very act of delivering seems likely to transform that system. As current arms reductions and a greater willingness to negotiate outstanding international differences appear to be the product of economic desparation, the future of rapprochement in the Asia-Pacific region will depend largely on Gorbachev's ability to survive the upcoming party congress and achieve some degree of success with *perestroika*.[22]

Omnidirectional coexistence

The course of economic reform is also central to any determination of China's future foreign policy. Like Gorbachev, Deng Xiaoping inherited a Stalinist style economy which was stagnant.[23] It was clear to Deng that a sustained programme of economic modernisation must be the state's highest priority. China's survival would depend largely on abandoning economic autarky, strategic confrontations and the export of revolution. Unlike Gorbachev, however, Deng enjoyed a number of advantages. Firstly, the need for reform had been dramatically highlighted by the chaos associated with the Great Proletarian Cultural Revolution (GPCR). While Russians had grown passive in the face of systemic arterio-sclerosis in the Soviet Union, the Chinese welcomed any possibility of relief from the anarchy of the late Maoist period. Secondly, the revolution had left much of the party apparatus in disarray and thus opposition to reform was undermined. Thirdly, the tradition of central planning was not nearly as entrenched or comprehensive as it was in the Soviet Union. And fourthly, Deng's likely opponents had been discredited.[24]

The economic modernisation programme in China seems likely to be more successful and far-reaching than the one in the Soviet Union. The household responsibility system has been particularly effective in the agricultural sector, the very sector that is the Russian 'Achilles' heel'. Similarly, the Chinese have been more innovative and successful in terms of integrating their economy into the world economic order. Like the Russians, they run a very real risk in exposing their economy of shortages to the inflationary effects of foreign competition, but unlike the Russians they have entered into almost 8,000 Sino-foreign joint ventures while the Russians have, thus far, entered into only 20. What is more the Chinese have effected sweeping economies in the realm of defence expenditure.[25] Whereas in 1973, 13 per cent of China's GNP was consumed by the military, the figure now stands at about 6 per cent and the Chinese have been able to reduce their armed forces by a reported one million men. This reduction reflects not only a post-Maoist reaction to the commanding position of the People's Liberation Army (PLA) in Chinese political affairs following the GPCR, but a major doctrinal shift from the concept of a people's war toward a professional military with modern technology. That shift in turn reflects the dominance of the pragmatic 'expert' rather than 'Red' Dengists and the realisation that mass consciousness cannot prevail in a war with the Soviet Union. What was needed instead (and it constituted somewhat of an *ex-post facto* justification for reduced defence budgets) was — to put it colloquially — an army that was leaner and meaner.[26] While the necessary and desired precondition for successful economic modernisation was a peaceful and stable international environment, the new style army with nuclear and conventional weaponry was predicated to a considerable degree (like the economy as a whole) on technical and economic co-operation with the United States. At the same time, as Gorbachev had noted at Vladivostok, there was a considerable complementarity between the Chinese and Soviet economies.[27] Thus the Chinese have begun to pursue what Harding has called a policy of 'omnidirectional peaceful co-existence', fostering the reduction of tensions with Washington and Moscow, and generally making foreign policy the handmaiden of economic modernisation.[28]

Sino-Soviet relations

It is a matter of historic magnitude that Gorbachev and Deng Xiaoping are moving their respective nations in much the same direction and this sense of common experience constitutes the backdrop to a significant rapprochement between the two superpowers. While the two nations view each other with suspicion and are never likely to be cordial allies they have made significant advances in the past year in reducing areas of tension.[29] Gorbachev's Vladivostok offers aside, it was probably the Chinese who contributed most to the rapprochement by their unilateral disarmament and their willingness to deal with the so-called 'Three Obstacles' on an individual rather than collective basis.

Hitherto China has been unwilling to normalise relations with the Soviet Union until such time as the Soviets withdrew from Afghanistan, the Vietnamese withdrew from Kampuchea, and the disputed riverine and mountain portions of the Sino-Soviet border were decided in China's favour. Although the Chinese were certainly sincere in their concerns, the Three Obstacles also served as a convenient device which enabled them to orchestrate the pace and extent of normalisation.[30]

Two of the three obstacles have now been largely overcome. The border question is ripe for resolution. Gorbachev indicated at Vladivostok that he was willing to adopt the Chinese interpretation of the Amur-Ussuri riverine frontier. Border teams are now examining that problem and the disputed Sino-Soviet frontier in the Tien Shan mountains in western China.[31] Some arms control agreement may also be in the offing which would involve the drawing down of a significant proportion of the 50-plus Soviet divisions, 2,500 aircraft and 1,200 nuclear missiles deployed against China. Some of these missiles, SS-20s, were the subject of the May 1988 Intermediate-range Nuclear Forces (INF) treaty although the variety and quantity of Soviet missiles make the elimination of the SS-20s largely academic. Nevertheless, having built up their Far Eastern land, sea and air forces relentlessly over a period of 20 years, the Soviets now appear interested — for economic and geopolitical reasons — in reducing their military presence in Siberia and the Far East.[32] That vast region contains a population roughly equivalent to that of Hong Kong. The Russians feel the same paranoia about these open areas that the Australians do in the presence of a billion Chinese and a historically aggressive Japan. The dilemma for the Russians is just how far to reduce their forces: too little, and they gain no economic or diplomatic advantage; too much, and they render themselves vulnerable to attack and undermine the legitimacy of their claim to be a genuine Asia-Pacific power.[33]

The second and third obstacles became more closely associated when the Russians, following the commencement of troop withdrawals from Afghanistan, proposed that the withdrawal (unilateral and without a formal guarantee of a successor regime) might constitute a model for the extrication of Vietnamese troops from Kampuchea. The principal players in that sorry and byzantine drama seem increasingly predisposed to negotiate. The Vietnamese, for their part, are in dire straits economically and politically. The Vietnamese economy is on the verge of collapse. Inflation is rampant, the black market is flourishing and a reported seven million people are on the brink of starvation in parts of northern Vietnam following two successive years of crop failures.[34] The reformist government of Nguyen Van Linh has an even greater need to embark on its own *perestroika*, to halt the flight of currency and to attract western investment. Here again the military-economic nexus is inescapable. Not only must Linh reduce the crushing burden of maintaining the world's fourth largest army (in one of the world's poorest countries) but he must terminate the nine-year-old occupation of Kampuchea if he is to persuade the Americans, the Japanese and financial institutions like the Asian Development Bank to invest in Vietnam. In the same way that the future economic development of the Far Eastern regions of the Soviet Union is predicated on reduced military expenditure and the attraction of foreign investment, so the survival of Vietnam is largely dependent on the same requirements.[35] If the economic argument were not sufficiently compelling the political one would make it so. For three years now, since Vietnam's successful dry season offensive against the Khmer Rouge in 1984-85, Hanoi has predicated its plan for a complete withdrawal of troops from Kampuchea by 1990 on the expectation (resonant of American ambitions in Vietnam two decades ago) that its Cambodian clients would consolidate their new regime and Vietnamese forces would be effectively replaced by friendly Cambodian units. The failure of that scheme has provided a strong incentive to the Vietnamese to try to negotiate their way out of the morass.[36]

For a long while the Vietnam 'obstacle' was seen simplistically as an antecedent to improved Sino-Soviet relations. In point of fact there has been a dialectical interplay between Sino-Soviet relations and the Vietnam-Kampuchea problem. The Chinese improved their relations with the Soviet Union significantly before any resolution of that problem was in sight and that improvement has almost certainly encouraged both players to eliminate the problem once and for all. The Vietnamese involvement in Kampuchea has been a costly and embarrassing exercise for the Russians. Not only have they had to subsidise the Vietnamese economy to the extent of US$3 million a day and more recently to buy grain on the open market for Hanoi, but their support of the Vietnamese occupation and the maintenance of significant naval and intelligence gathering facilities at Cam Ranh Bay and Da Nang have not endeared them to the Asean states.[37] For their part, the Chinese have long supported the Khmer Rouge, mobilised regional and global opposition to the occupation, and built up a very close security relationship with Thailand. They have also inflicted 'lessons' — in the form of military incursions or artillery bombardments of various intensities — on the Vietnamese. Their failure to inflict sterner lessons on their opponents in recent years suggests not only their changed domestic military priorities but their increased commitment to improved Sino-Soviet relations. At the same time the Chinese have displayed a greater flexibility toward an eventual negotiated settlement in Kampuchea. This flexibility may reflect in part a growing concern about the negative impact of close Chinese association with the Khmer Rouge in terms of that faction's association with the genocidal Pol Pot regime.[38] There are still hurdles in the way of a settlement even if the outlook is more optimistic than it has been before. Publicly at least, Hanoi has indicated its disdain for the Afghanistan withdrawal model. However, it is significant that the Vietnamese did not choose to embarrass the Russians by publicly requesting their support in the Sino-Vietnamese dispute over the Spratly Islands in the South China Sea. Had they done so it would have put the Russians in an awkward spot and given the Chinese an additional Sino-Soviet bargaining chip.[39]

In the latter part of May 1988 Hanoi announced the withdrawal of 50,000 troops from Kampuchea by the end of the year. It was clear that the announcement was timed in order to ensure the maximum political impact during the Soviet-American summit. Unlike earlier rotational 'withdrawals' and modest troop reductions this withdrawal does appear to constitute a significant military and diplomatic signal.[40] Faced with the upcoming Communist Party congress — the first since 1940 — Gorbachev is particularly anxious to cap his foreign policy success with a resolution of the Kampuchean problem. Accordingly, he has promoted the idea of the national reconciliation in Kampuchea. This slogan is apparently designed as much to assist in Kampuchea as it is to reassure his critics in Asean and win over Indonesia as an ally in steering Southeast Asian states away from an anti-Soviet stance. The Russians have been much more active of late on the diplomatic front, consulting with high-level representatives of Southeast Asian states and indicating their intention to bypass Hanoi in their dealings with the region. What remains unclear for the moment is just how much pressure Moscow has been able to bring to bear on Hanoi. Outwardly, the Vietnamese remain stubbornly independent, but it may very well be that the major troop withdrawal and the unwillingness to involve Russia over the Spratlys indicates the Soviet Union's hand.[41]

Japan

Another major factor in determining the degree of peace and stability in the Asia-Pacific region in the next decade is the course of Russo-Japanese and Sino-Japanese relations. The recovery and sustained growth of the Soviet economy is based in large part on the development of the vast untapped potential of Central Asia and Siberia. That region contains three-quarters of the country's minerals, fuel and energy resources, over one-half of its hydro-electric resources and about one-half its commercial timber reserves.[42] Improved Russo-Japanese relations might pave the way for substantial Japanese investment in the eastern half of the Soviet Union and would have the inestimable, additional advantage of providing greater security to the remote area in the face of a perceived resurgence in Japanese nationalism and militarism. For the moment, however, there seems little likelihood that Russian ambitions will be realised. Trade with Russia constitutes only 1.4 per cent of Japanese foreign bilateral trade and the Japanese seem in no hurry whatsoever to invest their money in technologically and politically risky ventures in the Soviet Far East.[43] Far more important than this financial chariness is the continued problem of the disputed

Northern Islands. For some time now (history of occupation is long and complicated) the Russians have occupied the islands of Etorofu and Kunashiri in the Kuriles and Shikotan and the Habomai Group. While the Japanese legal claim to the islands is stronger than the Soviet counterclaim the latter are not likely to cease occupancy since they constitute vital links in the defensive chain which surrounds the Sea of Okhotsk, Russian's primary Pacific SSBN (nuclear-powered ballistic missile submarine) bastion.[44]

The reduction of tensions appears far more likely in the Sino-Japanese relationship. Japan is China's second largest trade partner and Japanese economic and technical assistance plays a crucial role in China's programme of economic modernisation.[45] Furthermore, despite improvements in the Sino-Soviet relationship, China and Japan are both wary about Soviet political and military presence in Northeast Asia. The anti-hegemony clause in the 1978 Sino-Japanese treaty was clearly directed toward the Soviet Union. Furthermore, Russian support of North Korea, the KAL007 incident and the Russian naval build-up have stimulated Sino-Japanese anxieties over the years.

However, the Sino-Japanese relationship is not without its problems. The concerns are mostly Chinese. Beijing continues to worry about the growth of Japan's military potential despite Japanese promises and reassurances to the contrary.[46] Related is the textbook irritant in which the Chinese maintain that the Japanese are sanitising their aggressive role in China in World War II in their high school textbooks.[47] Japanese relations with Taiwan are also a problem. Although Japan severed diplomatic relations with Taiwan in 1972, Japanese-Taiwanese trade continues to flourish and Beijing has expressed annoyance that Japanese investment in Taiwan (US$1 billion in 1985) is greater than in China (US$365 million in 1985). Beijing is also uneasy about its continued trade imbalance with Japan (US$4.2 billion in 1986 in a two-way trade of US$15.5 billion). There is no short-term solution to this last-mentioned problem since it relates to the basic structure of the trade relationship, but China's long-term dedication to economic modernisation is too great to let the trade imbalance stand in the way. For their part the Japanese are alert to Chinese sensitivities and will almost certainly work towards a bigger and better share of the China market.[48]

Wild cards

There are two major wild cards in the Asia-Pacific equation — the Philippines and Korea. The Philippines raise three interrelated issues. First, will President Corazon Aquino survive? Second, will her reform programme be sufficient to drag the Philippine economy out of its feudal lethargy? And third, what will be the outcome of the 'bases' problem? What is perhaps remarkable is that President Aquino, an almost complete political ingenue, has survived as long as she has. For the most part the efforts to overthrow her have been farcical and she has indicated her ability to grow with the job. The economy, however, is still the slowest growing one in non-communist Southeast Asia. It is a country 'living under an illusion of prosperity'.[49]

While Mrs Aquino has accomplished the amazing feat of bringing an element of real democracy back into the Philippines government, the major question is whether she will be able to reform the economy in general and land tenure in particular before her momentum and the people's idealism fade. The economic problems she faces are formidable and involve corruption, population pressure, entrenched feudal interests and a communist New People's Army (NPA) insurgency.[50] The NPA, which has been growing steadily in size, is not winning in the provinces but it is not losing either. It represents a sentiment which finds expression in resistance to the renewal of the leasing arrangements for the American bases at Subic Bay Naval Base and Clark Air Force Base. 'Nowhere else,' the *Economist* noted, 'is the Philippine dilemma over its identity so acute'.[51] American personnel contribute US$350 million a year to the Philippine economy and the bases, which employ 69,000 Filipinos, have a payroll second only to the government itself. Although the leases expire in 1991, negotiations must take place now and it may be that the huge, US$5 billion to US$10 billion multinational economic recovery plan being considered by Washington is designed to keep Aquino in office and establish the right climate for the bases renegotiation.[52] Whatever the case, it seems likely that the Americans will pay substantially more for their use and may suffer operational constraints resulting from the desire of the Filipinos to express greater sovereign control and/or anti-nuclear policies. In the final analysis the bases will probably stay. Most of the Asean states publicly or privately support America's continued military presence in the area and even the Chinese want the US to stay as a counter-balance to Soviet power and a check on possible Japanese militarism.[53]

What makes the Korean peninsula so significant in terms of the Asia-Pacific region is that the interests of the Chinese, Americans, Russians and Japanese come together in that polarised and militarised corner of Northeast Asia. The Democratic People's Republic of Korea in the north is an eastern Albania, a Stalinist state 'ruled' by the Kim 'dynasty' which is wedded to *juche*, a concept of self-determination seen to be threadbare to all but the most fanatical.[54] Like other communist systems it has failed to deliver. Roughly 20-25 per cent of the GNP is spent on defence and the republic is known internationally for its lack of creditworthiness.[55]

To the south of the demilitarised zone (the most militarised zone in the world) lies South Korea, a nation of remarkable economic strengths and weaknesses. The South Korean economy is now the 17th largest in the non-communist world but it also has the third highest foreign debt in the world. The South Koreans have indeed accomplished an economic miracle in the past three decades but their economy is 'a candle in the wind', acutely vulnerable (because of their foreign debt and high debt-equity ratios) to shifts in exchange rates and changes in international demand.[56] For all their effort South Koreans are only half as well off as the average resident of Hong Kong or Singapore.

Like the Filipinos, the South Koreans are experimenting with democracy. President Roh Tae-Woo was the first president to come to office in South Korea through the democratic process. In June 1987 he enumerated an eight-point plan of political reform which included the promise to end authoritarianism and police state controls. The real question is will he be able to deliver. The military will be a major force for Roh to reckon with.[57] While war with the North is unlikely they dare not lower their guard. The South Korean armed forces are smaller than those of the North and the South Koreans spend only 6 per cent of their GNP on defence. But because South Korea is five times richer than the North the military gap is closing. Roh must try to deal with a huge foreign debt, demands for greater democratisation, periodic bouts of public unrest, and the political and military realities of a state of siege.[58]

Confusing and simplifying his task is the presence of the Americans. The United States maintains 40,000 troops in South Korea and they, depending on one's point of view, constitute a lightning rod or a trip wire. Recent student demonstrations in Seoul focussed on the removal of American forces and this may eventually come to pass though most Asia watchers see the American presence as a stabilising force. They subscribe to the trip wire theory that the North Korean regime, which friends and foes alike seem to consider a 'loose cannon', remains suitably restrained in its adventurism because of the likelihood of being drawn into a war with the United States. The South Koreans tend to find the continued American presence humiliating but the alternatives — the possibility of attack by North Korea or a more active Japanese military role in Northeast Asia — are not particularly attractive.[59]

The Russians view the Kim 'dynasty' with a considerable degree of wariness.[60] Pyongyang remains secretive and unpredictable. And the two powers are drifting farther apart ideologically as the Soviet Union courts the West. The Russians have provided the North Koreans with MiG-29s and in return the North Koreans have granted the Russians access to Wonsan and Nampo harbours and overflights between Vladivostok and Cam Ranh Bay.[61] Other than Mongolia, North Korea is Russia's only partial ally in North Asia and Gorbachev is not likely to cut it adrift, particularly when it serves Soviet interests to try to stabilise the peninsula. The Soviets no doubt hope that following the succession struggle, which some authorities predict will accompany Kim Il Sung's death, a more predictable, reform-minded regime will come into power in Pyongyang which will be less of a liability.[62] In the interval Moscow does not wish to be seen to be drawing too close to Pyongyang lest it work to the detriment of improved relations with Beijing and Seoul.

The Chinese have mixed feelings about the Koreas. Sensitive about their troubled borders (India, Burma, Vietnam, Tibet and the Sino-Soviet), the Chinese are eager to stay on good terms with Pyongyang. At the same time they see the future as lying with the South. Although trade is indirect, China's trade with South Korea now exceeds that with the Soviet Union.[63] South Korean technology may be more suitable for the Chinese than that from Japan and the Chinese see the South Korean economic model as one easier to emulate.

The Japanese also have a foot in both camps in the Koreas. The Japanese and the North Koreans do not have diplomatic relations, but Japan is North Korea's primary non-communist trade partner, accounting for more than two-thirds of North Korea's trade with the capitalist world.[64] South Korea and Japan have strong trade links although the size of South Korea's indebtness to Japan is a source of concern in Seoul. The Japanese and the South Koreans share the Americans as defence partners and the

Japanese view the stability of the Korean peninsula as inseparable from the issue of their own security.

The Northeast Asian military balance

The principal features of the Northeast Asian military balance in the past decade have been the continued qualitative and quantitative build-up of Soviet forces and the application of the American concepts of Forward Strategy and Horizontal Escalation.[65] The Soviets see the Pacific region as their third priority after a war on the Central Front in Europe or on the Sino-Soviet border. They have been drawn into the Northeast Asian region militarily in pursuit of Gorshkov's power projection and in response to the threats posed by China, Japan and the United States. The American threat is of particular concern becuase of the apparent American dedication to the idea of Horizontal Escalation; that is to say that Russian forces engaged on the Central Front would be thrown off balance and quite possibly defeated by the opening of a second front in the Far East. The Soviet build-up, which witnessed the growth of ground forces to approximately 56 divisions, a dramatic increase in the number of aircraft and the formation of the Pacific Fleet (the Soviets' largest), was symbolised by the establishment of the Far Eastern Theatre Command (TVD) in 1978. The TVD preceded similar commands in Europe and the Caucusus by six years and is responsible for co-ordinating military planning and operations.[66]

Since 1978 Soviet forces in the Far East have undergone some significant restructuring largely as a result of the work of Marshall Nikolai Ogarkov who has emphasised combined operations, improved C^3I (command, control, communications and intelligence) and better equipment. Ogarkov's initiatives have dovetailed neatly with Gorbachev's desire to effect economies and the overall result has been strategic continuity but a dedication to smaller, more efficient forces.[67]

Much of the strength of the Soviet Far Eastern forces lies in the SSBN fleet which operates primarily in the Sea of Okhotsk. For many years navalists commented on the fact that the geography of the Northeast Asian region severely limited the movements of Soviet naval vessels by obliging them to pass through narrow, interdictable, choke points. However, current thinking has tended to stand that argument on its head and suggests that the Soviet navy now enjoys an inestimable advantage, namely, the difficulty American SSN (nuclear powered [attack] submarine) skippers will face when they try to gain access to the SSBN 'bastions' like the Sea of Okhotsk.

One of the assumptions underlying the American Forward Strategy (which seeks to exploit US and allied maritime power to carry the war quickly and decisively against the enemy shore) is that US SSNs will be able to penetrate the bastions and detect and kill Soviet SSBNs. This assumption, however, is coming under increasing attack for a number of reasons. First, the Russians are building quieter submarines which will render their detection more difficult. Second, the Sea of Okhotsk is shallow, ice bound part of the year and unattractive as a sonar environment.[68] Third, it seems that the American anti-submarine warfare (ASW) advantage may be declining more rapidly than anticipated and that it will be much easier for the Russians to detect the penetrations on which the Forward Strategy is partly based. Equally vexing is the problem of threshold. If American SSNs do penetrate the Sea of Okhotsk successfully, how many Soviet SSBNs dare they destroy before the Russians are driven to stage some massive first strike retaliation?[69]

The other major assumption underlying the Forward Strategy is the willingness of America's Asia-Pacific allies to co-operate fully in wartime.[70] None is more crucial to any wartime scenario in Northeast Asia than Japan. The Japanese and the Americans are extraordinarily interdependent on one another economically (something which is certain to go on producing periodic bouts of tension) and are forging ever closer military links.[71] The Americans have long urged the Japanese to bear a greater part of the Northeast Asian defence burden and it now appears that the two nations have developed a division of labour which sees the Japanese expanding their defence responsibilities to include greater maritime air defence and control of sea lines of communication (SLOCs) out to 1,000 nautical miles from the home islands.[72]

These increased commitments are part of a significant transformation of the Japanese Self-Defence Forces (JSDF). While constitutional constraints still affect the operation of the JSDF, concern about the Soviet build-up, the disputed Northern Islands and the security of Japanese supplies of raw materials has led the Japanese to accelerate the modernisation and increase the size of the JSDF. The Japanese have broken the 1 per cent barrier of GNP on defence (more likely 1.6 per cent if North American Treaty Organisation [NATO] formulae are applied) and are now the world's six largest spender on defence. The growth of the JSDF also reflects Japan's increased economic and political stature in the world.[73]

It is a development, however, which has drawn mixed reviews. The Chinese have acknowledged the legitimacy of the JSDF and the South Koreans welcome its growth and would like somehow to co-operate with the JSDF but are uncertain how to grasp that nettle psychologically and politically.[74] The Russians are concerned about the increased size and efficiency of the JSDF (despite its very real weaknesses). Emotional generalisations about the revival of Japanese militarism are now a common feature of the Asia-Pacific press. Two things do seem certain: the JSDF will probably increase slowly in size and the Japanese will become increasingly autonomous and forceful players in Northeast Asia within the existing structure of US maritime strategy.[75]

Conclusion

This paper began by raising the issue of rapprochement: What is the likelihood of greater peace and stability in the Asia-Pacific region in the immediate future? A review of the domestic and foreign policies of the major players and their allies suggests that economic concerns will play a very powerful part in encouraging more peaceful conditions. The Russian, Vietnamese and Philippine economies are in trouble; the Chinese economy somewhat less so. It is in the best interests of all these players to foster conditions of stability in order to give effect to economic reform programmes. Having said that, the outlook in the first three nations is not particularly promising. Gorbachev's ability to turn an entrenched bureaucracy and apathetic society around is still very much in doubt. So long as he remains in office and so long as the restructuring campaign succeeds there is the likelihood that the Russians will be open to arms control negotiations and force reductions, even of an asymmetrical sort. In the long term if *perestroika* works the world could be less stable because the decline of the Soviet Union would have been halted. It is unlikely that Gorbachev will attract the investment and technology to make *perestroika* work. Some middle ground will probably be reached with the Russians muddling through and the current atmosphere of accommodation will fade away.[76]

The modernisation of China will most likely be successful and the Chinese, in the short term at least, will exploit the advantages of their pivotal position in the newly emerging trilateral superpower relationship. In the case of all of these countries the fundamental question is, can the leaders — Linh, Aquino, Roh, Gorbachev — stay the course. In the case of China it appears that Deng's supporters are sufficiently entrenched that the economic modernisation programme will continue after his death. The Sino-Soviet relationship will go on improving (thereby reducing tensions) but not to the extent where it would endanger the relationship between Beijing and Washington. Despite a recent cooling of that relationship as a result of the Iranian receipt of Silkworm missiles, both powers realise the huge advantages which accrue from a close working relationship.

The Vietnamese situation is problematical. It seems likely that with suitable face-saving formulae in place, the Linh regime will bow to the inevitable and to Russian pressure and withdraw from Kampuchea. Failure to do so would mean prolonged diplomatic isolation and financial collapse. In the Philippines each passing day means that the Aquino presidency is more secure. However, it seems that she is moving rightward and her failure to deliver on reform (and the same applies to Roh in South Korea) may make the Philippines one of the major areas of instability in the near future.

A growing sense of nationalism in both China and Japan could constitute an obstacle to what is likely to be one of the major power relationships in East Asia. The Russo-Japanese outlook is not promising. There are serious political and strategic obstacles in the way of an improved relationship between Tokyo and Moscow and there seems little prospect of improvement.

On the military front there will probably be more continuity than change. Indeed while much of this paper has emphasised major structural changes in the political and economic character of the great powers the forces of continuity should not be underestimated. Unlike the European region, the Asia-Pacific region is highly complex in terms of security arrangements. Whereas the European region is characterised by two major blocs — NATO and the Warsaw Pact — the Asia-Pacific region tends to be characterised by bilateral relationship. What is more, the fundamental asymmetry between the land-based and maritime forces of the opponents makes arms control negotiations even more difficult. It is also important to note that there is no unanimity whatsoever in terms of who constitutes the enemy.

The evidence suggests that most of the nations in the region would prefer to see the maintenance of the status quo in terms of American military dispositions. They would like to see the Americans remain in the Philippines, South Korea and Japan as a force of continuity and constraint. The strategic concepts underlying that presence, however, are now increasingly the subject of debate. The basic assumptions embodied in the Forward Strategy are held by many critics to be faulty and/or potentially destabilising.

It appears that we are at the beginning of the end; albeit a long end but an end nevertheless. The Americans have entered that predictable stage of imperial decline where they are calling for greater support from their allies. The Russians and the Chinese have entered a period of ideological decline where ideological justification becomes more tortured and contrived. The *Pax Americana* is drawing ever so slowly to a close as is much of the Marxist-Leninist experience as we have known it. Where does all this leave us? The opportunity for improved relations between the great powers in the Asia-Pacific region now seems greater than it has been for a very long time. By happy coincidence it suits all the players for domestic reasons to pull in their horns, make timely concessions and regroup. This atmosphere of conciliation, however, is based largely on a series of economic reform experiments which are not very likely to succeed. When their failure is recognised the Asia-Pacific region is likely to be increasingly unstable once again.

Afterword

This paper was written in June 1988. The ensuing six months have provided answers to some of the questions raised and confirm some of the conclusions reached with respect to the prospects for big power rapprochement. The outcome of the great Soviet experiment is still problematic though the relationship between economics and military contraction has been underscored graphically by Gorbachev's offer to reduce Soviet armed forces by half a million men. What this offer means in real terms is hard to say, but the fact that the suggested cuts came in the defence sector is symptomatic.

The suggested inter-relationship between economic restructuring and increased demands for political power appears to have been borne out in the Soviet Union. While Gorbachev has not only survived but consolidated his authority, he finds himself confronted with increasingly awkward situations in the Baltic Seas and Armenia. The demands for greater political autonomy resulting from the former and civil unrest arising in the latter would have been almost unheard of a decade ago, and taken along with developments elsewhere in Eastern Europe, constitute a further assault on the dictatorship of the CPSU. For the moment, the Armenian initiative has probably been lobotomised by the trans-Caucasian earthquake of December 1988, but Armenian political quiesence is likely to be temporary.

Elsewhere in Asia, the Vietnam-Kampuchea negotiations appear to be going nowhere quickly. A stay of execution has been effected in the Philippines in terms of an interim agreement regarding the American bases. Corazon Aquino seems well on her way to surviving her term in office but the outcome of the bases negotiations in

1991 appears marginally less promising than it did six months ago. Despite a brief flurry of diplomatic talk at the time of the Seoul Olympics in September 1988 the relationship between North and South Korea appears unchanged and largely unchanging. Not so the Sino-Soviet relationship, where a Deng-Gorbachev summit is in the offing. The Chinese economy continues to grow though at the risk of dangerous sectoral overheating while the American economy is still plagued by deficit problems and the debilitating effects of increasingly unsupportable defence expenditures. While not a carbon copy of the Reagan administration, the Bush administration is likely to maintain a fairly high degree of continuity in terms of its Asia-Pacific policies. American-Japanese relations are solid although trade, investment and military spending issues will continue to test the patience of Washington and Tokyo. The Japanese have continued their efforts to articulate a new trade/aid role for themselves in the region and have broken with the past to a degree by entering into multi-billion dollar negotiations with the Soviet Union over the construction of huge petroleum complex in Siberia.

A major concern expressed by regional experts is what will happen to rapprochement if there is a failure of the world economic order. Severe macroeconomic imbalance would quite clearly have profound security implications for the Asia-Pacific region. Global economic issues were not addressed in this paper though the ability of world economics to weather the October 1987 crisis suggests an increased resilience in the global economic system. Nevertheless, considered opinion suggests that the October crisis was a near run thing; that the house of cards was deeply imperilled. If it were to come tumbling down much of the projection outlined above would be rendered academic.

Rising expectations characterise the Asia-Pacific region. The ability of national leaders to deliver in the political and economic realms will be critical in terms of their survival and the survival of the political systems they represent. Economic and political ideals are not likely to be realised in the short to mid-term. Instead muddling through will probably be the order of the day. Nevertheless, for the moment there is a sense of optimism in the air, which, coupled with a willingness to entertain fairly bold political initiatives, bodes well for the prospects of rapprochement into the 1990s.

NOTES

This paper was made possible by the generous assistance of the Canadian Department of External Affairs in Ottawa and by the active support of three members of that department, David Peel, Paul Bennett and Glen Sheppy.

1. Michael Nacht, 'United States-Japanese Relations,' *Current History*, Vol 87, No 528 (April 1988), p149. The American share of the world GNP has fallen from 33 per cent (1960) to 22 per cent (1980s).
2. Harry Harding, *China's Second Revolution: Reform After Mao*, Washington: The Brookings Institution, 1987, pp 240-242.

3. Anon, 'Alas, Poor Marx,' *The Economist*, Vol 307, No 7549 (May 7-13, 1988), pp 12-13.

4. Stephen Kirby, 'The Two Koreas — Conflict or Compromise,' *Conflict Studies*, No 207, p30.

5. Thomas Walkom, 'Japan Quietly Builds Up Military Muscle,' *The Globe and Mail*, June 4, 1988, pD-3.

6. Amitav Acharya, 'The Asia-Pacific Region: Cockpit for Superpower Rivalry,' *The World Today*, Vol 43, Nos 8-9 (August-September 1987), pp 155-158.

7. Masahiko Asada, 'Soviet Security and Arms Control Initiatives and Objectives in the Pacific,' unpublished paper, p1.

8. Keith Suter, 'Australia's Defence Debate: The Dibb Report,' *RUSI Journal*, Vol 132, No 4 (December 1987), p55.

9. Sheldon Simon, 'Asean's Strategic Situation in the 1980s,' *Pacific Affairs*, Vol 60, No 1 (Spring 1987), p75.

10. Asada, p8.

11. Ross Babbage, 'The Future of the US Maritime Strategy and the Pacific Military Balance,' unpublished paper, p3.

12. Thomas Robinson, 'Soviet Policy in Asia: The Military Dimension,' *Soviet Foreign Policy*, Proceedings of the Academy of Political Science, Vol 36, No 4 (1987), p155.

13. Ramesh Thakur and Carlyle A Thayer, *The Soviet Union as an Asian-Pacific Power: Implications of Gorbachev's 1986 Vladivostok Initiative*, Boulder, Colorado: Westview Press, 1987, p3.

14. Thakur, p214. The text of the Vladivostok address is contained between pp 200 and 227.

15. Asada, pp 25-27.

16. Gary Klinworth, 'Gorbachev's China Diplomacy' in Thakur, p42.

17. Anon, 'The Soviet Economy,' *The Economist*, Vol 307, No 7545 (April 9, 1988), p3.

18. Anon, 'The Soviet Economy,' p3.

19. Natalie Gross, 'Glasnost: Roots and Practice,' *Problems of Communism*, Vol 36 (November-December 1987), p77.

Alain Besancon, 'Gorbachev Without Illusions,' *Commentary*, Vol 85, No 4 (April 1988), p51.

20. William Odum, 'How Far Can Soviet Reform Go?' *Problems of Communism*, Vol 36 (November-December 1987), p26.

21. Anon, '*The Soviet Economy*,' p18.

22. Marshall Goldman and Merle Goldman, 'Soviet and Chinese Economic Reform,' *Foreign Affairs*, Vol 66, No 3 (1987/1988), p566.

23. Goldman, p551.

24. Goldman, p559.

25. Klinworth in Thakur, p47.

26. Denis Simon, Review of *The Chinese Army After Mao* by Ellis Joffe, *Bulletin of the Atomic Scientists*, Vol 44, No 5 (June 1988), p46.

Tai Ming Cheung, 'Reaching For Detente,' *Far Eastern Economic Review*, Vol 140, No 22 (June 2, 1988), pp 34-35.

27. Klinworth in Thakur, p48.

28. Harding, p242.

29. For background see: Thomas Robinson, 'The New Era in Sino-Soviet Relations,' *Current History*,Vol 86, No 521 (September 1987), pp 241-244 and 303-304; Herbert Ellison, 'Changing Sino-Soviet Relations,' *Problems of Communism*, Vol 36 (May-June 1987), pp 17-29; and Gerald Segal, 'Sino-Soviet Detente: How Far, How Fast?' *The World Today*, Vol 43, No 5 (May 1987), pp 87-91.

30. Robert Horn, 'Soviet Policy in East Asia,' *Current History*, Vol 86, No 522 (October 1987), p322.

31. Klinworth in Thakur, pp 44-46.

32. Richard Solomon, *The Soviet Far East Military Buildup*, Dover, Massachusetts: Auburn House Publishing Company, 1986; Banning Garrett, 'Gorbachev's Reassessment of Soviet Security Needs: Implications for Northeast Asia,' Working Paper, No 27, Peace Research Centre, Canberra, 1988.

33. Robinson, 1987a, p158.

34. Barry Wain, 'Vietnam Squeezed by Crop Shortage and Currency Crisis,' *The Asian Wall Street Journal,* Vol 10, No 20, (May 16, 1988), p1 and 20.

Philip Smucker, 'Disillusioned Vietnamese Beg, Steal to Survive,' *The Globe and Mail* (June 16, 1988), pA-10.

35. Anon, 'Vietnam,' *The Economist*, Vol 307, No 7551 (May 21-27, 1988), p28. Clare Hollingworth, 'To Forestall Economic Collapse, Vietnam Will Pull Out of Cambodia,' *Pacific Defence Reporter*, Vol 17, No 11 (May 1988), p12.

36. Gareth Porter, 'Cambodia: Sihanouk's Initiative,' *Foreign Affairs*, Vol 66, No 4 (Spring 1988), pp 819-820.

John Le Boutillier, 'Coming to Terms With Vietnam,' *New York Times Magazine* (May 1, 1988), pp 48-51 and 73, 77-78.

37. Nayan Chanda, 'A Troubled Friendship,' *Far Eastern Economic Review*, Vol 140, No 23 (June 9, 1988), pp 16-19.

38. John Pedler, 'Kampuchea and Peace Prospects in Indochina,' *The World Today*, Vol 43, No 10 (October 1987), p176.

Porter, p823.

39. Anon, 'Relieved Ally,' *Far Eastern Economic Review*, Vol 140, No 22 (June 2, 1988), p13.

40. Anon, 'Vietnam,' p28.

41. Anon, 'Moscow's Cambodia Push,' *Asiaweek*, Vol 14, No 20 (May 13, 1988), pp 33-36; Michael Richardson, 'Storm Signals in the Spratlys,' *Pacific Defence Reporter*, Vol 17, No 11 (May 1988), p5; and Leszek Buszynski 'Gorbachev and Southeast Asia: Prospects for the 1990s,' unpublished paper, p6.

42. Ross Babbage, 'Soviet Strategic Dilemmas in the North Pacific in the 1990s,' unpublished paper, p1.

43. Wolf Mendl, 'Japan's Northern Territories: An Asian Falklands,' *The World Today*, Vol 43, No 6 (June 1987), p100.

44. Susan Lesley Clark, 'Soviet Policy Toward Japan,' *Soviet Foreign Policy*, Proceedings of the Academy of Political Science, Vol 36, No 4, 1987, p148.

45. Hong N Kim, 'Sino-Japanese Relations,' *Current History*, Vol 87, No 528 (April 1988), p153.

46. Kim, p154.

47. Anon, 'Japan and China: The War That Will Not Die,' *The Economist*, Vol 307, No 7549 (May 7-13, 1988), p30.

48. Kim, p179-180.

49. Anon, 'The Economist Survey of the Philippines,' *The Economist*, Vol 307, No 7549 (May 7-13, 1988), p7.

Mary Walsh, 'Improving Economy Fails to Solve Deep Problems,' *The Asian Wall Street Journal*, (May 16, 1988), p11.

50. Vyvyan Tenorio, 'Manila Employs New Tactics in War Against Rebels,' *The Globe and Mail* (June 16, 1988), pA-9.

51. Anon, 'The Economist Survey of the Philippines,' p17.

52. Robert Greenberger, 'US is Considering Huge Aid Package for the Philippines,' *The Asian Wall Street Journal Weekly* (May 16, 1988), p11.

53. Evelyn Colbert, 'United States Policy in Southeast Asia,' *Current History*, Vol 86, No 519 (April 1987), p146; Leszek Buszynski, 'The Philippines, Asean and the Future of the American Bases,' *The World Today*, Vol 44, No 5 (May 1988), p85; and Susumu Awanohara, 'Many East Asian Countries Want the US to Remain,' *Far Eastern Economic Review*, Vol 140, No 16 (April 21, 1988), pp 27-28.

54. James Cotton, 'Patriarchs and Politics: Prospects for the Korean Peninsula,' *Third World Quarterly*, Vol 10, No 1 (January 1988), p82.

55. Anon, 'The Economist Survey of South Korea,' *The Economist*, Vol 307, No 7551 (May 21-27, 1988), p5.

56. Anon, 'The Economist Survey of South Korea,' p17.

Selig Harrison, 'Dateline South Korea: A Divided Seoul,' *Foreign Policy*, No 67 (Summer 1987), p160.

57. Cotton, p92.

58. Kirby, p30.

59. Mark Clifford, 'Passages to Prosperity Strains US Ties,' *Far Eastern Economic Review*, Vol 140, No 19 (May 12, 1988), pp 19-21.

60. Babbage, 1988b. p3.

61. Asada, p8.

62. Cotton, p79. See also John McBeth, 'A Military Mystery,' *Far Eastern Economic Review*, Vol 140, No 14 (April 7, 1988), p38.

63. Kirby, p32.

64. Anon, 'Still There's Trade,' *The Economist*, Vol 307, No 7551 (May 21-27, 1988), p27.

65. Anon, 'Japan Watches Forces Build-Up,' *Jane's Defence Weekly*, Vol 9, No 19 (May 14, 1988), p975; Derek de Cunha, 'Soviet Naval Capabilities in the Pacific in the 1990s,' unpublished paper; Malcolm MacIntosh, 'Soviet Military Strategy and Operational Capabilities in the 1990s,' unpublished paper, pp 9-11.

66. MacIntosh, pp 16-26.

67. MacIntosh, pp 8-17.

Anon, 'Economics Force Cut-back in Naval Power,' *Jane's Defence Weekly*, Vol 9, No 12 (March 26, 1988), p600.

68. Babbage, 1988a, pp 19-21.

69. Babbage, 1988a, p17.

Bill Hayden, 'Security and Arms Control in the North Pacific, 'Working Paper, No 31, Peace Research Centre, 1988, p8.

70. Babbage, 1988a, p22.

71. Bernard Gordon, *Politics and Protectionism in the Pacific*, Adelphi Papers, No 228 (Spring 1988), pp 20-23; Nacht, p150; and Yoshihide Soeya, 'Japan's Defense Policy in the 1990s,' unpublished paper, p21.

72. Anon, 'The Allies: Time to Share the Burden,' *The Economist*, Vol 307, No 7549 (May 7-13, 1988), pp 23-24.

James Auer, 'Japan's Defence Policy,' *Current History*, Vol 87, No 528, (April 1988), pp 147-148.

73. Ron Matthews and Joanne Bartlett, 'The Stirring of Japan's Military Slumber,' *The World Today*, Vol 44, No 5 (May 1988), pp 79-82.

74. Soeya, p24.

75. Soeya, pp 25-26.

Walkom, pD-3.

76. T H Rigby and R F Miller, 'Domestic Determinants of Soviet Foreign Policy: Prospects for Change in the 1990s,' unpublished paper, p31.

BIBLIOGRAPHY

Acharya, Amitav, 1987, 'The Asia-Pacific Region: Cockpit for Superpower Rivalvy,' *The World Today*, Vol 43, Nos 8-9 (August-September), pp 155-158.

Anon, 1988, 'Economics Force Cut-Back in Naval Power,' *Jane's Defence Weekly*, Vol 9, No 12 (March 26), p600.

Anon, 1988, 'The Soviet Economy,' *The Economist*, Vol 307, No 7545 (April 9-15), (Special Section) pp 1-18.

Anon, 1988, 'Japan Watches Forces Build-up,' *Jane's Defence Weekly*, Vol 9, No 19 (May), p975.

Anon, 1988, 'Alas, Poor Marx,' *The Economist*, Vol 307, No 7549 (May 7-13), pp 12-13.

Anon, 1988, 'The Economist Survey of the Philippines,' *The Economist*, Vol 307, No 7549 (May 7-13), pp 1-18.

Anon, 1988, 'The Allies: Time to Share the Burden,' *The Economist*, Vol 307, No 7549 (May 7-13), pp 23-24.

Anon, 1988, 'Japan and China: The War That Will Not Die,' *The Economist*, Vol 307, No 7549 (May 7-13), p30.

Anon, 1988, 'Still There's Trade,' *The Economist*, Vol 307, No 7551 (21-27 May), pp 27-28.

Anon, 1988, 'Vietnam,' *The Economist*, Vol 307, No 7551 (May 21-27), p28.

Anon, 1988, 'The Economist Survey of South Korea,' *The Economist*, Vol 307, No 7551 (May 21-27), pp 1-28.

Anon, 1988, 'Relieved Ally,' *Far Eastern Economic Review*, Vol 140, No 22 (June 2), p13.

Asada, Masahiko, 1988, 'Soviet Security and Arms Control Initiatives and Ojectives in the Pacific.' Paper presented at the Conference on Maritime Security and Arms Control in the Pacific Region, University of British Columbia, Vancouver.

Auer, James E, 1988, 'Japan's Defence Policy,' *Current History*, Vol 87, No 528 (April), pp 145-148.

Awanohara, Susumu, 1988, 'Many East Asian Countries Want the US to Remain,' *Far Eastern Economic Review*, Vol 140, No 16 (April 21), pp 27-28.

Babbage, Ross, 1988a, 'The Future of the United States' Maritime Strategy and the Pacific Military Balance.' Paper presented at the Conference on Maritime Security and Arms Control in the Pacific Region, University of British Columbia, Vancouver.

Babbage, Ross, 1988b, 'Soviet Strategic Dilemmas in the North Pacific in the 1990s.' Paper presented at a conference on the Soviets in the Pacific in the 1990s, Australian National Univerity, Canberra.

Bacho, Peter, 1987, 'Rural Revolt in the Philippines,' Vol 40, No 2, pp 257-270.

Bell, Coral, 1987, *The Unquiet Pacific*, No 205, London: Centre for Security and Conflict Studies.

Besancon, Alain, 1988, 'Gorbachev Without Illusions,' *Commentary*, Vol 85 No 4 (April), pp 47-57.

Buszynski, Leszek, 1988a, 'The Philippines, Asean and the Future of the American Bases,' *The World Today*, Vol 44, No 5 (May), pp 82-85.

Buszynski, Leszek, 1988b, 'Gorbachev and Southeast Asia: Prospects for the 1990s.' Paper presented at a conference on the Soviets in the Pacific in the 1990s, Australian National University, Canberra.

Chanda, Nayan, 1988, 'A Troubled Friendship,' *Far Eastern Economic Review*, Vol 140, No 23 (June 9), pp 16-19.

Cheung, Tai Ming, 1988, 'Reaching for Detente,' *Far Eastern Economic Review*, Vol 140, No 22 (June 2), pp 34-35.

Clark, Susan Lesley, 1987, 'Soviet Policy Toward Japan,' *Soviet Foreign Policy*, Proceedings of the Academy of Political Science, Vol 36, No 4.

Clifford, Mark, 1980, 'Passage to Prosperity Strains US Ties,' *Far Eastern Economic Review*, Vol 140, No 19 (May 12), pp 19-21.

Cloughley, Brian, 1988, 'Storm Signals in the Spratlys — Challenge For Vietnam,' *Pacific Defence Reporter*, Vol 13, No 11 (May), pp 6-7.

Colbert, Evelyn, 1987, 'US Policy in Southeast Asia,' *Current History*, Vol 86, No 519 (April), pp 145-179.

Cotton, James, 1988, 'Patriarchs and Politics: Prospects for the Korean Peninsula,' *Third World Quarterly*, Vol 10, No 1 (January), pp 79-94.

de Cunha, Derek, 1988, 'Soviet Naval Capabilities in the Pacific in the 1990s.' Paper presented at a conference on the Soviets in the Pacific in the 1990s, Australian National University, Canberra.

Dexiang, Jin, 1987, 'Some Observations on Southeast Asian Peace and Security in the 1990s.' Paper presented at a workshop on Peace and Security in Southeast Asia and Southwest Pacific in the 1990s, Bangkok.

Dibb, Paul, 1983, 'The Soviet Union as a Pacific Power,' *International Journal*, Vol 35, pp 234-250.

Ellison, Herbert J, 1987, 'Changing Sino-Soviet Relations,' *Problems of Communism*, Vol 36 (May-June), pp 1-29.

Esterline, John H, 1988, 'Hanoi Report,' *ORBIS*, Vol 31, No 1 (Winter), pp 97-106.

Garrett, Banning, 1988, 'Gorbachev's Reassessment of Soviet Security Needs: Implications fr Northeast Asia,' Working Paper, No 27, Peace Research Centre, Australia National University, Canberra.

Goldman, Marshall and Merle Goldman, 1987/88, 'Soviet and Chinese Economic Reform,' *Foreign Affairs*, Vol 66, No3, pp 551-573.

Gordon, Bernard K, 1988, *Politics and Protectionism in the Pacific*, Adelphi Papers, No 228, London: International Institute of Strategic Studies.

Greenberger, Robert, 1988, 'US is Considering Huge Aid Package for the Philippines,' *The Asian Wall Street Journal Weekly* (May 16), pp 11.

Gross, Natalie, 1987, 'Glasnost: Roots and Practice,' *Problems of Communism*, Vol 36 (November-December), pp 69-80.

Harding, Harry, 1987, *China's Second Revolution*, Washington: Brookings Institute.

Harrison, Selig S, 1987, 'Dateline South Korea: A Divided Seoul,' *Foreign Policy*, No 67 (Summer), pp 154-175.

Hayden, Bill, 1988, 'Security and Arms Control in the North Pacific.' Working Paper, No 31, Peace Research Centre, Australian National University, Canberra.

Hiebert, Murray, 1988, 'Reforming Pains,' *Far Eastern Economic Review*, Vol 139, No 11 (March 17), pp 20-21.

Hollingworth, Clare, 1988, 'To Forestall Economic Collapse, Vietnam Will Pull Out of Cambodia,' *Pacific Defence Reporter*, Vol 17, No 11 (May), pp 12-14.

Horn, Robert C, 1987, 'Soviet Policy in East Asia,' *Current History*, Vol 86, No 522 (October), pp 321-324 and 338-340.

Kim, Hong N, 1988, 'Sino-Japanese Relations,' *Current History*, Vol 87, No 528 (April), pp 153-156 and 178-180.

Kirby, Stephen, 1988, 'The Two Koreas — Conflict or Compromise?' *Conflict Studies*, No 207, London: Centre for Security and Conflict Studies.

Le Boutillier, John, 1988, 'Coming to Terms with Vietnam,' *New York Times Magazine* (May 1), pp 48-51 and 73, 77-78.

MacIntosh, Malcolm, 1988, 'Soviet Military Strategy and Operational Capabilities in the 1990s.' Paper presented at a conference on the Soviets in the Pacific in the 1990s, Australian National University, Canberra.

Matthews, Ron and Joanna Bartlett, 1988, 'The Stirring of Japan's Military Slumber,' *The World Today*, Vol 44, No 5 (May), pp 79-82.

McBeth, John, 1988, 'A Military Mystery,' *Far Eastern Economic Review*, Vol 140, No 14 (April 7), p38.

Mendl, Wolf, 1987, 'Japan's Northern Territories: An Asian Falklands?' *The World Today*, Vol 43, No 6 (June), pp 99-102.

Nacht, Michael, 1988, 'United States-Japanese Relations,' *Current History*, Vol 87, No 528 (April), pp 149-152, 184-185.

Nishihara, Masashi, 1987, 'Maritime Co-operation in the Pacific: The United States and its Partners,' *Naval War College Review*, Vol 40, No 3 (Summer), pp 37-41.

Odom, William E, 1987, 'How Far Can Soviet Reform Go?' *Problems of Communism*, Vol 36 (November-December), pp 18-33.

Pedler, John, 1987, 'Kampuchea and Peace Prospects in Indochina,' *The World Today*, Vol 43, No 10 (October), pp 173-176.

Porter, Gareth, 1988, 'Cambodia: Sihanouk's Initiative, *Foreign Affairs*, Vol 66, No 4 (Spring), pp 809-826.

Richardson, Michael, 1988, 'Storm Signals in the Spratlys — Revised Fears of Chinese Expansion,' *Pacific Defence Reporter*, Vol 17, No 11 (May), p5.

Rigby, T H and R F Miller, 1988a, 'Domestic Determinants of Soviet Foreign Policy: Prospects for Change in the 1990s.' Paper presented at a Conference on the Soviets in the Pacific in the 1990s, Australian National University, Canberra.

Robinson, Thomas W, 1987a, 'Soviet Policy in Asia: The Militry Dimension, '*Soviet Foreign Policy*, Proceedings of the Academy of Political Science, Vol 36, No 4.

Robinson, Thomas W, 1987b, 'The New Era in Sino-Soviet Relations,' *Current History*, Vol 86, No 521, pp 241-304.

Rusk, James, 1988, 'Defensive Diplomacy,' *Globe and Mail* (June 4), pp 1-3.

Scalapino, Robert A, 1987, 'Asia's Future,' *Foreign Affairs*, Vol 66, No 1 (Fall), pp 77-108.

Segal, Gerald, 1987, 'Sino-Soviet Detente: How Far, How Fast?' *The World Today*, Vol 43, No 5 (May), pp 87-91.

Simon, Denis, 1988, Review of *The Chinese Army After Mao* by Ellis Joffe, *Bulletin of the Atomic Scientists*, Vol 44, No 5 (June), pp 46-48.

Simon, Sheldon, 1987, 'Asean's Strategic Situation in the 1980s,' *Pacific Affairs*, Vol 60, No 1 (Spring), pp 73-93.

Soeya, Yoshihide, 1988, 'Japan's Defence Policy into the 1990s.' Paper presented at the Conference on Maritime Security and Arms Control in the Pacific Region, University of British Columbia, Vancouver.

Solomon, Richard, 1986, *The Soviet Far East Military Buildup*, Dover, Massachusetts: Auburn House Publishing Company.

Smucker, Philip, 1988, 'Disillusioned Vietnamese Beg, Steal To Survive,' *The Globe and Mail* (June 16), pA-10.

Suter, Keith, 1987, 'Australia's Defence Debate: The Dibb Report,' *RUSI Journal*, Vol 132, No 4(December), pp 55-62.

Thakur, Ramesh and Carlyle Thayer, 1987, *The Soviet Union as an Asian-Pacific Power: Implications of Gorbachev's 1986 Vladivostok Initiative*, Boulder, Colorado: Westview Press.

Tenorio, Vyvyan, 1988, 'Manila Employs New Tactics in War Against Rebels,' (June 16), pA-9.

Tritten, James J, 1988, 'Scenarios of Nuclear Escalation Dominance and Vulnerability.' Paper presented at the Conference on Maritime Security and Arms Control in the Pacific Region, University of British Columbia, Vancouver.

Vatikiotis, Michael and Rodney Tasker, 1988, 'Slow Boat to China,' *Far Eastern Economic Review*, Vol 140, No 20 (May 19), p42.

Walkom, Thomas 1988, 'Japan Quietly Builds Up Military Muscle,' *The Globe and Mail*, (June 4), pD-2-3.

Walsh, Mary, 1988, 'Improving Economy Fails to Solve Deep Problems,' *The Asian Wall Street Journal Weekly*, (May 16), p11.

Willey, Fay, 1988, 'Hands Across the Border,' *Newsweek*, (April 11), p53.

Xiang, Hoang, 1988, 'A View From Beijing,' *International Affairs*, Vol 3, pp 146-158.

Arms control in the North Pacific: Problems and prospects

ANDREW MACK
Head, Peace Research Centre, Australian National University, Canberra

Introduction

PROGRESS towards regional arms control in the North Pacific over the past 40 years has been virtually non-existent. There is no equivalent in the Pacific region to Europe's Mutual and Balanced Force Reduction (MBFR) talks, or to the Conference on Security and Co-operation in Europe (CSCE); and the negotiations which eventually led to the 1987 Intermediate-range Nuclear Forces (INF) Treaty initially ignored the Asian deployments of Soviet INF systems completely.

There are no extant North Pacific regional arms control agreements — like the Antarctica Treaty, the Treaty of Tlatelolco or the South Pacific Nuclear Free Zone (SPNFZ) Treaty — and there has been little regional interest in negotiating the only two regional nuclear-free zone proposals (for Northeast and Southeast Asia) which have been mooted from time to time. There are of course many arms control agreements to which regional powers are party — for instance, the Non-Proliferation Treaty and the Partial Test Ban Treaty (see Table 1 for details) — but these treaties are all global in scope and do not relate to any specifically regional security concerns. The fact that European security issues should have been the focus of so much attention from the arms control community, while those of the Pacific have received so little is unfortunate, since the need for arms control is demonstrably greater in the Pacific than in the more stable European region.

Issues

Why has progress towards regional arms control in the North Pacific been so lacking? There is no simple answer to this question, but there are a number of important differences between the North Pacific region and Europe which make progress towards arms control even more difficult to achieve in the former than in the latter.

Territorial disputes

In sharp contrast to Europe, there remain many outstanding territorial disputes in the North Pacific: between the Soviet Union and Japan; North and South Korea; Thailand and Laos; China and the Soviet Union; and China, Vietnam and the Philippines over islands in the South China Sea. They reflect in part the fact that there was no Yalta-type settlement in the region at the end of World War II, and in part the legacy of European and Japanese colonialism. As long as these disputes remain unresolved they provide a rationale for arms build-ups, a source of tension and sometimes overt conflict between the opposing parties. As such they constitute a barrier towards progress in force reductions and inhibit the negotiation of confidence building measures.

The North Pacific also, and again the contrast with Europe is obvious, encompasses a number of indigenous insurgencies — in Kampuchea, Burma, Thailand, Indonesia (in Timor and Irian Jaya) and the Philippines. Such conflicts can, and sometimes do, increase tension with neighbouring states, which in turn hampers any confidence building process.

Military build-ups

If limiting the growth of military expenditure is an important arms control objective, the need would seem to be greater in the North Pacific than in Europe. Military expenditure in the Far East as a whole (excluding China and the Soviet Union) grew at 4.4 per cent between 1982 and 1985 (compared with a growth rate of 2.9 per cent in the previous three years) and Asian states are buying some of the most modern weapon systems currently available. By contrast, the rate of growth in military expenditure in the European NATO (North Atlantic Treaty Organisation) countries during the first five years of the 1980s was well under 3 per cent.

The military build-up in the region has a variety of causes. At one level, it is an ongoing response to the so-called Nixon Doctrine which, in 1969, called on regional allies of the US to take increased responsibility for their own defence in regional conflicts. The US withdrawal from Vietnam also severely undermined regional confidence in America's reliability as an ally. As Singapore's First Deputy Prime Minister, Dr Goh Keng Swee, stated in 1979:

> None of the Asean states believes that it can depend on military intervention by the US should a communist power mount aggression either directly, or by proxy... The US does not appear to have recovered from the trauma of Vietnam.[1]

Lack of confidence in America's reliability as an ally, coupled with concern over the Soviet build-up in the region, the revolutionary victories in Indochina in the mid-1970s, and the subsequent Vietnamese invasion and occupation of Kampuchea, provided the rationale for increased military build-ups among the pro-Western states of the region. The rapidly growing economies of these states allowed them to sustain the increased defence outlays.

At the superpower level, the military build-up has been dramatic. On the Soviet side it includes a doubling of Soviet ground forces, a near-doubling of Soviet surface combatants and a six-fold increase in fighter aircraft since the mid-1960s.[2] Following a period of relative stagnation in the 1970s, there has been a corresponding build-up on the US side. In the late 1980s, the Soviet Union remains the predominant land power in Asia, while, notwithstanding the Soviet naval build-up, the US retains naval superiority. Both sides command formidable land-based air power.

The deployment of modern sea-launched, nuclear-armed, land-attack cruise missiles has particularly serious implications for regional security which are dealt with in detail later. The US Tomahawk[3] and its Soviet counterparts, the SS-N-21 and the SS-NX-24,[4] effectively transform attack submarines into quasi-strategic weapons platforms capable of dispatching missiles over 2,000 kilometres of ocean to strike deep into enemy territory. The land-atttack version of the Tomahawk has a range of 2,600 kilometres, and the SS-N-21 has a range of some 3,000 kilometres[5] — the same range as the Soviet 'strategic' SS-N-6 which is covered by Strategic Arms Limitation Talks (SALT) agreements. The range of other Soviet and American tactical naval nuclear delivery systems (with the exception of carrier-borne aircraft) is measured in tens or hundreds of kilometres.[6]

Although the sea-launched Tomahawk is virtually identical to the ground-launched cruise missile which is being destroyed under the terms of the INF treaty, neither it, nor its Soviet counterparts, are covered by any arms control agreements, nor are they the subject of any ongoing negotiations.

These missile deployments provide a good illustration of the so-called 'action-reaction' phenomenon where new force deployments on one side function to legitimise those on the other side — Tomahawk deployments were justified in part as a response to Soviet SS-20 deployments in the region.[7] Achieving force level reductions in such a context is extremely difficult. The 'action/reaction' process inevitably generates mutual suspicion, hindering the achievement of even modest confidence-building measures.

The 'action/reaction' phenomenon is not restricted to increases in force levels. It is also evident in the exercise patterns of the superpowers in the region. Both US and Soviet exercises in the region are growing larger and more provocative. Indeed, as Reinhard Drifte has observed, 'All military powers in the region are increasing the number and size of milirty manoeuvres and conducting them in closer proximity to the borders of the adversary'.[8] Just a few examples, drawn primarily from a recent study by William M Arkin, illustrate the highly provocative nature of naval operations in the Pacific during much of the 1980s:[9]

- September 1982, the US Navy holds its first multiple carrier battle group operation in the North Pacific since World War II. US ships come within 500 miles of the Soviet coast provoking, for the first time, simulated cruise missile attacks from Backfire bombers of Soviet naval aviation.
- 1982-83, the US Navy holds the first fullscale surface exercises in the Sea of Japan in 13 years and operates attack submarines in the Sea of Okhotsk for the first time ever.
- August 1984, the Soviets conduct a large scale amphibious landing on the Soviet-held island of Sakhalin. This is widely assumed to be a simulation of an attack on the northern Japanese island of Hokkaido.[10]
- November-December 1984, five US carrier battle groups take part in the largest peacetime exercise since World War II. Two carriers manoeuvre within 50 miles of the Soviet naval base at Vladivostok. This action, according to a Pentagon official, generated 'the most vigorous reaction' from the Soviets to an American deployment of this kind since World War II.[11]
- 1984, Japanese Self-Defence Forces (JSDF) aircraft scramble 944 times in response to provocations by Soviet military aircraft; in 1975 the JSDF scrambled only 305 times. In December 1987, a Soviet TU-16 bomber penetrates Japan's airspace. For the first time in the long history of Soviet provocations a Japanese fighter uses tracer ammunition to fire warning shots against the intruder.[12]
- April 1985, a Soviet task force stages the largest exercise ever conducted by the Soviet Navy in the Pacific.[13]
- August 1986, the US Navy begins regular carrier deployments in the Bering Sea.
- February 1986, the Soviet Navy carries out its first ever anti-carrier exercise in the South China Sea.
- September 1986, the US Navy conducts the largest naval operations ever in the Sea of Japan.
- January 1987, US Marines carry out an amphibious landing on Shemya Island in the Aleutians for the first time since World War II.

Superpower exercises with allies have also been getting bigger throughout the 1980s — this has been most obviously the case with the massive US/South Korean 'Team Spirit' exercises which by the second half of the 1980s were involving some 200,000 service personnel.[14] Japan, via the basing facilities it provides for the US, is becoming increasingly involved in these exercises.

In 1987, Pacific Command Commander-in-Chief, Admiral Hays, announced that the Soviets had 'recently conducted their first ever combined operations with the North Koreans'.[15] US/Japan strategic co-operation has also been growing steadily. In 1980, the Japanese Maritime Self-Defence Force took part in the biannual RIMPAC exercise for the first time. By 1986, the level of Japanese participation (relative to 1980) had increased three-fold in terms of personnel and more than four-fold in ship numbers, and Japanese submarines had participated for the first time. In 1981, US and Japanese forces took part in combined exercises for the first time. In October 1986 a total of 13,000 Japanese and American military personnel participated in 'Keen Edge 87'.

There is no doubt that each superpower sees the other's exercises as provocative, and that each responds to these perceived provocations by countermoves — which generate counter-countermoves and so forth. There is also little doubt that the tension and suspicion which such exercises generate are a major obstacle to confidence building.

Asymmetry in alliance and force structures

The nature of alliance structures in the North Pacific creates unique problems for regional arms control. In Europe, NATO and the Warsaw Pact provide institutional structures within which common alliance arms control policies can be worked out. In the Pacific, however, there are no equivalent organisations. Both the US and the Soviet Union have a series of bilateral relationships with their regional allies and the nature of those relationships hampers prospects for achieving even modest progress towards regional arms control. Suppose, for example, the US and the Soviet Union were to contemplate mutual regional force reductions. In formulating a negotiating position, the Soviets would be anxious to ensure that a force reduction agreement would not put the Soviet Union at a strategic disadvantage. They would therefore have to take seriously the possibility that a war with the US could see the Soviet Union fighting against Japan — and possibly China and South Korea as well. So the Soviets would wish Japanese forces (and possibly those of China and Korea) to be taken into account in any negotiations. Prudent US negotiators, on the other hand, would have to assume that, in a war with the Soviets, the US might have to fight alone. They would therefore resist any Soviet attempts to have Japanese (or other) friendly forces taken into account.

There are no obvious solutions to the problems generated by asymmetric threat perceptions. As Gerald Segal has recently noted:

> In Asia there is no simple balance of power... There are in fact *several* balances of power and needless to say this is a nightmare for arms control. Do the superpowers simply count each other's forces or must allowance be made for the Soviet threat to China? But then is China not potentially a threat to the United States as well? How are Soviet 'swing forces' counted: are they to be included in the Asian or European balance? And... do you count Vietnam as part of the Soviet camp? A messy picture, and one that essentially defies any region-wide arms control.[16]

In Europe, at least at the conventional level, this third party problem does not exist.[17]

Equally problematic is the radical asymmetry in force structure between the superpowers in the North Pacific. Even in Europe, where the force structures of the two alliances are more symmetrical, negotiations on force level reductions are hampered by the difficulty in working out agreed trade-offs for different weapons systems. In the North Pacific, the asymmetric force structure problem might seem to be almost insuperable. US strength in the region is primarily maritime, while the Soviets are relatively weak at sea yet very strong on land. Moreover, even if agreements in force level equivalence could be reached, the exercise would have been to a large degree pointless since approximately 90 per cent of Soviet land-forces in

Asia are not directed against the US at all, but against China. If Soviet land forces are to be significantly reduced in the region it is more likely to be via an agreement with China than with the US.

Regional versus global arms control agreements

It should not be assumed that regional arms control is always a goal worth pursuing. The arguments for negotiating exclusively European limits to INF systems, for example, never had much appeal in Asia. The description of the Soviet SS-20s as 'Euromissiles' when some 500 plus SS-20 warheads were targetted against Asia, was not only inaccurate but reflected yet again the marked Eurocentric bias of the Western arms control and security communities. Some Asian governments had feared that Soviet SS-20s negotiated out of Europe would finish up adding to deployments already in Soviet Asia. But attempting to resolve the problem of Asian INF deployments by negotiating a separate regional INF agreement would have been of little utility since the US did not deploy what were counted as INF systems in the Pacific theatre.[18] Thus there were no INF reductions which the US could have made in return for cuts in Soviet SS-20 deployments — a fact which would have given Moscow no incentive to negotiate a regional INF agreement. Given this, the US determination to hold out for a *global* rather than a regional approach to the INF negotiations was surely correct.

It is worth noting that, for Asia, the global INF agreement which was finally signed in Washington in December 1987, represented a very considerable concession from Moscow. It will eventually involve the removal of all the SS-20 missiles currently deployed in Soviet Asia — missiles which are capable of striking targets in China, Japan, Korea and even as far afield as the Philippines. The US will not be required to remove any nuclear weapon from the region in return. The Soviets will be able eventually to cover most of the targets previously covered by SS-20s with the new and relatively slow-flying SS-N-21 cruise missiles. These are, however, being deployed more slowly than originally envisaged by the US.

It is difficult to specify hard and fast rules for determining whether or not superpower arms control negotiations should be conducted globally or regionally, but a number of guidelines suggest themselves:

- If the negotiations have to do with force levels they should preferably be global — this is a principle already accepted (for obvious reasons) for nuclear strategic systems — that is, those with an intercontinental range.
- Negotiations should generally *not* be conducted at the regional level if the systems in question can be moved rapidly and easily from theatre to theatre (for example, Backfire bombers). Without this proviso, whatever force levels were negotiated in an agreement covering one theatre could rapidly be exceeded in a crisis by reinforcements from another theatre.[19]
- Regional negotiations on conventional force level reductions (for example, MBFRs) in Europe make sense in principle because NATO assumes that the Soviets (for a variety of reasons) do not have a 'swing strategy' for shifting forces

from the Far East TVD (theatre of military operations) to Europe in time of war. The most obvious candidates for force level reductions in the North Pacific are China and the Soviet Union (where some reductions have already taken place), and North and South Korea.

- Even where attempting to seek global arms control agreements makes more sense than regional agreements, regional *initiatives* for global agreements may still be worthwhile.
- Confidence building measures (CBMs) may be implemented regionally without the problems which regional force level reductions generate.

Operational arms control and confidence building measures.

There is much greater scope in the North Pacific for what is sometimes called 'operational arms control' than for force level reductions. 'Operational arms control' refers to those measures which seek to control particular military operations and deployments which are seen as destabilising — that is, likely to undermine policies of crisis avoidance and crisis control. Such measures are often referred to as confidence building measures — although in many cases they would be more aptly described as tension reducing measures, since it may be possible to reduce tension without increasing confidence. Not all CBMs involve constraints on military operations or deployments; many are simply concerned with increasing 'transparency' — that is, with the provision of information (for example, advance notification of exercises), or with improving communications (for example, the 'Hotline').

The most obvious precedent for a major operational arms control agreement in the North Pacific would be that which emerged in 1986 from the Stockholm Conference on Disarmaments in Europe (CDE), an offshoot of the Helsinki/Stockholm CSCE. For the past two decades the Soviets have been making arms control proposals for Asia which bear some resemblance to the Helsinki/Stockholm model. The first such proposal — for a 'Collective Asian Security System' — came from Soviet Leader Leonid Brezhnev in 1969. However it was widely seen in the region as designed simply to achieve '...the encirclement of China and promote the expansion of Soviet influence in Asia'.[20] Under Gorbachev, the Soviets have called for an Asian Security Conference, invoking the successful CSCE model as an example of what could be achieved in a confidence building forum. The Gorbachev proposal has been met in the region with less overt hostility than Brezhnev's Collective Asian Security idea.

However, for Japan, China and Korea, there are fundamental problems with the Helsinki/Stockholm model — namely that in Europe the CSCE negotiating process was predicated on the agreed assumption that all territorial as well as other major disputes between the participating states had essentially been resolved. This is certainly *not* the case in the North Pacific where sovereignty issues are a major source of conflict. Japan, for example, will not accept an arms control process which starts from the assumption that territorial disputes between regional states have been resolved. It is precisely such a dispute, involving the so-called Northern Territories, which constitutes the major source of conflict between Tokyo and Moscow.[21]

The same is true for China, which has *inter alia*, ongoing territorial disputes with the Soviet Union. In China's case, however, the concessions on the border dispute and the troop withdrawals from Mongolia which were announced by Gorbachev at Vladivostok in July 1986, together with the Soviet withdrawal from Afghanistan and progress in resolving the Kampuchea conflict, should permit Sino-Soviet relations to continue to improve and should also increase the chances that CBMs can eventually be successfully negotiated between the two countries.

North Korea has refused to agree to a number of US proposals for confidence building, not so much because the measures themselves were inherently objectionable, but because agreeing to negotiate them could be seen as *de facto* recognition of the legitimacy of the US presence in South Korea which the North rejects.

It is clear, however, that the Soviets now recognise that the CSCE model simply cannot be applied to Asia without modification. Thus although Mr Gorbachev had proposed a Stockholm-type conference for the Pacific in his much-reported speech in Vladivostok in 1986, a year later he was far more diffident about the idea. In an interview with the Indonesian newspaper *Merdeka* in July 1987, Gorbachev was asked whether he still supported the proposal. He replied:

> In Vladivostok I suggested a sort of working hypothesis or, better to say, an invitation to discussion. And the only reason I referred to Helsinki is that so far the world community has had no other experience of the kind. This does not mean, of course, that the European experience can automatically be transplanted to Asia and the Pacific.[22]

There is, however, no reason in principle why some modest regional confidence building measures — for instance, exchange of data on military forces or advance notification of exercises — should not be negotiated independently on the far more difficult question of territorial disputes. The need for such measures is clear — particularly in the vital area of open-ocean naval exercises to which the CSCE negotiations in Europe did not apply anyway.[23]

The superpowers and North Pacific arms control

Apart from proposing various CBMs between North and South Korea, the US has shown almost no interest in promoting arms control measures for the region. Washington has either ignored or dismissed various Soviet arms control proposals. Soviet overtures are seen as either lacking in seriousness and/or intended to disadvantage the US militarily. The US Arms Control and Disarmament Agency (ACDA) is not even *studying* proposals for regional arms control in the North Pacific.[24] And, in the critical area of maritime strategy, it is clear that the US Navy believes that naval superiority coupled with a forward offensive strategy is a more efficacious means of achieving US security objectives than naval arms control.

America's allies in the region have not sought to pressure the US into seeking regional arms control agreements — again in marked contrast to the situation in Europe. This is, in part, because regional governments share many US threat perceptions and security objectives, and in part because until recently they had little interest in arms control as a means of enhancing regional security. (One exception to this is the active support that Indonesia and Malaysia have given to the idea of creating a Southeast Asian Nuclear-Weapons-Free Zone).

In contrast to the US and its allies, the Soviets *have* advanced a considerable number of regional arms control proposals in addition to the Asian Security Conference proposal. But, at least until recently, these proposals have either been at such a high level of generality as to be virtually empty of meaning, or so obviously one-sided that they would have had little chance of being accepted, even as a basis for negotiation. Moscow's proposal for anti-submarine warfare (ASW)-free zones in the region is an example of the Soviets' frequently self-serving approach to arms control.

The Soviet Union seeks to protect the ballistic missile submarines which it deploys in the North Pacific by keeping them in highly defended bastions — the Sea of Japan and the Sea of Okhotsk. The US fears that should an arms control agreement banning ASW activities in the bastions be implemented, the Soviet attack submarines (SSNs), which currently protect Soviet missile submarines (SSBNs), could be redeployed to a wide variety of offensive tasks — including attacks on allied sea lines of communication (SLOCs).

The US protects its quieter (and therefore less easy to detect) missile submarines primarily by concealing them in the open ocean where relatively few US SSNs are deployed to protect them. The creation of ASW-free zones would thus release far greater numbers of Soviet SSNs to take part in offensive missions than it would release US SSNs. Not surprisingly the Soviet proposal has little appeal in Washington. This is not to say that the idea of ASW-free zones is without merit — safeguarding second-strike, submarine-based retaliatory capabilities has always been regarded as a *sine qua non* of strategic stability. But if the Soviets had wished their proposal to be taken seriously they should have indicated a willingness to make significant concessions in other areas. It has been suggested that the ASW-free zone proposal would be more equitable if the Soviets were prepared to make reductions in the number of SSNs they deploy. With an ASW-free zone in place, Soviet SSNs would no longer be needed to counter the US Hunter-Killer submarines hunting Soviet SSBNs and could therefore be reduced in number without upsetting the strategic *status quo ante*. But this option would have little appeal to the Soviets since they would be reluctant to believe that the US would *in fact* adhere to a commitment not to attack Soviet SSBNs in their sanctuaries in a war. Compliance with agreements on ASW-free zones is also extremely difficult to verify with confidence.

The ASW-free zone proposal fits into the wider Soviet approach to naval arms control which was outlined in a series of proposals in a letter from Andrei Gromyko to United Nations Secretary General Perez de Cuellar at the Conference on Disarmament in Geneva in 1984 and reiterated by Marshal Sergei Akromeyer, chief of staff of Soviet armed forces in September 1988.[25] The Soviet proposals included proscriptions on naval activities in areas of conflict or tension, proscriptions on great power long-range naval deployments for extended periods, withdrawal of ships equipped with nuclear weapons from parts of the Pacific, and limits on overseas naval bases.[26]

There is little doubt that many of these measures *would* reduce tensions but, in the case of the North Pacific, they would do so primarily by excluding the US Navy from large parts of the region. The various measures, if implemented, would constrain US naval operations very considerably; those of the Soviet Union hardly at all. This alone was reason enough for the US to reject the idea.

The problem of sea-launched cruise missiles

The deployment of long-range, land-attack, sea-launched cruise missiles (SLCMs) has a number of serious implications for regional security in the Pacific. The US is currently reluctant to negotiate limits on SLCMs. Officials cite difficulties in verifying differences between conventionally and nuclear-armed variants of the missile as a reason for resisting what would in effect be a naval INF agreement. But while verification difficulties are very real they do not necessarily pose an insuperable barrier to an agreement.[27] Nor do they constitute the only reason for the US lack of interest in reaching a SLCM agreement.

Currently the US has a lead both in numbers of deployed land-attack SLCMs and in SLCM technology, and a major reason for the lack of US enthusiasm for naval INF negotiations is that a treaty could negate the current US advantage. However the claim that limits on SLCMs would necessarily be counter to US security interests is unpersuasive.

The Navy's case for land-attack SLCMs — as a 'strategic reserve' and as a war-fighting theatre weapon — is made with some force. But Navy arguments rarely give much weight to the implications of SLCMs for strategic stability, nor do they consider how the balance of military advantage will be affected when the Soviets also deploy modern land-attack SLCMs in large numbers.

The Soviet SS-N-21 commenced deployment in 1988, and the supersonic SS-NX-24 may be operational by the end of the decade — in other words the Soviets are catching up. By the mid-1990s, according to British naval analyst Desmond Wettern, the Soviets may have deployed as many as 1,500 SS-N-21s (plus an unknown number of SS-N-24s).[28] The US, on the other hand, plans to produce less than 800 of the nuclear-armed land-attack variants of the Tomahawk. Furthermore, there is a greater number of militarily significant US targets in range of Soviet SLCMs based in the Pacific, than Soviet targets in range of Pacific-based US SLCMS. Thus, without an agreement banning or controlling land-attack SLCMs, the US could find itself both relatively more threatened and relatively more vulnerable than the Soviet Union in future.

Deployment of long-range land-attack SLCMs by both superpowers will provide the Soviets with a dual incentive to increase their long-range power-projection capability in order to:

(a) Attack the continental US with Soviet SLCMs; and
(b) Attack US SLCM platforms which threaten the Soviet Union from as far as 2,000 kilometres from the Soviet mainland.

It is not clear how this is in the US strategic interest. The inability of SLCM launches to be detected by early-warning satellites, the inadequacy of other early-warning systems, the lack of effective anti-SLCM defences, and the 'one shot kill' capability of the missiles themselves, also undermines crisis stability. Notwithstanding their long flight time, the relative undetectability and lethality of SLCMs makes them well suited to damage-limiting preemptive strike missions. This fact also makes the platforms that deploy them targets for preemption in turn under the same damage-limitation logic.

In other words, without limits on SLCM deployments there is a real possibility, not only that the US will lose its current lead in SLCM technology and deployments, but that crisis stability will have been undermined at the process. If the US takes a long term view then the case for controls, or even an outright ban, on long-range land-attack SLCMs is persuasive.

Grounds for optimism

Notwithstanding the general lack of US enthusiasm for regional arms control and the self-serving nature of many past Soviet proposals, there are some grounds for optimism.

First, as Douglas Stuart has argued,[29] the decline in bipolar hostility has created new opportunities for resolving old and destructive conflicts. It has, for example, enabled China to play a constructive role in concert with Japan and the US in attempting to lower tensions on the Korean peninsula.[30]

Second, there is growing interest within the region in *non-military* solutions to security problems. This arises, in part, because a considerable number of Asian security studies institutes, often with close ties to national governments, have been established over the past three decades and have '...gradually developed the institutional and intellectual infrastructure required for analysing and formulating substantive arms control initiatives'.[31] Interaction between scholars in the Asian institutes and comparable institutes in the US and Europe, has increased both Asian understanding of arms control and Western understanding of Asian security issues. Some governments within the region are paying greater attention to arms control than was previously the case, although few show much interest in *regional* arms control issues.

Third, if we take a historical perspective, there is no doubt that a number of regional security problems have become less salient over the past three decades. Relations between the Asean states, for example, have improved to such a degree that Asean is now sometimes described as a 'pluralistic security community' — a marked change from the hostile relationships of the 1950s and 1960s. Relationships between the two Koreas have improved somewhat during the past two decades and, since 1978, China has become less hostile towards a number of arms control measures — particularly the Non-Proliferation Treaty. However, China's current arms export drive — which has included the sale of long range ballistic missiles to Saudi Arabia — is causing considerable concern. Finally, and perhaps most importantly, there have been the Gorbachev proposals for enhancing regional security. Some of these, as noted earlier, have been self-serving, but others — the troop withdrawals from Mongolia and the concessions to China on the Amur River dispute announced at

Vladivostok in 1986 — are highly encouraging. The shift in Moscow's approach to *global* arms control questions, evident in a new willingness to make concessions on a wide variety of arms control issues (such as on-site verification of treaty compliance) is also an encouraging portent for regional arms control. It suggests that the Soviets may in future be increasingly willing to support arms control and confidence-building measures in the North Pacific which enhance *common* security in the region and not just the security of the Soviet Union.

Specific arms control measures

Given that there are signs in at least *some* areas that the prospects for arms control are improving, it may be helpful to examine a number of the most frequently discussed arms control proposals for the region.

Nuclear-weapons-free zones

Nuclear-weapons-free zones (NWFZs) are essentially CBMs. None of the extant zones (for the South Pacific, Latin America and the Antarctica) has required any reduction in nuclear force levels or the removal of nuclear weapons from the zone area. Indeed the remoteness of these zones from areas of superpower confrontation and nuclear deployments is a major reason for their succesful negotiation. The fact that the proposed North Pacific Zones (for Southeast and Northeast Asia) are located in areas of considerable strategic significance for both superpowers constitutes a major barrier to their implementation.

The most powerful opposition to the North Pacific NWFZ proposals has come from the US, which sees maritime NWFZs as a manifestation of the 'nuclear allergy' or 'Kiwi Disease'[32] which, if permitted to spread, would constrain the military operations of the US (a maritime power) more than those of the Soviet Union (a land power). The 'nuclear allergy' is also seen as posing a threat to the cohesion of western alliance systems.

The NWFZ proposals for the North Pacific also confront strong regional opposition. The Northeast Asian zone proposal would, if implemented, remove US nuclear weapons from South Korea without any corresponding reduction on the Soviet side. The Soviets do not, of course, have any nuclear weapons in North Korea. This is not to argue that seeking to remove nuclear weapons from the Korean peninsula is a bad idea, simply that the proposals for doing so have thus far been so one-sided that they were bound to be rejected. More serious proposals would have called not only for US nuclear weapons to be removed, but also for a parallel reduction in the offensively-deployed North Korean conventional forces against which the US nuclear weapons are supposedly deployed. Without such a *quid pro quo* the unilateral removal of US nuclear weapons could generate intense domestic pressures for South Korea to build its own bomb. After the Carter Administration announced its intention to remove US nuclear weapons from the peninsula in 1977, there were warnings from the South Korean government that it would consider the acquisition of an independent South Korean nuclear capability. Carter reversed the decision and the nuclear weapons are still in place.

The Southeast Asian NWFZ (SEANWFZ) proposed by Indonesia at the Committee on Disarmament in Geneva in 1982 has been consistently supported by only one other Asean country — Malaysia. Whatever theoretical merit SEANWFZ may have as a security-enhancing measure, it suffers from a fatal political defect. Less than half of the Asean countries which would be party to it presently support it. The states which oppose the idea (principally Singapore and Thailand) argue that unless Indochina is included in the zone area, SEANWFZ would disadvantage the US more than it does the Soviet Union. But Asean will not negotiate with Indochina until the Kampuchean conflict is resolved in such a way that the Asean states would again have a Kampuchean government in Phnom Penh which they recognise as legitimate and with which they could negotiate. But even overcoming this not inconsiderable political hurdle would still not assuage US concerns. The US would reject any agreement which it perceived as threatening its presence at the Clark and Subic Bay bases in the Philippines. Even if the Soviet facility at Cam Ranh Bay were equally affected by a SEANWFZ proposal, the US would still oppose the zone idea since the Soviet facilities in Vietnam are far less important strategically than the US facilities in the Philippines. The US has already made clear its opposition to any 'trade-off' proposal which would see the US lose its bases to the Philippines in exchange for the Soviets quitting Cam Rahn Bay. Over and above these immediate concerns would be the abiding US fear that the 'nuclear allergy' could spread, threatening the solidarity of regional alliance structures.

Force level reductions and 'tacit arms control'

There seems little dissent from the proposition that near-term reductions in force levels between the superpowers confront almost insuperable difficulties arising from the nature of regional alliance structures, from the asymmetries in superpower forces in the region, and from the quite different missions of those forces.

This is not to say that reductions in force levels in the region are impossible, simply that they are unlikely to take place between Moscow and Washington in the near future. Force reductions between the Soviet Union and China are, however, a real possibility. This is so despite the fact that Beijing has persistently rejected Soviet proposals for formal MBFR-type negotiations on the grounds that the imbalance of forces had first to be rectified by unilateral Soviet cuts.

In fact forces have already been reduced along the Sino-Soviet border. Between 1984 and 1985, China's military strength along the border was cut from 74 to 66 divisions, while the level of readiness of Soviet forces has been reduced very considerably since 1976.[33] Compared with the absence of progress after many, many years of the MBFR negotiations in Europe, the Sino-Soviet border reductions are a considerable achievement. Such 'tacit arms control' is both an effect, and in turn a cause, of improved security relationships. It is, unfortunately, a little-studied process. Tacit arms control has the advantage that, if a state chooses (for whatever reason) to make unilateral cuts in its force levels — as China has done — its action cannot be presented as having resulted either from weakness or coercive bargaining by its opponents.

Other examples of tacit arms control include the restraint which both superpowers exercised in providing advanced weapons systems to North and South Korea in the 1970s. This mutual restraint continued until the US commenced selling F-4 and F-5 fighters to the South in the early 1980s; F-16 sales followed in the mid-1980s. The Soviets responded by selling MiG-23s to the North.

Unilateral restraint can even operate in war — both China and Vietnam, for example, eschewed the use of airpower in their 1979 border war.

The possibility of informal restraint and unilateral arms control initiatives is particularly important in Asia where there is neither much interest nor expertise in the formal European approach to arms control.

MBFR-type talks are also possible in principle between the two Koreas, but are unlikely to take place without a real decrease in tension between the two sides. However, a return to the tacit understanding which existed between Moscow and Washington prior to the 1980s not to supply advanced weapons systems to the opposing sides would be a step in the right direction. In addition the changing military balance in favour of the South may remove one major objection Seoul has always offered to the MBFR-type proposals advanced by Pyongyang in the past — namely that any agreement risked freezing a military imbalance in the North's favour.

CBMs for crisis prevention and crisis stability

'Operational arms control' seeks to promote tension reduction and confidence building. It seeks above all to create a political climate which lessens the chance of crises occurring and which enhances crisis stability — which reduces the incentives to go to war in those crises which cannot be prevented. The difference between measures designed to enhance crises prevention and those designed to strengthen crisis stability is considerable. The former would include *political* CBMs — for example, statements of peaceful intent and non-aggression pacts — such as that agreed on between China and Burma in 1960, or the Treaty of Peace and Friendship signed by China and Japan in 1978. 'No first use' pledges and those clauses in NWFZ treaties which require nuclear weapon states not to make nuclear threats against treaty states are also examples of political CBMs. The Soviets, who believe that crisis avoidance is more important than crisis control, have long stressed political CBMs.

The problem with political CBMs is that when they are most needed — that is, when suspicions and tensions are high — they are least likely to be believed. When suspicion and tensions are low, political CBMs are far more credible — but also far less necessary.

CBMs intended to increase crisis stability (as against crisis avoidance) aim to minimise the possibility of surprise attack, and reduce the incentives for pre-emption in crises and escalation in war. They include such minimal steps as exchanges of information designed to increase the 'transparency' of rival force postures. Without reasonably accurate knowledge of an opponent's force levels, prudent 'worst case' defence planners will tend to assume the worst of that opponent's intentions and that his military production lines are working at full capacity. The quite unjustified US concerns about 'bomber gaps' and 'missile gaps' in the 1960s provide a classic example of 'worst case' thinking. They led to an unwarranted US strategic build-up in the 1960s and indicate how lack of 'transparency' may have a destabilising effect.

'Transparency' can be increased co-operatively — by open publication of data on defence manpower and hardware levels; or unilaterally — via so-called 'national technical means' of surveillance, for instance, satellites. More intrusive *information measures* would involve exchanges of observers to monitor force levels, the output of military factories and the conduct of military exercises.

Notification measures can also help assuage suspicion and build confidence. These include the notification of military exercises — which may help indicate that the exercises are not preparations for aggression — and notification of weapon tests.

A third type of CBM, the *communication measure*, is designed to increase communications between the opposing parties — particularly during a crisis. The 'Hotline' agreement of 1963, the improved 'Hotline' agreement of 1971, and the recent US/Soviet agreement to establish nuclear risk reduction centres are obvious examples. According to Masashi Nishihara, a 'hotline' was set up between North and South Korea in 1971 — a rare example of an European-type CBM being established in Asia.[34] More recently, following the KAL 007 tragedy, an agreement was signed between the Soviet Union, the US and Japan which is intended to minimise the probability of such an event recurring.

Most CBM proposals in the North Pacific have focussed on Korea. For example, in April 1984 the US proposed to North Korea:

(1) Restoration of the non-military character of the demilitarised zone (DMZ) by pulling forces back and removing heavy weapons from the area;
(2) Regular inspection by teams composed of neutral nations to ensure the non-military character of the DMZ;
(3) Prior notification by the North as well as the South of military exercises; and
(4) Mutual assignment of observers to such exercises.[35]

None of these proposals, nor any of the large number of counter-proposals from the North Korean side, has thus far made much headway, primarily because CBMs of this type require a certain minimum level of confidence between the parties. In Korea, where enhancing deterrence is still accorded top priority, such confidence is lacking. In the long term, however, there seems no reason in principle why the type of process which eventually led to a quasi-detente between the two Germanies could not also take place in Korea.[36]

More far-reaching CBMs include those *deployment measures* which proscribe or restrict *types* of weapons from being deployed or which place limits on weapons deployment (or non-deployment) in particular areas. Demilitarised zones, battlefield nuclear-weapons-free zones and anti-submarine warfare free zones, are some frequently discussed examples. The physical separation of forces which such zone proposals involve, increases warning time, makes surprise attack more difficult and decreases the risk of minor clashes occurring. (Such clashes, which can easily escalate out of control, are more likely to arise when forces are in close proximity). The 1972 US/Soviet Agreement on Prevention of Incidents on the High Seas, is an example of another type of *deployment measure*. The aim of this latter agreement was to reduce the number of incidents between rival navies engaged in close surveillance of each other's operations and exercises. But although the agreement is widely considered to have been a success[37] there were still some 30 to 40 'potentially dangerous incidents' between US and Soviet naval vessels in 1982-83.[38] The increasingly provocative nature of current superpower exercises in the Pacific is likely to increase the risk that more of such incidents will take place. Expansion of the 1972 Incidents at Sea agreement to the Pacific region was suggested by Gorbachev in his speech at Krasnoyarsk on September 16, 1988.

Advocacy of CBMs is predicated on the assumption that the real risk of war arises from inadvertence rather than premeditated aggression. Given that assumption, the task of CBMs is to increase the flow of information between the opponents in order to reduce the level of prejudice and suspicion. The better the information, the more apparent the non-aggressive intentions of the other party will become. The removal of mutual fears of aggressiveness removes the rationale for preventive and pre-emptive war.

One obvious problem with the CBM approach is that the underlying assumption about the basically benign intentions of the other party may be wrong. If the other party *is* bent on aggression, attempts to gain his confidence will, at best, be a waste of time. Worse, they may amount to appeasement — which was Chamberlain's painful lesson at Munich. If unprovoked aggression is a real threat, then the central security task must be that of enhancing deterrence. This in turn will require the enhancement of warfighting strategies.[39] It is thus easy to see how *in certain circumstances* some CBMs will be perceived as, at best, irrelevant; at worst, dangerous. It is this factor above all others which makes the achievement of a CBM regime between the superpowers in the North Pacific so difficult. Nowhere is this more evident than in the case of Maritime Strategy in the region.

The Maritime Strategy in the Pacific

Both superpowers have created offensively oriented force structures and warfighting strategies designed to enhance deterrence and fight wars effectively should deterrence nevertheless fail. Offensive force structures and strategies do not, in themselves, indicate an aggressive intent. But although such force structures may be intended only to be used *in response* to aggression, they can also be used *for* aggression. Prudent 'worst case' defence planners in rival states who are confronted with capabilities that *could* be used for aggression must take seriously the possibility that they *would* be used for that purpose. It is basically for this reason that offensive force structures and strategies almost invariably generate suspicion and tension, as well as create incentives for pre-emption in crises and escalation in war. Offensive force structures and strategies are characteristic of an approach to security which subverts confidence building and generates what Robert Jervis has called 'security dilemmas' — wherein an increase in one nation's security decreases the security of other nations.[40]

The US Maritime Strategy is a classic example of an offensively oriented strategy designed to enhance deterrence. It is based on the premise that if the Soviets can be made to believe that the US will prevail in a war, they will be deterred from starting one in the first place. And if war cannot be prevented it is clearly better to win than lose. The Maritime Strategy plays a particularly important role in the Pacific theatre.[41]

The US Navy argues that in order to prevail, in order to force the Soviets to terminate war on terms favourable to the US, it must deploy and use its forces in a highly offensive manner. The Maritime Strategy is thus designed to 'go for the jugular', to 'bottle up' the Soviet fleet before it can surge out to sea, to 'kill the archer before he releases his arrows' and to win 'the battle of the first salvo'. Offence is seen as the best form of defence and to prevail, it is necessary to 'carry the fight to the enemy'. The Maritime Strategy is seen as epitomising 'the best tradition of naval warfare's offensive spirit'.[42]

The military advantages which the offensive operations of Maritime Strategy are alleged to offer have been challenged by John Mearsheimer and others.[43] But most of the critical commentary has dealt with the North Atlantic rather than with the Pacific, so it is perhaps worth making some points which relate in particular to the latter theatre.

First, the defence of allied SLOCs is less important in the Pacific than the Atlantic simply because there are no massive allied land forces which would need to be supplied and reinforced during a war in the Pacific theatre. Moreover, over the last several decades there has been a proliferation of cargo ships (most under flags of convenience), without a concomitant increase in numbers of submarines available to attack those ships. Commerce warfare is, therefore, much less likely to make a decisive military impact on any future conflict than it did during World War II. In commerce warfare, *numbers* of submarines are critical and by the mid-1990s the Soviets will have less than 60 SSNs and diesel submarines available *globally* for both SLOC interdiction and attacking US SSBNs — not enough to cut the flow of vital supplies along allied SLOCs.[44] According to an Atlantic Council study published in 1979, 'only about 12 submarines, seven of them obsolescent, would be available for the interdiction of ports and sea lines of communication in the entire Pacific and Indian Oceans'.[45] According to Desmond Ball, the Soviets would have 14 SSNs for SLOC interdiction in the Pacific.[46]

There are also many opportunities in the Pacific for evasive routing of shipping in order to evade detection — and thus interdiction. The prospects for avoiding detection would be further enhanced by the destruction of Soviet ocean surveillance and target acquisition assets. Such assets would very probably be attacked or jammed at an early stage in any superpower confrontation. Allies' ASW assets could then be concentrated around the 'focal areas' of major ports — these areas would become the most likely hunting grounds for Soviet SSNs once Soviet open-ocean surveillance capabilities had been degraded. US and allied resort to such 'defensive sea control' tactics would be facilitated by the fact that US ASW assets would then be operating in friendly waters either out of range of Soviet combatants or defended from them. 'Offensive sea control' — keeping Soviet SSNs pinned down in the bastions of the Seas of Japan and Okhotsk — places US ASW assets at a far greater risk and risks escalation by threatening Soviet SSBNs.

Second, the Maritime Strategy is predicated on the assumption that allies will co-operate in its execution. But if the US were involved in a conflict in Europe and decided to widen the war by making the Soviet Union's Pacific bases targets for 'horizontal escalation' it is by no means certain that Japan (which would inevitably be involved) would co-operate. The US is committed to the defence of Japan; Japan is under no similar obligation to aid US military operations against a third party.

Third, the strategy of 'horizontal escalation' assumes that the Soviets can and will swing forces between their Far East TVD and other theatres. But this assumption ignores or underestimates the importance of a number of highly salient facts. Thus:

- The Soviets may choose, like Churchill in World War II, to pursue a 'Europe first' strategy, in which case the US will have deployed assets against the Far East while the Soviets concentrate their capabilities on the primary theatre. *Or* the Soviets might 'horizontally escalate' in turn. If the US attacked Soviet Pacific bases during a war in the Gulf region, for example, the Soviets might respond by attacking Berlin.
- It is difficult to 'swing' ground forces back and forwards between the Soviet Far East and European theatres. Moreover, the interdiction of the two highly vulnerable rail links between East and West would be a less costly means of preventing forces being 'swung' between theatres than attacking Soviet bases in the Far East TVD, and one less fraught with risks of escalation. Attempting to move men and material between the two theatres by sea would be virtually impossible in wartime — apart from being extremely slow.
- Quite apart from being difficult to move, Soviet Far East forces are 'pinned' to a large degree by their missions in the region. Those forces which *can* be easily swung from theatre to theatre — like the Backfire bombers — can be kept in the Far East theatre by the mere *threat* of attack. Such a threat could be provided by a carrier battle group on station in the Pacific just out of range of the Backfires.[47]

In other words the Maritime Strategy tactic of 'horizontal escalation' is predicated on assumptions about military efficacy which are highly questionable. But the more important issue from an arms control perspective is the Maritime Strategy's potential impact on crisis avoidance and crisis stability. This is almost wholly negative.

The Maritime Strategy and arms control

The logic which underpins the Navy's offensive strategy is antithetical to the core objectives of 'operational arms control' for the following reasons.

First, the US has long encouraged the Soviet Union to put more of its strategic nuclear warheads at sea on the grounds that this is more stabilising.[48] The tactic of attacking Soviet missile submarines in their defensive North Pacific bastions which the Maritime Strategy prescribes, not only negates this stability-enhancing objective, but also poses real risks of nuclear escalation.[49]

Second, 'horizontal escalation' makes the North Pacific (particularly Japan) hostage to instabilities in other parts of the world. A longtime goal of arms control has been to reduce the incentives for escalation; the advocates of 'horizontal escalation' see strategic virtue in precisely the opposite. Moreover, whereas US policy in the past has sought to contain conflicts, the Maritime Strategy seeks to expand them globally.

Third, the offensive thrust of the Martime Strategy *must* appear to Soviet defence planners to be highly threatening. If this is doubted consider how the US would respond if major battle groups of Soviet naval combatants were to be deployed in offensive exercises 50 nautical miles from US naval bases at San Diego or Bangor. There can be no doubt that the US would find such exercises both provocative and threatening. Yet the US has practised just such exercises 50 nautical miles offshore from Vladivostok, the Soviet Union's major naval base in the Pacific.

Clearly if a nation adopts an offensively oriented strategy like the Maritime Strategy — or Soviet *blitzkrieg* tactics against NATO on the Central Front in Europe — its military commanders will wish to practise that strategy. They will, therefore, be opposed to any operational arms control measures which seek to prevent realistic training exercises simply on the grounds that such exercises are 'provocative'. Enhancing deterrence, they will argue, requires the enhancement of warfighting capabilities and the 'realistic' practice of the wartime missions of those capabilities. It is primarily for this reason that superpower military exercises in the North Pacific have become bigger, broader in scope and more provocative throughout the 1980s.

The US Navy opposes operational arms control precisely because it *would* constrain exercises which are perceived as essential to warfighting and hence to deterrence. The Navy made its opposition to naval arms control clear to the UN experts' group preparing a report on naval arms control in 1984-85. Navy hostility to any limitations on its global role is well known and not new. In 1971, when the Nixon Administration was developing its proposal for an agreement on incidents at sea it was made clear to the Soviets that the US was:

> ...not willing to discuss any type of limitations upon submarine operations, any type of distance limitations, or any type of limitations on operations.[50]

The logic of the Navy's case against operational arms control is clear. If CBMs constrain exercises which are deemed necessary to enhance warfighting, and if enhanced warfighting is seen as necessary to maintain and bolster deterrence, then it follows that CBMs can actually undermine deterrence and in so doing increase the risk of aggression. In 1987, US Secretary of State George Shultz explicitly warned that 'so-called confidence-building measures' weaken deterrence. Shultz invoked the spectre of 1930s appeasement as a reason to reject such measures.[51]

The case against CBMs is, however, predicated on a highly questionable assumption. Proponents of the Maritime Strategy assume what needs to be demonstrated — namely that unprovoked Soviet aggression is the most important security problem which the US confronts, and that deterrence therefore needs enhancing. But no persuasive evidence has been produced to show that this is the case. When the Navy's conventional wisdom is challenged, which happens rarely, the traditional response is that the Soviet threat in the Pacific has grown. The evidence cited for the existence of this allegedly increased threat is the Soviet Union's massive military build-up in the Pacific over the past 20 years.

The facts of Soviet build-up are not in dispute, but they do not necessarily indicate an increased threat of aggression. If Soviet forces are allocated to the various missions they would have to fulfil in wartime, there is *no* excess of Soviet capability over wartime requirements. Indeed most naval analysts believe that, compared with the US, the Soviets are relatively weak in the North Pacific — which is precisely why Soviet Asia is seen by the US Navy as an ideal target for 'horizontal escalation'.

It is also worth noting that Soviet conventional naval forces in the Pacific are not really suited to, or intended for, long-range power projection in the region, or for attacking the home ports of the US, or for mounting major invasions against regional powers. Notwithstanding its increased blue-water capability, the Soviet Navy remains primarily configured for what are essentially defensive missions — protecting Soviet missile submarines in their bastions and defending against US attacks on the Soviet homeland.[52] According to the US Defence Intelligence Agency, the primary missions of the Soviet Pacific Fleet are 'to protect the Pacific flank of the Soviet Union, to help secure the Delta SSBN launch areas and provide limited interdiction'.[53] Moreover according to highly placed Australian defence sources the amount of time that Soviet major combatants spend 'out of area' — that is, away from the seas of Japan and Okhotsk and the waters around the Kamkatcha peninsula — has been halved over the past three years.[54]

In other words, there is at least a *prima facie* case for seeing the core rationale for the Soviet build-up in the North Pacific as being defensive. There is certainly room for debate on this question, but there is in fact a more compelling reason for doubting the proposition that the Western deterrent posture in the Pacific needs enhancing.

If we assume that both the Soviets and the Americans are rational — at least in the minimal sense of seeking to avoid unwinnable wars — then it would seem to follow that the risk of *unprovoked* aggression by one superpower against the other, or its allies, is very low. The very existence of nuclear weapons, the ability of each side to destroy the other no matter which strikes first, the fear that it may be impossible to prevent either a conventional conflict crossing the nuclear threshold, or a limited nuclear war from escalating to the holocaust level — all of these factors combine to provide the necessary and sufficient conditions for what has been called 'existential deterrence'.[55]

In fact almost all strategic analysts concur that the most likely cause of a superpower war is *not* unprovoked aggression, but a crisis which gets out of hand and draws the superpowers into a confrontation which they had not sought. As former US Chief of Naval Operations and architect of the Maritime Strategy Admiral James D Watkins has put it, '...if war with the Soviets ever comes, *it will most likely result from a crisis which escalates out of control*'.[56] Captain Linton Brooks, another leading proponent of the Maritime Strategy, has argued that the most plausible path to war would be, 'A modern equivalent of the downward spiral of August 1914 during a European crisis, perhaps one growing out of an extra-European situation...'[57] Insofar as these claims are true, it follows that the *primary* security task should not be to enhance deterrence against the minimal risk of unprovoked aggression, but rather to reduce the risks of inadvertent war. In the nuclear age the most salient lesson of history derives not from Hitler, Munich and appeasement, but from Sarajevo and the outbreak of World War I.

Here we confront a fundamental problem. Since deterrence strategies are designed to prevent deliberate, premeditated aggression, they are — by definition, almost — of little utility in preventing unintended wars. But the real danger with offensively oriented strategies designed to deter aggression is that they may actually *increase* the risk of war by inadvertence. Such strategies and their associated force postures undermine strategic stability by generating incentives to preempt in crises and to escalate once hostilities commence. Their tendency to increase mutual fear and suspicion also constitutes a major barrier to achieving far-reaching confidence building and other arms control measures.

The Navy seems particularly insensitive to the risks of instability inherent in the Maritime Strategy. Asked if the controversial tactic of attacking Soviet missile submarines at the outset of a conventional war was destabilising, former US Navy Secretary, John Lehman replied, 'Maybe, maybe not. That's for the Soviets to decide'.[58] And when Congressional Research Service analyst Ronald O'Rourke questioned members of the Strategic Concepts Group (OP-603) — 'the Navy Office responsible for articulating and defending the Navy's maritime strategy'[59] — their responses consistently downplayed the risks involved. Thus it was claimed that:

(a) The Soviets would not see US strategic ASW operations against their SSBNs as provocative; and
(b) If they *did* see these operations as provocative they would not respond with nuclear weapons.[60]

In O'Rourke's account these Navy strategies go to great lengths to deny that extraordinary risks may be involved in the anti-SSBN strategy. They also appeared unaware of a fundamental contradiction which the strategy contains.

The ASW campaign against Soviet SSBNs is intended to shift the nuclear 'correlation of forces' against the Soviet Union so that resort to nuclear weapons becomes a less attractive option for Moscow.[61] This in turn is supposed to enhance the prospects for war-termination on 'favourable terms'[62] to the US — that is, it is supposed to increase the chances that the Soviets will lose. In other words the Navy is arguing that the effects of its anti-SSBN strategy would make a major contribution to the defeat of the Soviets, while simultaneously claiming that anti-SSBN operations constitute neither a provocation nor any incentive for the Soviets to use nuclear weapons in response.[63] Either claim *could* be true, but it simply defies credibility to argue that both can be true at the same time.

Navy enthusiasm for offensive operations and the persistent rejection of more defensively oriented strategies, would seem to derive more from what Jack Synder has called 'the ideology of the offensive' and Stephen Van Evera has described as the 'cult of the offensive' than from a dispassionate assessment of alternatives.[64] But whatever the reason for the commitment to offensive strategies there is no doubt that it constitutes a formidable barrier to naval arms control in the region.

Conclusion

As the foregoing discussion will have made abundantly clear, achieving progress towards arms control in the North Pacific will not be easy. But however far one believes that an arms control process could or should go, Barry Blechman's recent proposal for the creation of an International Commission on the North Pacific should surely be welcomed.[65] The commission would be made up of delegations representing the interested states and have a small international staff. Dr Blechman argues that:

> Establishment of the commission would represent a critically important first step in the establishment of an arms control regime for the North Pacific. By agreeing to establish the organisation, participating governments would be signalling their desire to enhance their mutual security and reduce the risk of conflict. The commission would provide an institutional backbone for the entire arms control process, as well as an organisational vehicle for developing the mechanisms of potential future arms control agreements. The commission would provide a neutral forum for the discussion and negotiation of mutually-acceptable confidence-building measures and, conceivably, other types of arms control arrangements. It could also be used for the airing of grievances, complaints, or differences in interpretation of agreements in force.[66]

Such a forum would, in other words, create for the first time an institutional structure within which a wide range of security problems and possible arms control solutions to those problems could be explored in detail.

In the short term it may be possible to negotiate some very limited CBMs — an agreement on exchanges of military data or on the advance notification of military exercises, for example. Further modest progress may be possible if the political will is present and if political relationships within the region do not deteriorate. In the longer term, if there is increasing appreciation within the region that inadvertent war between the superpowers is the fundamental security problem and that some current military policies exacerbate that problem, then quite far-reaching measures of operational arms control could eventually be implemented.

NOTES

1. Cited in Michael Richardson, 'The influence on the Asean community of Australian-American security relations', *Australian Outlook* (December 1984) p 196.
2. See Paul Dibb, 'The Soviet Union as a Pacific Military Power', *Working Paper No 81* (Strategic and Defence Studies Centre, Australian National University, Canberra, August 1984), pp 7-9.

3. By the end of fiscal year 1989 Tomahawk will be deployed on 104 US naval combatants, submarines as well as surface vessels. The number will rise to 198 when deployment is completed. 758 of the 3,994 Tomahawks will be nuclear-armed.
4. Deployment of the SS-N-21 commenced in early 1988. The SS-NX-24 is currently in an advanced stage of development. An air-launched version of the SS-N-21, the AS-15, has been operational for some time. The US Tomahawk is deployed on both surface combatants and submarines; the Soviet SLCMs are only deployed on submarines.
5. US Department of Defence, *Soviet Military Power 1987* (US Government Printing Office, Washington D C, 1987), p 38.
6. The longest range US naval tactical nuclear weapon after the Tomahawk is the SUBROC with a range of 55 kilometres; the longest range Soviet systems after the SS-N-21 and SS-NX-24, are the SS-N-12 and SS-N-19 which both have a range of 550 kilometres.
7. The 'action/reaction' process is rarely the simple tit-for-tat process depicted in some of the models of arms race dynamics of the 1960s. The interactive process is much more diffuse and complex than the models suggest but real enough nevertheless.
8. Reinhard Drifte, 'Arms control and the superpower balance in East Asia' in Gerald Segal (ed), *Arms Control in Asia* (Macmillan, London, 1987), p 23.
9. William M Arkin, 'The nuclear arms race at sea', *Neptune Papers* No 1 (October 1987), p 2 and p 14.
10. Drifte, 'Arms control and the superpower balance in East Asia', p 23.
11. Cited in Derek da Cunha, 'The rationale for the build-up of Soviet naval power in the Pacific', unpublished MSS, Department of International Relations, Australian National University, June 1987.
12. *Ibid*, p 24. On the TU-16 incident see Robert Horiguchi, 'Soviet snooper finds a sting in the air', *Pacific Defence Reporter* (March 1988).
13. *Ibid*, p 40, footnote 11.
14. US participation in 'Team Spirit' has levelled off over the past few years and there is some evidence that during the late 1980s both sides are being more circumspect in their exercises. The highly provocative behaviour of the early and mid-1980s has apparently been curbed.
15. Arkin, 'The nuclear arms race at sea', p 14.
16. Gerald Segal, 'Introduction' in Gerald Segal (ed), *Arms Control in Asia*, pp 4-5.
17. The problem has, of course, been very evident in the past with respect to nuclear arms control negotiations — the Soviets having argued that French and British strategic systems be taken into account in US/Soviet negotiations. The US has successfully denied the Soviet demand.
18. Sea-launched cruise missiles do not count as INF systems even though they are virtually identical to the ground-launched cruise missile (GLCMs) which *do* count as INF systems, and air-launched cruise missiles (ALCMs) which count as *strategic* nuclear systems.
19. Even with systems that can be switched rapidly from theatre to theatre there may be an argument for such an agreement as a confidence building measure. Most nuclear-weapons-free zone proposals are of this type.
20. Drifte, 'Arms control and the superpower balance in East Asia', pp 30-31.

21. The dispute is over four islands between Hokkaido and Sakhalin occupied by the Soviet Union and claimed by Japan. The islands, which straddle the eastern exit from the Sea of Okhotsk where Soviet missile submarines are based, have considerable strategic significance.

22. 'Mikhail Gorbachev's Replies to Questions Put by the Indonesian Newspaper *Merdeka*', July 21, 1987 (Novosti Press Agency Publishing House, Moscow, 1987), p 10.

23. The Soviets have already offered such a data exchange in Europe.

24. According to Michael Guhin, Counsellor of the US Arms Control and Disarmament Agency at a seminar hosted by the Strategic and Defence Studies Centre, Australian National University, Dec 16, 1987.

25. See Michael Parks, 'Soviets offer plan to avoid naval clash', *The Daily Yomiuri* (Sept 7, 1988).

26. Cited in Drifte, 'Arms control and the superpower balance', p 32.

27. See Rose E Gottemoeller, *Land Attack Cruise Missiles* (Adelphi Paper No 226, International Institute of Strategic Studies, London, Winter 1987/8) p 33 for description of some of the verification techniques which might be employed.

28. Desmond Wettern, 'Sub-launched cruise missiles', *Journal of Defence and Diplomacy* (November 1987), p 15.

29. Douglas Stuart, 'The international context of Asian arms control' in Segal (ed), *Arms Control in Asia*, p 172.

30. The decline in bipolar hostility has also created some new problems. China's rapprochement with Japan, symbolised by the 1978 Sino-Japanese Peace and Friendship Treaty, caused considerable alarm in the Soviet Union and led to an accelerated build-up of Soviet forces in the disputed Northern Territories — a build-up which has caused tension between Tokyo and Moscow.

31. Stuart, 'The international context of Asian arms control', p 172.

32. So called because of New Zealand's anti-nuclear policy which led to the rupture in the ANZUS alliance in 1985.

33. See Gerald Segal, 'Arms control and Sino-Soviet relations' in Segal (ed), *Arms Control in Asia*, pp 44-45.

34. Masashi Nishihara, *East Asian Security and the Trilateral Countries* (New York University Press, New York, 1985), p 67.

35. Cited in Drifte, 'Arms control and the superpower balance in East Asia', p 35.

36. See Hans Gunter Brauch, 'Germany and Korea — Changes in the international system and implications for both divided countries: Assessments and policy prospects for the 1980s' in Chong-ki Choi (ed), *Peace and Stability in Northeast Asia: Achieving International Order Without Violence* (Korean Institute of International Studies, Seoul, 1985).

37. See Sean M Lynne-Jones, 'A quiet success for arms control: Preventing incidents at sea', *International Security* (Spring 1985).

38. See 'Superpowers manoeuvring for supremacy on high seas' *Washington Post*, April 4, 1984. Prior to the treaty the rate of incidents was more than 100 a year.

39. It does not, however, follow that such warfighting strategies have to be offensively oriented. The question of which is the most efficacious way of actually fighting a war is not one that can be answered *a priori*. For a discussion of this issue see Andrew Mack, 'Defence versus offence: The Dibb Report and its critics', *Australian Outlook* (April 1987).

40. See Robert Jervis, 'Co-operation under the security dilemma', *World Politics* (January 1978).

41. The following discussion of the Maritime Strategy draws on Andrew Mack, 'The Soviet-American Conflict', in M Alagappa (ed), *In Search of Peace: Confidence Building and Conflict Reduction in the Pacific* (Institute of Strategic and International Studies, Kuala Lumpur, 1988).

42. Jan Breemer, 'US Maritime Strategy: A reappraisal', *Naval Forces*, No 8 (1987), p 73.

43. See John J Mearsheimer, 'A strategic misstep: The Maritime Strategy and deterrence in Europe', *International Security* (Fall 1986) and Joshua M Epstein, 'Horizontal escalation: Sour notes of a recurrent theme', *International Security* (Winter 1983-84).

44. Karl Lautenschlager, 'The submarine in naval warfare, 1901-2001', *International Security* (Winter 1986-87), p 135.

45. Paul Dibb, 'The Soviet Union as a Pacific military power', *Working Paper No 81* (Strategic and Defence Studies Centre, Australian National University, Canberra, August 1984), p 11.

46. See Desmond Ball, 'Some implications of 50 per cent reductions in strategic nuclear-forces for sea-based systems' (Strategic and Defence Studies, Australian National University, June 1988) p 9.

47. See Epstein, 'Horizontal escalation', for an extended critique of many of the assumptions underpinning 'horizontal escalation'.

48. Since submarines are relatively invulnerable they do not provide tempting targets for pre-emptive attacks from the enemy and because submarine missiles are still relatively inaccurate they cannot be used for pre-emptive strikes against 'hardened' targets in the enemy's homeland. The combination of submarine invulnerability and lack of submarine missile accuracy provides incentives for *neither* side to pre-empt and thus enhances crisis stability. Current US strategy is to make Soviet missile-firing submarines more vulnerable and US submarine launched missiles more accurate (with deployment of the D-5 missile). Both developments are destabilising.

49. This is not to say that the Soviets would be likely to launch their submarine-based missiles, but use of tactical nuclear weapons against the highly threatening US carrier battle-groups (which cannot easily be disabled by conventional attacks) or against the attacking US SSNs, is a real possibility. See Mearsheimer, 'A strategic misstep' and Barry Posen, 'Inadvertent nuclear war: Escalation and NATO's Northern Flank', *International Security* (Fall 1982).

50. Anthony F Wolf, 'Agreement at Sea: The United States-USSR Agreement on Incidents at Sea', *The Korean Journal of International Studies* (Summer 1978), p 63.

51. George Shultz, 'Meeting the challenge of change in the Pacific', address given at Stanford Cornerstone Centennial Academic Convocation, Stanford University, California, May 14, 1987.

52. The deployment of long-range land-attack SLCMs on both sides will, however, give the

Soviets an incentive to deploy their forces both more offensively and further afield.

53. Cited in William M Arkin and Richard W Fieldhouse, *Nuclear Battlefields: Global Links in the Arms Race* (Ballinger, Cambridge, 1985) p 14.

54. Cited in Mara Moustafine, 'Soviets not a military threat to us: Beazley', *Australian* (March 21, 1988).

55. On 'existential deterrence' see McGeorge Bundy, 'Existential deterrence and its consequences' in Douglas Maclean (ed), *The Security Gamble: Deterrence Dilemmas in the Nuclear Age* (Rowman and Allanheld, Totowa, 1984).

56. See Admiral James D Watkins, 'The Maritime Strategy', *Proceedings* (January 1986). Special Maritime Strategy Supplement, p8. (Emphasis added).

57. Captain Linton F Brooks, 'Naval power and national security: The case for the Maritime Strategy', *International Security* (Fall 1986), p 69.

58. Interview with John F Lehman, *Arizona Republic* (March 29, 1987).

59. Ronald O'Rourke, 'Nuclear escalation, strategic anti-submarine warfare, and the Navy's Forward Maritime Strategy', (Congressional Research Service, Library of Congress, Washington D C, Feb 27, 1987), p CRS-3.

60. *Ibid*, p CRS-viii. Linton Brooks does concede that the SSBN strategy carries 'some risk' of escalation but insists that this is 'acceptable' since it offers 'a unique means of gaining war termination leverage'. See Brooks, 'Naval power and national security', p 81.

61. See Watkins, 'The Maritime Strategy', p 14.

62. *Ibid*, p 13.

63. See O'Rourke, 'Nuclear Escalation' p CRS-xi and Tom Stephanick, 'Attacking the Soviet sea-based deterrent; Clever feint or foolhardy manoeuvre?', *FAS Public Interest Report* (June-July 1986) p 8.

64. Jack Synder, *The Ideology of the Offensive: Military Decision Making and the Disasters of 1914* (Cornell University Press, Ithaca, 1984) and Stephen Van Evera, 'The cult of the offensive on the origins of the First World War', *International Security* (Summer 1984).

65. Barry M Blechman, 'Confidence building in the North Pacific: A pragmatic approach to naval arms control' in Andrew Mack and Paul Keal (eds), *Security and Arms Control in the North Pacific* (Allen and Unwin, Sydney, forthcoming). A longer version of this paper was published as *Working Paper No 29* (Peace Research Centre, Australian National University, Canberra, February 1988). The paper was first presented by Dr Blechman at a conference on 'Security and arms control in the North Pacific' hosted by the Peace Research Centre at the Australian National University in August, 1987).

66. *Ibid*, p 28.

Confidence-building measures for the Asia-Pacific: The relevance of the European experience

TREVOR FINDLAY
Senior Research Fellow, Peace Research Centre, Australian National University, Canberra

THE idea that states can reach agreements, either formal or informal, to build mutual confidence and reduce conflict, is as old as the idea of the nation-state itself. Cultural exchanges, state visits, the establishment of diplomatic relations, the formation of regional organisations, in fact any measure designed to increase mutual trust between nations, could be described as a 'confidence building measure'.

In arms control parlance, the term 'confidence building measure' or CBM has however assumed a more specific meaning since first appearing in a United Nations General Assembly resolution in December 1955.[1] One of the most comprehensive definitions has been devised by James Macintosh of York University in Toronto. He defines confidence building measures as:

(1) A variety of arms control measures entailing
(2) state action
(3) that can be unilateral but more often either bilateral or multilateral
(4) that attempt to reduce or eliminate misperceptions about specific military threats or concerns (often having to do with surprise attack)
(5) by communicating adequately verifiable evidence of acceptable reliability to the effect that those concerns are groundless
(6) often (but not always) by demonstrating that military and political intentions are not aggressive
(7) and/or by providing early warning indicators to create confidence that surprise would be difficult to achieve

(8) and/or restricting the opportunities available for the use of military forces by adopting restrictions on the activities and deployments of those forces (or crucial components of them) within sensitive areas.[2]

Such measures, even before they had a name, were included in a wide variety of international agreements dating at least as far back as the 1688 Treaty of Munster, which called for the effective demilitarisation of the east side of the Rhine through the razing of fortresses.[3]

The establishment of an entire 'regime' of confidence building measures has however only been achieved in the past 13 years by the states of Europe through what is known as the 'CSCE process'. The negotiating mechanisms for this process have been the Conference on Security and Co-operation in Europe (CSCE) and its offshoot, the Conference on Confidence and Security Building Measures and Disarmament in Europe (CCSBMDE or, for short, CDE). A separate but related set of talks, the Mutual and Balanced Force Reduction (MBFR) Talks have been conducted in Vienna during the same period. Although confidence building measures were included in MBFR's original mandate, it has concentrated on negotiating troop reductions. It has failed to achieve either. The European states are currently holding discussions to decide how the envisaged second stage of the CDE can be handled and how the MBFR talks can be rejuvenated. The current idea is that so-called Conventional Stability Talks (CST) should be initiated to replace MBFR. These would examine both conventional reductions and more complex confidence building measures. The precise link between Conventional Stability Talks and the CSCE process has yet to be agreed on.

The idea that the successful CSCE experience might be used as a model for the Asia-Pacific region has been stimulated by Soviet General Secretary Mikhail S Gorbachev. At Vladivostok in July 1986 he proposed:

> ...a Pacific conference along the lines of the Helsinki conference, with the participation of all countries gravitating towards the Ocean, as an objective, if rather remote one.[4]

While the Soviets have subsequently retreated from the idea, it is nonetheless apposite that the states of the Asia-Pacific region should examine the European experience, since it has produced the only existing model of a comprehensive CBM regime.

The CSCE/CDE model

The Conference on Security and Co-operation in Europe is an ongoing 35-nation forum involving all the states of Europe except Albania, plus Canada and the United States.[5] The original proposal for such a conference came from the Soviet Union, which was anxious to obtain legitimacy for itself and its allies in Eastern Europe.

The major event which paved the way for CSCE was the September 1969 election of Willy Brandt as Chancellor of the Federal Republic of Germany and his subsequent policy of *Ostpolitik* towards the Eastern bloc. This included treaties with the Soviet Union and Poland, recognising their post-war borders and thus their incorporation of pre-war German territories, the 1972 Treaty on the Basis of Intra-

German Relations and the admission of the two Germanies to the United Nations in 1973.

A start to the CSCE process was contingent upon the commencement of talks on troop reductions (MBFR), favoured by the North Atlantic Treaty Organisation (NATO) as a means of reducing alleged Soviet conventional preponderance in Europe. Eventual Western agreement to the commencement of CSCE was in effect a trade-off for Eastern agreement to participate in MBFR. Such an agreement was possible because of the growing detente between the superpowers, signalled by the signature of SALT I (Strategic Arms Limitation Treaty I) in May 1972. It was at the SALT I summit meeting that the Soviets tentatively agreed to start preliminary talks on MBFR in return for Western agreement to commence preliminary CSCE talks in the summer of 1972 in Helsinki.[6]

The first formal CSCE conference, held in Helsinki between 1973 and 1975, produced the Helsinki Final Act, a non-binding political declaration representing a compromise between the aspirations of three European groupings: the West, the Socialist bloc and the neutral/nonaligned (NNA). So-called Basket I of that accord outlined principles to guide relations between states; Basket II contained provisions on commerce, industrial co-operation, science and technology; Basket III dealt with human rights; and questions relating to security in the Mediterranean were tacked onto the end. Subsequent review meetings at Belgrade, Madrid and Vienna have assessed the implementation of the accord.

While all elements of the Helsinki Final Act can be viewed as attempts to increase confidence and reduce the likelihood of war, Basket I contained specific military measures, which have become known officially as CBMs, to be undertaken by the parties. The most significant and only obligatory confidence building measure to emerge from Helsinki was the obligation of all CSCE participants to give 21 days advance notice of military manoeuvres exceeding 25,000 troops, independently or combined with any possible air or naval components.[7] Additional CBMs, such as invitations to observers to watch such manoeuvres and more onerous notification requirements, were voluntary. The two participating states whose territories extend beyond Europe — the Soviet Union and Turkey — were exempt from all CBMs at distances beyond 250 kilometres from their frontiers with other European participating states.

In 1983 the Madrid follow-up meeting of the CSCE agreed to a conference in Stockholm, to be known rather misleadingly as the Conference on Disarmament in Europe, to negotiate further confidence and security building measures (CSBMs). The idea was an amalgam of proposals by France and the Soviet Union. At American insistence the conference was restricted to confidence building measures, rather than conventional disarmament, in an effort to avoid undermining the MBFR talks.

By the time the conference convened in early 1984, the international situation was bleak, with all other arms control talks suspended or cancelled, including MBFR, START (Strategic Arms Reduction Talks) and INF (Intermediate-range Nuclear Forces), and the prospects for future agreements remote. Canadian delegation leader Thomas Delworth describes this as ‘the era of megaphone diplomacy, because the microphones at all conference tables (except the CDE) had been turned off'.[8]

Not until three years later, following a major Soviet concession on on-site inspection, was agreement reached at the CDE. According to Swedish representative Johan Tunberger, agreement was finally achieved because:

> The domestic political situation within some key states as the Stockholm Conference approached its guillotine helped to bring the agreement about. To put it in a nutshell: it seems to me as if the superpowers, as it were, needed a sufficiently important agreement in September (1986) and that this need coincided with a more permanent wish amongst most other participating states to see the CSCE process inch forward.[9]

A principal contributing factor was the need of the new Soviet leader, General Secretary Gorbachev, to demonstrate his *bona fides* in the arms control field. Other factors include the relative lack of publicity given to the talks plus the fact that it was working to a deadline imposed by the Madrid review conference.[10]

The 1986 Stockholm Agreement is a much meatier affair than the Helsinki Accord. While not a treaty (it requires neither signature nor ratification), the agreement is, unlike the Helsinki Accord, politically binding.[11] It provides for:

- Notification of military activities involving more than 13,000 troops or 300 tanks;
- The extension of advance notification to 42 days;
- An exchange of annual calendars of notifiable military activities;
- Notification of exercises involving more than 40,000 trooops two years in advance;
- Mandatory invitations to observers to observe military activities involving 17,000 troops or more;
- The right of on-site inspection, without a right of refusal, to verify compliance; and
- A declaration relating to the non-use of force.

In contrast to the Helsinki Final Act, the Stockholm Agreement applies these CSBMs in the entire European area 'from the Atlantic to the Urals', except in the cases of Turkey (to which the area of application remains that agreed on at Helsinki) and Albania (which had not participated in the talks).[12] The implementation of the agreement is proceeding well. On August 28-30, 1987, the US successfully conducted, under the agreement's provisions, its first-ever on-site inspection of Soviet troops exercises on Soviet territory.[13]

Applicability of the European experience to the Asia-Pacific

The direct application of the Helsinki/Stockholm model to the Asia-Pacific region is problematic. Gorbachev himself has noted:

> In Vladivostok I suggested a sort of working hypothesis or, better to say, an invitation to discussion. And the only reason I referred to Helsinki is that so far the world community has had no other experience of the kind. This does not mean, of course, that the European experience can automatically be transplanted to Asia and the Pacific.[14]

It is self-evident that every international agreement is a product of its time and place and cannot be emulated exactly elsewhere. The CSCE process is largely attributable to unique historical circumstances, such as *Ostpolitik*, the flowering of detente and the rise to power of General Secretary Gorbachev. It is also clear that the CSCE process is a problematic model, having been almost derailed on several occasions, most notably by the human rights/security nexus enshrined in the Helsinki Final Act. The Stockholm Agreement, while being a major advance in the evolution of CBMs, is itself not entirely exemplary. It fails, for instance, to cover air and naval movements unless these are associated with land exercises; it ignores mobilisation procedures; and it lacks a consultation procedure to assist verification of compliance.

The major problem in attempting to duplicate the European model in the Asia-Pacific lies, however, in the stark differences between the two regions.

Geopolitics

It is the geopolitical differences which are immediately the most striking. Europe is a self-contained sub-continent, an obvious regional entity, whereas the Asia-Pacific region comprises a vast ocean ringed with countries as different and as geographically distant as Australia, the Philippines and Korea. There is, moreover, no agreed definition of the Asia-Pacific region. Such a situation has implications for the area of application of a regional security regime, for the choice of participants in the negotiations and for the type of measures negotiated.

The area of application problem. The Europeans had problems agreeing on the area of application of their security regimes. The Soviet concession at Stockholm that Europe in fact reached all the way to the Urals only came after some years of negotiation. In the MBFR talks several months were lost arguing over whether Hungary should be included in the zone of application.

In the case of the Asia-Pacific, however, the problems are greatly magnified. While there would appear to be a consensus that a security regime for the region should not include the Latin American states of the eastern Pacific rim, or the South Pacific island states with their meagre armed forces, the exclusion of other areas is more contentious. For instance, should North America be included? As in the European negotiations, the US and Canada are likely to refuse to include their own territory in the area of application, on the grounds that it is not the North American side of the Pacific that has the security problem. Indeed, there would be little practical value in including North America in a land-based CBM regime. The vast distance between the North American and Asian mainlands itself provides sufficient warning of surprise attack involving land-based forces. Hence, one of the main aims of CBMs — warning of surprise attack — is rendered unnecessary. Insofar as there is a threat to the Soviets and Chinese from North America, it is naval and aerial, not land-based.

The Soviets may insist of course for political reasons, and on the grounds of equity, that at least Alaska and western Canada be included in any Asia-Pacific land-based CBM regime. This may not be such a bad concession for the West to make —

if the Soviets were to agree to include all their territory from the Pacific seaboard west to the Urals. This would mean that the whole of the Soviet Union would be subject to three different regimes — those of Helsinki, Stockholm and the Asia-Pacific.

At the other extremity of the Asia-Pacific region, Australia and New Zealand are unlikely to be serious contenders for inclusion in the area of application. As island states, they do not share contiguous borders with others, they are not directly involved in any regional conflicts and their military capabilities are not well suited to aggressive pursuits.

In purely geopolitical terms the most cohesive area in the Asia-Pacific region comprises the Asian land mass and the island states in proximity to it. This area, which is also in greatest need of confidence building and tension-reduction activities, comprises the Soviet Far East, Japan, the two Koreas, China, Taiwan, Mongolia, the three Indochinese states (Vietnam, Laos and Kampuchea), Thailand and the Philippines.

Whether any or all of the Asean (Association of Southeast Asian Nations) states should be included in the area of application is a vexed question. While they are significant regional actors, mutual confidence between them is already high and their co-operative activities grow yearly. A security problem does however exist between the Asean states and those to their north. One of the Asean states, Thailand, borders on a major area of instability in the Asia-Pacific region — Indochina. The Indochinese states would be likely to insist in any case on Thailand being constrained by any regional security obligations to which they themselves were subject. Moreover, several Asean members are involved in boundary disputes with China, Vietnam and Kampuchea resulting from the Exclusive Economic Zone provisions of the Law of the Sea and island claims predating that treaty.[15] Any Asia-Pacific security regime may therefore ultimately need to include the Asean states. An alternative, applied by the CSCE to the non-European Mediterranean littoral states, would be to admit them as observers in any regional security negotiations.[16]

The participation question. As in the European case, the states to which CBMs are to apply may not be the only states involved in negotiating such measures. In the Asia-Pacific region, an obvious participant in any talks — because of its status as a superpower and nuclear-weapon state, as well as its being a significant regional actor — is the US. Two non-regional nuclear-weapon states, France and Britain, would be likely to seek at least observer status, if not a negotiating role. The positions of Australia, Canada and New Zealand are more ambiguous. While unlikely candidates for inclusion in any area of application, they could play a role as mediators or as a 'third force' in negotiations but without a vote at the conference table.

A key advantage — perhaps the only one — that the Asia-Pacific region has over Europe, is that relatively few states would be eligible to be members of a regional negotiating forum. Including Canada and the US, there are only 14 Asia-Pacific countries north of the equator. In any event the number will certainly never amount to the 35 nations involved in the CSCE. As evidenced by the fate of the multilateral disarmament bodies in Geneva, which have steadily increased in size and complexity, the more states involved in negotiations, the harder it is to reach agreement — although this may be ameliorated somewhat by the existence of more or less informal negotiating blocs.

Sea vs land. A major geopolitical difference between the European and Asia-Pacific regions, which would critically affect the content of any negotiations regarding the latter, is the extent and pivotal role of the ocean in the Asia-Pacific. While in Europe the North Atlantic plays a vital role in NATO strategy, including facilitating re-supply of US forces, the US has considerable land-based power in place on the European continent. In the Pacific the US is predominantly a naval power facing the predominantly land-based power of the Soviet Union and China. Hence the reluctance of the US to consider CBMs which would constrain naval activities in the Pacific — and the Soviet willingness to propose such measures.

As Holdren and Lodgaard put it :

> A geopolitical asymmetry that is a significant barrier to naval arms control is the circumstance that the Soviet Union is predominantly and inherently a land power, meaning that most of its central interests lie in regions to which it has direct access to land, while the United States is fundamentally a maritime power, separated by oceans from its main allies as well as major markets and resource suppliers.[17]

These global asymmetries are heightened in the Asia-Pacific region since the US has only the slightest of toeholds on the Asian mainland (in South Korea), in contrast to Europe, where it occupies a major forward-deployed position on the Central Front (in West Germany).

The European model moreover provides no precedent for naval CBMs for the Pacific since, even in Europe, the ocean was precisely the area excluded from CBMs — at US insistence. While some naval activities do fall within the purview of the Helsinki and Stockholm agreements, this only occurs where they are relevant to major military exercises on land. The West favoured a 'functional approach' whereby CBMs would apply only to those military activities in the adjoining sea area and air space that were functionally linked with notifiable activities on land. The East argued for a 'geographical approach', maintaining that independent air and naval activities that affected European security in any way should be subject to notification.[18]

In theory there is no reason why an agreement relating to the Pacific could not include naval CBMs. Indeed it is the area in which the need for CBMs would appear most pressing, particularly in regard to nuclear-armed vessels. As Professor Desmond Ball notes:

> ...there are good reasons for believing that the first use of nuclear weapons could take place at sea, and for concern that the escalation dynamics of nuclear warfare in this theatre are far less constrained than those that would attend nuclear operations on land.[19]

In practice, the adoption of naval CBMs would involve a major change of position by the US Navy, and indeed by the Soviet Navy, whose real position on naval CBMs has never been tested in actual negotiations. As William Arkin has noted:

> The US Navy (and the other nuclear powers) have a strong aversion to any prohibitions on naval operations. In fact, they have made the 'right' to conduct operations on the high seas and in territorial waters a prerequisite for their support for any kind of confidence building measures (even on land) or for the existence of nuclear free zones covering ocean areas.[20]

Even if the superpowers were amenable to naval CBMs, they are more likely to want to negotiate them bilaterally than in a multilateral forum, particularly CBMs that affect their nuclear deployments, and to apply them globally rather than regionally.

It may be however that ultimately the European CSCE process itself will pave the way for naval CBMs in the Pacific region. The Soviet Union has already announced that it will be pressing the idea of naval CBMs at whatever European security forum is established to replace MBFR and carry forward the work of the CDE. John Borawski sees possible benefits for the West in the Soviet proposal:

> ...given the fact that a Warsaw Pact ground thrust would be *preceded* by a massive air strike, air and naval measures are hardly inapposite to European security considerations and may be to NATO's advantage.[21]

The problem in applying this logic to the Pacific is that under current US Naval doctrine, the so-called Maritime Strategy, it could be the US which would be launching such an attack, preceded by air and naval measures. Under the doctrine of 'horizontal escalation', facilities in Soviet Asia might be attacked even if the original conflict had begun in Europe.[22]

Another problem with naval CBMs is that the ocean is not sovereign territory. This would not matter in the case of agreements like the 1972 Incidents at Sea Agreement which simply affect the way naval vessels operate. However those CBMs involving geographical limitations, such as excluding anti-submarine warfare operations from particular areas, would have implications for the Law of the Sea. Any CBMs negotiated by the regional states that affected rights under the Law of the Sea would need to be agreed on and adhered to by virtually all other states.[23] This would, in theory, complicate the process of concluding agreements.

One solution would be to forward draft agreements to the UN General Assembly for its approval. This is the current procedure for agreements reached by the limited membership of the multilateral disarmament body in Geneva, the Conference on Disarmament. In practice, most states are likely to go along with any agreement that is reached between such a powerful group of countries as those found in the North Pacific. However, one would imagine the European powers, especially the French and British, insisting on their prerogatives. Other seekers of great power status, such as India and Brazil, could also prove difficult in the UN General Assembly over what they would see as attempts to legislate for part of the 'common heritage of mankind'.

While some initial naval CBMs for the Asia-Pacific region cannot be ruled out, more far-reaching measures are clearly problematic.

Political/defence culture

The political make-up of the Asia-Pacific region also allows few parallels with

Europe. There is, for instance, no shared political culture between the Asia-Pacific countries as there is in Europe. However much the 35 CSCE states are divided on ideological, political and socio-economic grounds, they still share a common culture of European diplomacy and a *lingua franca* of arms control negotiations stretching back at least a century. As Gerald Segal puts it, 'arms control is a "game" that Europeans have been playing for hundreds of years in various guises'.[24] In the nuclear age Europeans have a shared feeling that they have to either swim or sink together. There also is a long history in Europe of surprise attack — Hitler's *blitzkreig* being just the latest example — which threatened to or did engulf the whole continent in war. This has created a defence culture that has concentrated on preparedness against surprise attack and which has therefore grasped the significance of confidence building measures. Efforts to establish a European security regime go back at least as far as the Congress of Vienna in 1815. Diplomatic manoeuvrings that preceded the initiation of the Helsinki process can be traced back to Soviet Foreign Minister VM Molotov's 1954 proposal for a 'General European Treaty' on collective security.[25]

There is no such common culture in the Asia-Pacific area or historic momentum towards collective security. Democratic Japan, socialist China and divided Korea for instance have little enough in common with one another, much less with the Soviet Union and the US. There is little evidence of a 'sink or swim' mentality in the area. One only has to contrast the attitudes of the two Koreas with that of the two Germanies to see this. Nor is there a range of small states, a cohesive group of influential allies, or a collective of nonaligned states in the Pacific to help goad the superpowers into a Helsinki-type negotiating forum as there was in Europe. There is no history of repeated surprise attack back and forth across a vast plain in *blitzkreig* style. China's misfortune, for example, was to be pressed on all sides, nibbled away from the sea by the Europeans and carved up, although never conquered, by the Japanese. Unlike Europe, proposals for arms control in East Asia do not have a long legacy, the earliest Soviet initiative being Leonid Brezhnev's much reviled proposal for an Asian Security Conference in June 1969.[26]

It would be wrong however to suggest that the Asia-Pacific countries do not understand the concept of confidence building measures or lack the capability to negotiate them. As Douglas Stuart points out:

> Key Asian governments have gradually developed the institutional and intellectual infrastructure for analysing and formulating substantive arms control initiatives.[27]

Gerald Segal makes a good case that the states of Asia were engaged in tacit confidence building measures long before the term was invented by the West.[28] The problem is not that Asian states are unable to negotiate CBMs, but rather that such measures are not considered useful tools of national security policy. Clearly many more Asian governments, bureaucracies and military establishments need to be persuaded of the benefits of CBMs before they will be willing to negotiate such measures. At the very least the potential of CBMs needs to be unambiguously demonstrated. In this regard the successful implementation of the Stockholm Agreement should provide an ongoing example of what can be achieved by CBMs and give greater confidence to Asian governments contemplating such measures.

Political/territorial questions

Another major political difference between Europe and the Pacific — one often seen as completely ruling out a CSCE-type arrangement for the latter — is that the Europeans have largely disposed of the outstanding territorial questions arising from World War II, principally by setting them in concrete. The CSCE process was openly perceived by the Soviets as legitimising the territorial and ideological boundaries resulting from the war and lowering expectations that the two Germanies might ever be reconstituted as one nation.

In the Asia-Pacific region such a process has not yet taken place. World War II has not even officially ended for the Soviets and the Japanese, locked as they are in an apparently unresolvable dispute over the Northern Territories. Across the straits, Korean reconciliation seems not much closer than at the end of the Korean War. Neither of the Koreas are members of the United Nations. The peninsula remains, in Bruce Cumings' words, 'a Cold War island in a post-Cold War sea'.[29] China, with Hong Kong and Macao within reach, is unlikely to lessen its claim to Taiwan. In Indochina, the Vietnamese occupation of Kampuchea and the lingering threat of a resurgence by a Pol Pot-led Khmer Rouge is an enduring threat to regional stability. Then there are the Sino-Soviet border disputes (although recent concessions by the Soviets have eased this problem) and competing claims on the Spratly Islands in the South China Sea.

While the purely territorial disputes, such as the Northern Islands and Sino-Soviet border disputes are certainly not conducive to harmonious international relations in the Pacific, it is not clear why they should necessarily rule out a European-style CBM process in the region. After all, the CSCE process has managed to envelop a major territorial dispute between three of its participants — Turkey, Cyprus and Greece.

The dispute between Britain and Spain over Gibraltar, while not so fiery, is another example. Japanese commentator Masahiko Asada notes that the Northern Territories question, for instance, 'should not be a stumbling block to introducing CBMs'.[30] It is quite possible to imagine a Helsinki process that simply aimed at establishing CBMs without making any attempt to tackle or freeze territorial disputes. One could argue that CBMs are even more necessary in a region where territorial claims persist.

A more intractable problem in the Asia-Pacific is not territorial disputes, which can to some extent be set aside for the purpose of negotiating CBMs, but disputes over the very existence of particular regional actors. It is a prerequisite for face-to-face negotiations of the CSCE variety that there at least be mutual recognition and diplomatic relations between the states involved. While all the states of Europe have diplomatic relations with one another (the exception being Albania which does not participate in the CSCE), there are major gaps in diplomatic relations between the Asia-Pacific states. These are mostly the result of ongoing political conflicts but in some instances the result of sheer neglect.

True, there have been some improvements of late. The US recently restored diplomatic relations with Mongolia and lifted a ban on American diplomats talking to North Korean officials in certain circumstances.[31] China has established diplomatic relations with Laos.[32] The establishment of diplomatic relations between other states in the region is, however, impossible in the absence of broader political reconciliation between them.

The two Koreas, China, Taiwan and Kampuchea all fall into this category. Although the two Koreas have at least sat opposite each other (albeit intermittently) at the same negotiating table at Panmunjom for over 30 years, Pyongyang has repeatedly rejected calls for cross-recognition by the North and South, most notably when suggested in 1975 by Henry Kissinger.[33] As for China and Taiwan, as long as each adheres to its 'one China' policy they are unlikely to appear together at an Asia-Pacific conference. Since Taiwan is never likely to be part of a CSCE-type arrangement unless as a reunified part of China, it could end up becoming the (involuntary) Albania of an Asia-Pacific CSCE. Finally, since there is no international consensus on which government represents the people of Kampuchea, there can be no Kampuchean delegation at any Asia-Pacific security conference.

As Masahiko Asada points out, the successful negotiation of CBMs requires at least a modicum of confidence between the parties. Even if region-wide diplomatic cross-recognition was achieved, this would not necessarily bring about orderly, constructive negotiations on a CBM regime. For example, the attendance of the two Koreas at a CSCE-type negotiating forum could easily sour the atmosphere unless a certain degree of confidence had been established beforehand. Even in the event that the two Koreas were on speaking terms, the North Koreans may not be any more amenable to CBMs in a multilateral forum than they have been in a bilateral or trilateral context. Pyongyang has for instance rejected a US proposal that it observe the annual Team Spirit exercises.[34] It has also rejected American proposals for more formal CBMs — apparently because it sees such measures as conferring legitimacy on the US 'occupation' of South Korea.[35] One advantage of a multilateral forum may be that in a larger grouping the North Koreans may feel less isolated and paranoid and more amenable to CBMs, especially those not directed specifically at the Korean peninsula.

Balance of power

Another, more specious, argument that has been used to question the possibility of a Helsinki process taking place in the Asia-Pacific region, is the existence of several 'balance of power' equations, as opposed to just one in Europe.

There are sound arguments against this proposition. First, the Europeans did not have a simple balance of power to contend with. Neither NATO nor the Warsaw Pact are monolithic in a negotiating context (the most notable 'renegades' being France and Romania). The European neutral/nonaligned group constitutes another complicating factor in the equation (note the roles of Switzerland, Ireland and Malta). Second, while a complicated balance of power situation may make the negotiation of troop or arms reductions more complex, because of the difficulty of striking equitable bargains, this does not apply in the case of CBMs. Confidence building measures do not degrade the military capability of states, but rather help reveal intentions. Hans Gunther Brauch defines CBMs as particular forms of arms control:

> ...which do not directly affect the size, weaponry and structure of military forces and weapons of war. Instead CBMs aim at increasing trust and confidence between two hostile sides, making the intentions and actions of each clearer and more predictable to the other.[36]

While some allowance may be made for contiguous areas, as was done in the case of Turkey and the Soviet Union in the Helsinki Accord and Turkey in regard to the Stockholm Agreement, CBMs are applied equally to all states within a given geographical area, regardless of their size or place within a 'balance of power'. Allowing for differences in the openness of the societies involved, CBMs should, by increasing transparency, have equal benefits for all parties. As Barry Blechman notes:

> A particular value of CBMs is that their negotiation can bypass questions of relative military capabilities, where problems of quantification, verification, and asymmetrical perceptions of threat can bog down discussions. CBMs aim directly at assessments of intent, regardless of actual capabilities.[37]

By contrast, an MBFR-type process of armed force reductions in the Asia-Pacific would have to address directly the power disparities and competing balances within the region.

Verification

A further reason sometimes given for the impracticability of arms control in Asia is the assumed difficulty of verification. Since CBMs tend to be either self-verifying, as in the case of states permitting observers at military manoeuvres, or verifiable by so-called 'national technical means' such as satellites, verification should not be too daunting a task. The two superpowers would be involved as a matter of course and would be likely to assist their allies and co-operate with each other in verifying third party compliance with any agreement, including troop reductions. In any case the region contains several advanced industrial powers, most notably Japan and South Korea, which could add technical muscle to any regional verification effort. In the CSCE and MBFR cases most of the states involved also had no national technical means of verification of their own.

Absence of the neutral/nonaligned

Another difference between Europe and the Asia-Pacific region is the absence from the latter of a group of neutral or nonaligned countries. Geographically these European states act as useful buffers between the two rival blocs, a role that is itself a form of confidence building. In the establishment of a regional security regime, these states can help prod the aligned states into negotiations, act as hosts and mediators once negotiations commence and help verify agreeements reached.

The success of the Helsinki/Stockholm Conference — and indeed the advent of CBMs in Europe in the first place — was partly due to the persistence and ingenuity of the neutral/nonaligned group.[38] During the Stockholm Conference they chaired working groups, presented detailed proposals and sought compromises between East and West.[39] Also of some significance in breaking down bloc stereotypes were the activities of Ireland, which participates in the CSCE as a Western country, and Romania, renegade of the Socialist group. Romania, for instance, was the only Warsaw Pact country enthusiastic about CBMs from the outset, largely because such measures can provide early warning of Soviet (rather than NATO) attack.[40]

On the other hand the European NNA group is extremely heterogeneous, containing states with such widely diverging views on security as Sweden, Cyprus and Liechtenstein. In some respects this diversity enhanced the NNA role. As Hanspeter Neuhold explains:

> It may take the NN[A] delegations a rather long time to agree among themselves. Since the main positions adopted within the CSCE framework as a whole are frequently upheld in the NN[A] group as well, a solution eventually acceptable to the [NNA] will probably also be approved by the other 26 participating states.[41]

In other cases NNA diversity blocked progress in the Helsinki/Stockholm process. Malta for instance managed to prolong the agony of meetings by injecting Mediterranean issues into the proceedings at every turn. Switzerland, which relies heavily on the mobilisation of large reserve forces for its defence, strenuously resisted any CBMs that would affect mobilisation procedures.[42] The absence of such CBMs is a major flaw in the Stockholm Agreement.

No matter how active, committed, ingenious or united the NNA is, however, the outcome of major security negotiations must in the last resort be determined by the great powers, particularly the superpowers. As Neuhold points out, during the early days of the Stockholm talks, East-West relations were too strained and the gulf between the positions of the two blocs too wide for the NNA to engage successfully in 'bridge-building'. The final phase, Neuhold says, 'was negotiated on a bloc-to-bloc basis, with the two superpowers dictating the course of events and the NN[A] on the sidelines'.[43] This is corroborated by Borawski.[44]

The Asia-Pacific has no neutral/nonaligned grouping. While Indonesia and Malaysia are formally members of the Nonaligned Movement, Indonesia is hobbled in any mediatory role by the lack of depth in its relations with the Soviet Union and by its suspicion of China, while Malaysia may be constrained by its defence relationship with Britain, Australia and New Zealand. Neither country has any tradition of mediating international conflicts (although Indonesia has recently hosted talks on the Kampuchea question). Given the contradictory role of the NNA in the CSCE process however, the absence of a similar Asian-Pacific group may not be a drawback to the negotiation of CBMs in that region. Australia, New Zealand and Canada, though clearly aligned, are not participants in any regional conflict and might therefore play a role equivalent to that of the NNA in Europe.

Lack of a venue and/or forum

Finally, there is no obvious venue or forum in the Asia-Pacific area for talks to take place. This is not a trivial matter. Many negotiations have faltered over the question of a venue. Europe offers many, including Geneva, Vienna and Stockholm. Similarly Australia was at an advantage in having the South Pacific Forum in which to launch its proposal for a South Pacific Nuclear Free Zone.

The importance of an appropriate forum for talks can hardly be overemphasised. While establishment of a forum prior to participants agreeing on what is to be discussed may seem like 'putting the cart before the horse', the experience of the Helsinki/Stockholm process does not bear this out. In both the Helsinki and Stockholm cases the negotiators had little idea of the shape of the future agreement or even if agreement could be reached at all. The conference was swamped with a huge range of proposals from all sides but managed to sort through them successfully.

An Asian-Pacific CSCE?

Given the differences between Europe and the Asia-Pacific, it would seem that the Helsinki/Stockholm model, at least for the forseeable future, is not applicable to the latter region. The divisions between several key states in the region are too great and the individual security needs of each country too disparate to contemplate a region-wide 'confidence building' regime of the Helsinki/Stockholm variety at this stage. Rather, it may be more appropriate that CBMs be negotiated for subregional purposes. These would be applied to the particular security problems or areas where confidence building is most needed. Such areas are:

(1) Ocean areas of the Pacific, especially the Northwest Pacific, where the danger of inadvertent naval confrontations in crisis situations is greatest. Naval CBMs could be applied either to the North Pacific as a whole or to particular areas such as:
   - The Sea of Japan and/or the waters around Korea; the key negotiating states would be the US, the Soviet Union, Japan, China and the two Koreas.
   - The Spratly Islands; negotiations would involve China, Vietnam, Malaysia, Indonesia and the Philippines.

(2) The Korean peninsula, where the danger of war in the region is greatest. Existing US proposals for CBMs provide a good basis for negotiations between the US, China and the Koreas.

(3) The Sino-Mongolian-Soviet triangle, where troop withdrawals have already created some momentum for peace and where land-based CBMs of the Stockholm variety could be useful in consolidating this trend; the negotiators would be China, Mongolia and the Soviet Union. Even if only the Helsinki model were followed — whereby manoeuvres involving 25,000 troops or more within 250 kilometres of their borders were notified — this would be a significant beginning.

(4) The Sino-Vietnamese border, where CBMs could help lessen both states' fear of surprise attack. These could be extended to the other Indochinese states and Thailand (especially the Thai/Kampuchean border) once the Kampuchean problem is settled.

Apart from these partial subregional measures, the most likely area for a future comprehensive CBM regime in the Asia-Pacific region is the Northwest Pacific. This would require both land-based and naval CBMs and involve Japan, the Koreas, China, the Soviet Union and the US.

A North Pacific security forum?

One way to begin the process of bringing international order to the Asia-Pacific region through confidence building measures would be to establish a forum for discussions on CBMs to begin. Establishment of such a body could act as a confidence building measure in its own right. As the former head of the Canadian delegation to the CDE has said of that forum:

> It can... be argued that the Stockholm Conference was in itself a kind of confidence building measure and that it both contributed to a better East-West atmosphere while becoming the beneficiary (in turn) of this process of improvement.[45]

The Blechman proposal

Barry Blechman, former Assistant Director of the Arms Control and Disarmament Agency (ACDA) during the Carter Administration, has proposed the establishment of an International Commission on the North Pacific. Such a body would serve as a forum for discussions, a centre for negotiations and an institutional arrangement to administer any agreements concluded.[46] It would distribute the political burden of proposing arms control initiatives to all participants, help depoliticise regional arms control issues by channelling discussion into technical aspects and permit states to show interest in regional arms control without committing themselves to any particular proposal.[47] As to substantive matters, Blechman suggests that the commission could begin by examining the possibility of maritime 'rules of the road' for the Pacific. This could eventuate in a multilateral version of the US-Soviet 1972 Incidents at Sea Agreement. Notification of naval exercises and invitation of observers to such exercises could also be considered.

A mixed commission on North Pacific CSBMs

It might be preferable to establish a wider forum that could examine, at an expert rather than diplomatic level, both land-based and naval CBMs for the North Pacific region. At least at the outset it could be a 'mixed commission' comprising both governmental and nongovernmental representatives. This would enable, for instance, the two Koreas to send delegates in the guise of academics, thereby ensuring their participation. It would also enable Western CBM specialists to participate in their private capacities, thereby providing a plurality of Western views.

Such a commission would be principally a forum for Asian-Pacific states to educate each other on the issue of CBMs, discuss the relevance of such measures to the region's security needs and any obstacles that might block their implementation. It could study the record of Stockholm and seek advice from the CSCE on the functioning of European CBMs. Most importantly it would focus at least some regional attention on the idea of CBMs in the hope that such ideas might filter up to the governmental level in the form of concrete proposals.

A key question is who would initiate a proposal for the establishment of any kind of regional forum on CBMs. Clearly Soviet proposals for such schemes are still greeted with scepticism in the region. The US is not likely to support, much less propose, such an idea in the absence of regional pressure to do so. (The US administration is not even studying Pacific arms control issues). China still feels too inexperienced in the arms control field to initiate any such proposal.[48] Japan is constrained by regional memories of its Greater East Asia Co-Prosperity Sphere during World War II. Canada is unlikely to take a lead, since it is 'only now beginning to come to grips with its Pacific identity'[49] and allegedly 'does not even have a policy on Pacific arms control'.[50]

Australia supports the development of CBMs for the Asia-Pacific region.[51] Former Foreign Minister Bill Hayden proposed at the annual Australia/US ministerial talks in Washington in June 1988 that the two superpowers consider CBMs for the North Pacific. He also offered Australian assistance in developing such measures. While New Zealand has also officially described itself as 'well placed to lead in this area', its strained relations with the US preclude it from having much influence in Washington.[52] The biggest disadvantage that Australia and New Zealand have is that they are not North Pacific powers. Any proposals they might make run the risk of being dismissed as interference in areas outside their immediate region.

In view of the reluctance of the North Pacific states to seriously consider arms control proposals for their region, it is probably necessary for non-governmental organisations and individuals, especially the arms control and security studies community, to provide impetus for the idea of a regional forum on CBMs. Such activity should seek to take advantage of the current sea change in international relations.

If there is one lesson of the CSCE process that must be learned by the states of the Asia-Pacific region, it is that they need to take advantage of (possibly temporary) improvements in superpower relations if regional security endeavours are to succeed. The Helsinki accord was concluded in the heyday of detente, while the Stockholm Conference successfully took advantage of a renewed Soviet willingness to improve relations with the West. The current warming of relations between the US and the apparent willingness of the Soviet Union to achieve solutions to regional conflicts have already brought about the beginnings of a Soviet withdrawal from Afghanistan, better Sino-Soviet relations, movement on Kampuchea, the withdrawal of Soviet SS-20s from Asia and a breakthrough in the Eastern bloc's diplomatic boycott of South Korea (by Hungary). The late 1980s may provide the perfect diplomatic 'hot-house' for Asia-Pacific security initiatives, such as confidence building measures, to reach fruition.

NOTES

1. UN Resolution 914X of Dec 16, 1955, on the 'Regulation, limitation and balanced reduction of all armed forces and all armaments'. (John Borawski, *From The Atlantic To The Urals*, Pergamon/Brasseys, London, 1988, p 32.)
2. James Macintosh, *Confidence (and Security) Building Measures in the Arms Control Process: A Canadian Perspective*, Arms Control & Disarmament Studies No 1, Arms Control & Disarmament Division, Department of External Affairs, Ottawa, 1985, p 7.
3. *Ibid*, p 17.
4. Text of Speech by Mikhail Gorbachev in Vladivostok, July 28, 1986, reprinted in Ramesh Thakur & Carlyle A Thayer (eds), *The Soviet Union as an Asian-Pacific Power*, Westview Press/Macmillan Australia, Boulder & South Melbourne, 1987, p 223.
5. CSCE participating states are: Austria, Belgium, Bulgaria, Canada, Cyprus, Czechoslovakia, Denmark, Finland, France, the German Democratic Republic, the Federal Republic of Germany, Greece, the Holy See, Hungary, Iceland, Ireland, Italy, Liechtenstein, Luxembourg, Malta, Monaco, the Netherlands, Norway, Poland, Portugal, Romania, San Marino, Spain, Sweden, Switzerland, Turkey, the Soviet Union, Britain, the US and Yugoslavia.
6. Jonathan Dean, *Watershed in Europe*, Lexington Books, Lexington, Massachusetts, 1987, p 105.
7. Document on Confidence Building Measures and Certain Aspects of Security and Disarmament, included in the Final Act of the Conference on Security and Co-operation in Europe, Aug 1, 1975, Part I.
8. Thomas Delworth, 'Between Stockholm & Vienna: The Stockholm Conference & the CSCE Process', in Karl E Birnbaum & Bo Huldt (eds), *From Stockholm to Vienna: Building Conference & Security in Europe*, Conference Papers 9, Swedish Institute of International Affairs, Stockholm, 1987, p 1.
9. Johan Tunberger, 'An NN-Perspective on the Stockholm Agreement', in Birnbaum & Huldt, p 57.
10. Dean, p 198; Delworth, p 2.
11. Sverre Lodgaard, 'The Stockholm CSBMs & The Future of the CDE', PRIO Report 9/87, International Peace Research Institute, Oslo, 1987, p 155.
12. *Ibid*, p 157.
13. *Arms Control Today*, October 1987, p 29.
14. 'Mikhail Gorbachev's Replies to Questions Put by the Indonesian Newspaper *Merdeka*', July 21, 1987, Novosti Press Agency Publishing House, Moscow, 1987, p 10.
15. See Chapter 4, 'Critical issues in marine policies' in *Asia-Pacific Report: Trends, Issues, Challenges*, East-West Centre, Honolulu, 1987-88, p 49.
16. These were Egypt, Israel, Lebanon, Libya, Morocco, Syria and Tunisia.
17. John P Holdren & Sverre Lodgaard, 'Naval Forces: Arms Restraint & Confidence Building', PRIO Info No 3, International Peace Research Institute, Oslo, August 1988, p 4.

18. C A Namiesniowski, 'The Stockholm Agreement: An Exercise in Confidence Building', Background Paper No 14, Canadian Institute for International Peace & Security, Ottawa, September 1987, p 4.

19. Desmond Ball, 'Nuclear War At Sea', *International Security*, Vol 10, No 3, Winter 1985/86, p 3.

20. William Arkin, 'The Nuclear Arms Race At Sea', Neptune Papers No 1, Institute for Policy Studies/Greenpeace, Washington DC, October 1987, p 28.

21. John Borawski, 'Practical Steps for Building Confidence in Europe', *Arms Control Today*, March 1988, p 17.

22. Barry Blechman, 'Confidence Building in the North Pacific: A Pragmatic Approach to Naval Arms Control', Peace Research Centre Working Paper No 29, Peace Research Centre, Australian National University, Canberra, February 1988, p 7.

23. Article 95 of the 1982 Law of the Sea Convention provides that 'Warships on the high seas have complete immunity from the jurisdiction of any state other than the flag state'.

24. Gerald Segal, 'Arms Control In Asia', *Arms Control*, Vol 8, No 1, May 1987, p 83.

25. Borawski, *From the Atlantic to the Urals*, p 1.

26. Mahakiko Asada, 'Confidence Building Measures in East Asia', *Asian Survey*, Vol XXVIII, No 5, May 1988, p 495.

27. Douglas Stuart, 'The International Context of Asian Arms Control', in Gerald Segal (ed), *Arms Control in Asia*, Macmillan Press, London, 1987, p 172.

28. Segal (ed), *Arms Control in Asia*, p 16.

29. Bruce Cumings, 'Power and Plenty in Northeast Asia', *World Policy Journal*, Vol V, No 1, Winter 1987-88, p 102.

30. Asada, p 496.

31. Robert A Manning, 'Moscow's Pacific Future: Gorbachev Rediscovers Asia', *World Policy Journal*, Vol V, No 1, Winter 1987-88, p 76.

32. Special Broadcasting Service (SBS) news, Sydney, May 25, 1988.

33. Byung-joon Ahn, 'Changes in North Korea and its Relations with South Korea', in *New Directions in East-West Relations — German and Korean Perspectives*, Institute of East and West Studies, Yonsei University, Seoul, 1987, p 381.

34. Segal, 'Arms Control in Asia', *Arms Control*, p 90.

35. In April 1984 US Secretary of State George Shultz proposed:

- Restoration of the non-military character of the Demilitarised Zone (DMZ) by pulling back and removing heavy weapons from the area;
- Regular inspection of the DMZ by teams composed of neutral nations to verify its non-military character;
- Prior notification by both North and South of military exercises;
- Mutual assignment of observers to such exercises.

(Paul Keal, 'Implications for Northeast Asia' in Thakur & Thayer [eds], p 70).

36. Quoted in Heinz Vetschera, *Confidence Building Measures (CBMs) and European Security*, Institute for Strategic Research, National Defence Academy, Vienna, June 1986, p 45.

37. Blechman, p 14.

38. Hanspeter Neuhold, 'The Stockholm Conference: A Neutral & Nonaligned Perspective' in Birnbaum & Huldt, p 48. The NNA group comprises Austria, Cyprus, Finland, Liechtenstein, Malta, Monaco, San Marino, Sweden, Switzerland and Yugoslavia. The Holy See and Ireland are in a class of their own.

39. An example was the neutral/nonaligned proposal of Nov 15, 1985, known as SC 7. It was the product of nine months of intensive work led by Sweden but with active Austrian and Swiss input. (Borawski, *From the Atlantic to the Urals*, pp 77-78).

40. Borawski, *From the Atlantic to the Urals*, p 13.

41. Hanspeter Neuhold, 'The Stockholm Conference: A Neutral & Non-Aligned Perspective' in Birnbaum & Huldt, p 45.

42. *Ibid*, p 42.

43. *Ibid*, p 50.

44. See Borawski, *From the Atlantic to the Urals*, p 96.

45. Delworth, p 2.

46. Blechman, p 27.

47. *Ibid*, p 29.

48. See Alistair I Johnston, 'China & Arms Control in the Asia-Pacific', paper delivered to the Conference on Maritime Security & Arms Control in the Pacific Region, Vancouver, Canada, May 19-20, 1988.

49. John M Lamb, 'Pacific Arms Control: An Agenda For Canada', paper presented to the Conference on Maritime Security & Arms Control, Vancouver, Canada, May 19-20, 1988, pp 14-15.

50. *Sydney Morning Herald*, April 9, 1988.

51. *Australian Financial Review*, *The Australian* and *The Age*, June 30, 1988.

52. *Pacific Defence Reporter*, February 1988, p 27.

Peace, international security and co-operation in Northeast Asia and the Asia-Pacific

A V SERGIEV
Senior advisor, Policy Planning Department, Ministry of Foreign Affairs, Soviet Union

SINCE the First Asia-Pacific Roundtable in Kuala Lumpur to discuss problems of strengthening security and building confidence in the Asia-Pacific region in January 1987, many international developments have taken place in which the Soviet Union took an active part. The new political thinking has made it possible to formulate a new concept of Soviet foreign policy based on the conclusion that despite its highly contradictory nature the world today is an integral entity whose individual parts are interdependent. Such interdependence of different countries calls for peaceful coexistence, co-operation and political settlement of acute problems as well as preventing the risk of outbreak of a nuclear catastrophe. The overall Soviet policy course is aimed at broadening dialogue and co-operation with all countries and at improving the international situation as a whole. This course has been confirmed at the 19th All-Union Conference of the Communist Party of the Soviet Union (CPSU) in Moscow.

The summit meetings between the General Secretary of the CPSU Central Committee Mikhail Gorbachev and the President of the United States Ronald Reagan in Washington and Moscow were major international developments. Their main outcome is the deepening of the political dialogue between the Soviet Union and the US covering all key problems of bilateral and international relations. Purposeful efforts by the two sides have made possible further progress in the field of arms limitation and reductions. The exchange of instruments of ratification in Moscow put into effect the treaty on the elimination of Soviet and US intermediate-range and shorter-range missiles signed earlier in Washington. This treaty is history's first international agreement providing for the elimination of two classes of nuclear armaments in the Soviet Union and the US. This in fact is tantamount to the beginning of efforts to build a world free of nuclear weapons. The summit meeting in Moscow recorded convergence of the positions of the two sides on a number of aspects of reducing strategic offensive arms in conditions of preserving the Anti-Ballistic Missile (ABM) Treaty, of reductions in conventional arms and armed forces in Europe, limiting and stopping nuclear testing and banning chemical weapons.

The Moscow summit as well as Soviet-US summitry in general have enlarged in recent years the possibilities for improving the general atmosphere and contributed to shaping a favourable political climate in international relations. What is now taking shape is a brand new, fundamentally new, qualitatively new, international situation.

We are glad that essentially all states including countries of the Asia-Pacific region have positively assessed the signing by the Soviet Union and the US of the Intermediate-range Nuclear Forces (INF) Treaty. In fact all nations also support the efforts of the Soviet Union and the US aimed at reaching agreement on strategic arms reductions. The outcome of those contacts no doubt affect the situation in the Asia-Pacific.

The situation in the Asia-Pacific has developed in a quite contradictory way. On the one hand there are positive trends and serious shifts in healthy directions; on the other hand, continuing conflicts and a dangerous level of military confrontation. There are, however, reasons to point out that there still prevails a tendency toward the relaxation of international tensions and improvements in the situation. One can hardly deny that Soviet peace initiatives have played an important part in recent years in promoting this tendency. The participants in the Asia-Pacific Roundtable meetings know the Soviet concept of security in the Asia-Pacific region. It was outlined in Gorbachev's speech in Vladivostok and in his answers to questions put to him by the Indonesian newspaper *Merdeka*. The essence of this concept is the pooling of efforts of all countries of this vast region, co-operation and full respect for every nation's right to live as it chooses and to settle its problems independently in conditions of peace. Our approach to settling those problems is a *highly constructive* one.

Soviet initiatives relating to the Asia-Pacific region are an important part of the concept of the comprehensive international security system, put forward earlier by the Soviet Union. In short they include the following:

- Settling regional conflicts;
- Curbing proliferation and buildup of nuclear arms in Asia and the Pacific;
- Commencing negotiations on reducing naval activity in the Pacific, first of all that of ships carrying nuclear weapons;
- Resuming negotiations on making the Indian Ocean a zone of peace;
- Beginning stage-by-stage radical reductions in armed forces and conventional armaments in Asia to the limits of reasonable sufficiency; and
- Holding practical discussions on confidence building measures and non-use of force in the region.

Soviet proposals that build on numerous peace initiatives of other countries, socialist as well as non-aligned states, and existing positive diplomatic experience of the past years, have created a real opportunity for all countries of the Asia-Pacific region to participate on the basis of equality in the general process of improving the international situation and to lend their authority to disarmament efforts. Foreign policy actions of our country have clearly demonstrated in recent years our willingness to search, persistently and patiently, for solutions that would open up the way toward mutually acceptable arrangements on the key issues of security in the Asia-Pacific region and thus to co-operate in the closest possible manner with all the states of this region.

It is known that the Soviet Union agreed to include its medium- and shorter-range missiles deployed in the Asian part of our country, in the general agreement on elimination of the nuclear armaments of this type. This is essentially the first practical step towards nuclear disarmament in the Asia-Pacific region. We have declared our willingness to accept a commitment not to increase the number of aircraft carrying nuclear weapons in the Asian part of the Soviet Union, if the US did not deploy additional nuclear weapons able to reach Soviet territory. Part of the Soviet military contingent has been withdrawn from the Mongolian People's Republic. Soviet military units are being increasingly withdrawn from Afghanistan in pursuance of Geneva accords.

Further changes for better relations between the Soviet Union and China in the political, economic and cultural fields have great significance for improving the international situation. Their trade and economic co-operation is generally developing successfully. We highly appreciate China's contribution in removing the threat of nuclear war and in enhancing peace and international security. It is with satisfaction that one can note that efforts of our two largest socialist nations in the international arena have largely a similar thrust. The Soviet Union and China take similar approaches to a number of key international problems. The Soviet Union consistently conducts a policy of establishing confidence, expanding political dialogue, and enhancing mutually beneficial and good-neighbourly co-operation with China.

The public in the Far East and other regions are well aware of the latest positive initiatives by North Korea. To name but a few, one could mention proposals to withdraw all types of US nuclear weapons and troops from South Korea, to turn the Korean Peninsula into a nuclear-free zone, to work out a declaration on non-aggression between North and South Korea, to found a democratic federated Korean republic through dialogue and negotiations between the parties involved. Last year Pyongyang proposed holding high-level military and political talks between North and South Koreans to discuss such issues as mutual renunciation of major military manoeuvres, phased reductions in armed forces on both sides, economic and interparliamentary talks, and negotiations on other topical issues related to easing the tensions on the Korean Peninsula. If implemented, those proposals would make a real contribution to ensuring peace and security in Korea and the Asia-Pacific.

Vietnam, Kampuchea and Laos have given fresh impetus to their efforts at improving relations with China and the Association of Southeast Asian Nations (Asean) in order to turn Southeast Asia into a region of peace, stability and co-operation. Thanks to the realistic and flexible stance of the government of the People's Republic of Kampuchea and of the socialist nations in Indochina a new situation is emerging in Kampuchean affairs that offers good prospects for national reconciliation. Another trend in recent years is in expanding political contacts between India and China. Their moves for better relations have become an important aspect of the international situation in Asia.

In the context of further development of external political ties of the Soviet Union we attach great political significance to the visits to the Soviet Union by Malaysian Prime Minister Dato' Seri Dr Mahathir Mohamad last summer, then Thai Prime Minister Prem Tinsulanon last May, and former Indonesian Minister of Foreign Affairs Mochtar Kusumaatmadja.

Many other developments that have recently taken place, including in the Asia-Pacific countries, demonstrate greater aspirations for more durable peace and security and for ridding humankind of the yoke of nuclear weapons. The Rarotonga Treaty has been worked out declaring the South Pacific ocean a nuclear-free zone. The Soviet Union has become the first nuclear power to join the Rarotonga Treaty that has proclaimed the establishment of that region's first nuclear-free zone.

Japan is our neighbour and an influential factor of world politics in its own right. Developing ties with Japan is a long-term objective of our future policy. In his talk with a Japanese Socialist party delegation on May 6, 1988, Gorbachev stressed two aspects in the Soviet approach to relations with Japan, that is, we are prepared to improve relations on the basis of post-war realities and no expectations should be entertained that we would ever be forcing our friendship on the Japanese. Gorbachev said that 'The Soviet people, the Soviet leadership favour friendship with the Japanese people, with Japan... If we actively develop our relations, if we seek to make them friendly, one kind of future is in store for us. If we choose to embark upon another path, we'll get another kind of future. The role that our relations will play in attaining global progress and universal security will be contingent on this. Let us start restructuring our relations and not allow them to spin along some broken record grooves, playing a few bars of the same tune over and over again but failing to produce a complete song' (*Pravda*, May 7, 1988).

On the whole there are positive changes in the international situation in general and in the Asia-Pacific region in particular. But at the same time, it is neccessary for all nations to exert greater efforts in promoting that process. In Northeast Asia as well as throughout the world, nations are facing two strategic problems: First, to expand and enhance disarmament and second, to build international security on a qualitatively different basis.

Global nuclear disarmament is directly related to the problem of ensuring security in Asia and the Pacific. In our opinion, one of the major objectives for the international organisations must be to work out and design a disarmament concept based on the idea of an integral and interdependent world with its individual regions. Consolidating international security in the Asia-Pacific region is a major policy of ours pursued in its own right. The Soviet Union has undertaken not to be the first to use nuclear weapons and is prepared to conclude a convention offering greater security guarantees to non-nuclear nations, an agreement about non-deployment of nuclear weapons in the territories of those nations where now there are no nuclear weapons. Our country stated on numerous occasions that the Soviet Union will not use nuclear weapons against those nations which refused to produce and obtain them and do not have them in their territories. The Soviet Union is prepared to conclude an agreement with any non-nuclear nations to this effect.

The Soviet Union is fully prepared to give up its status of a nuclear power if other nuclear nations do likewise. Meanwhile our country is ready to make drastic cuts in practical manifestations of this status, in particular to support the establishment of nuclear-free zones and to provide relevant guarantees to the states participating in them. Nuclear-free zones are important in that they can be instrumental in reducing the scope of nuclear preparations and disengaging nuclear forces of confronting alliances thereby scaling down the threat of nuclear conflict. The establishment of those zones helps build international confidence, strengthens stability in nuclear power relations and bolsters the nuclear weapon non-proliferation regime.

In this sense we attach great importance to the proposal put forward by North Korea to turn the Korean peninsula into a nuclear-free peaceful zone as well as the desire of Asean countries to turn Southeast Asia into a nuclear-weapons-free zone. These proposals, if implemented, would contribute to freeing mankind from the threat of nuclear war. The question of establishing a nuclear-weapons-free zone in Southeast Asia is under active discussion by the Asean countries. At the insistence of peace advocates, provisions have been included in the new Philippine constitution to the effect that the Philippines, acting in its national interests, pursues the policy of having no nuclear weapons on its territory. Australia and New Zealand are supported by the international public at large in their vigorous opposition to French nuclear testing in the Pacific.

At the same time the Soviet Union is pressing for drastic reductions in armed forces and conventional armaments in Asia to levels of reasonable sufficiency. Reducing naval confrontation in oceans and seas is, indeed, an urgent problem nowadays. After all, today's confrontation line runs essentially in the areas where navies are in contact with one another. In our view, proceeding from the integral nature of the disarmament process, in future it will be impossible to leave aside the problems of how to limit the activities of, and make cuts in the navies, and it seems that these problems should be initially resolved at the regional level. Mikhail Gorbachev's speeches in Vladivostok, Murmansk and Belgrade dwelt on these problems more than once. He offered detailed proposals on limiting naval activities in the Indian and Pacific Ocean areas. These relate, in particular, to proposals on limiting the zones of naval activity of warships carrying nuclear weapons so that they do not approach the coast of another country within the striking range of their nuclear weapons, limiting anti-submarine rivalry and prohibiting anti-submarine activities, including aerial anti-submarine activities, in certain zones.

The first stage of limited naval activities could consist of implementing confidence building measures in the naval field. They could include advance notifications of transfers and manoeuvres of naval and associated air forces, limitations on the number, scale and zones of exercises, invitations for observers to such exercises and information exchanges. As a confidence building measure it would be advisable to compare data on naval forces and capabilities, to discuss principles of using naval forces and to compare the goals of naval exercises and manoeuvres. Indeed, the Stockholm Conference has provided a unique experience in this field, which could be used in the negotiations in Northeast Asia as well. All these ideas could be tested in the North Pacific and later extended to its southern part and other countries of the region.

As is well known, all states are interested in making sea lanes reliable and secure. For this purpose zones of lower density of armaments and of enhanced confidence could be established on major international ocean lanes and offensive forces and weapons could be withdrawn from such zones. As far as ensuring security at sea is concerned, we should be guided by the concept of non-offensive defence in order to preclude the risk of surprise attack and large-scale offensive activities at sea. We believe that the time is ripe for the Soviet Union together with the US and other nuclear powers to notify on the basis of reciprocity that their warships calling at foriegn ports carry no nuclear weapons on board.

It may be recalled that the Soviet Minister for Foreign Affairs Eduard Shevardnadze at the Third Special Session of the UN General Assembly on problems of disarmament expressed the view that it would be desirable to create a United Nations naval force made up of units provided by the UN Security Council permanent members. The Soviet Union proposes convening a special international conference on these issues with initial discussions to be held at the United Nations at a multilateral meeting of military experts and then at a special meeting of the UN Security Council.

The Soviet Union believes that mutual withdrawal of foreign troops and military bases from the territories of other countries is an important element of strengthening international security. This question has a special political urgency for the Asia-Pacific region. The Soviet Union proposes that foreign military presence and foreign military bases in foreign territories be eliminated by the year 2000. These problems could be solved gradually, taking into account regional characteristics and genuine needs for security and defence. Where the presence of troops is really necessary to maintain peace, these troops should be provided by the United Nations.

Further on, as the process of arms limitation and disarmament evolves and expands and as more and more countries participate in this process, undoubtedly new effective forms of control will be called for and the United Nations will have an ever greater role to play in that process. Naturally, security problems (preventing conflicts and wars) are not the only field for co-operation. Common and parallel interests of various states in Northeast Asia include many issues of expanding economic co-operation, including global problems of today. It is known that it is the economic contradictions that are today the main source of political and military conflicts. Let me emphasise that the economic interests of the Soviet Union — both global and regional, that is, in the Asia-Pacific region — do not run counter to the economic interests of the US, Japan and China. It is no secret that the main economic competitor of the US in this region is Japan rather that the Soviet Union. In an effort to become an active participant in economic relations within the Asia-Pacific region, the Soviet Union does not seek to 'oust' any country from the region or to undermine that country's economic interests there. Indeed, frankly speaking, our country (even if it wanted to) does not have economic capabilities to do that. The Soviet Union's international economic security programme rejects neocolonialist methods but does not require the demolition of historically evolved economic ties based on legitimate interests of various countries.

The programme for peace and security in the Asia-Pacific region put forward by Mikhail Gorbachev in Vladivostok envisages the development of stable, equal and mutually beneficial economic co-operation among all states of the region, which serves as a sound basis for enhancing trust and understanding among them. We believe it necessary to integrate the eastern region of the Soviet Union, which at present lags far behind other regions of the country in terms of the scale and rate of economic development, into the systems of international division of labour. In accordance with the resolutions of the 27th CPSU Congress a long-term government programme for the comprehensive development of the Far Eastern economic region, the Buryat Autonomous Republic and Chita region up to the year 2000 was adopted. The programme provides for higher growth rates (compared to the country's overall rates) in the fields of housing, communal and social construction, industrial production, export capabilities of the Far East and Transbaikal regions and for an improved food-producing industry in the region. It includes measures to use natural resources rationally and protect the environment. It is planned to develop a highly effective economic complex in the Far East, which will become an integral part of the system of national and international division of labour.

The restructuring of the Soviet economic mechanism and, in particular, its foreign economic activities, clears the way for the development of the Soviet Far East's international economic ties. The growing economic independence of enterprises, the right to establish direct links with foreign partners and the setting up of joint ventures provide propitious conditions for intensifying their foreign economic contacts, expanding their commercial relations and co-operation with socialist, developing and developed capitalist countries in the Asia-Pacific region. The Asia-Pacific countries have to tackle problems in the areas of environmental protection and power engineering, public health and education, exploitation of oceanic resources and utilisation of outer space for economic purposes. It is difficult for a single country or even a limited group of countries to resolve those problems. The need to co-ordinate and rally efforts is evident.

In relying upon its economic, scientific and human potential the Soviet Union is willing to participate in joint projects which would allow the peoples of the Pacific to live in greater dignity and security. We are firm in our belief that the establishment of broad, equitable and mutually beneficial co-operation among all Asian states is a sound guarantee for removing the threat of war and improving the political climate in the Asia-Pacific. The foreign policy conclusion is that interstate relations should not give priority to existing discrepancies and differences, but taking into account

region, its continuing security presence and its commitment to an open international trading system.

It is against this background and with this perspective that we should take up today's subject. To deal adequately with the subject of confidence building measures in the Asia-Pacific region and to assess their applicability to it, we should, first, ascertain if confidence is indeed lacking in the region and, second, understand why. A good beginning is to identify the underlying sources of tensions. Throughout the region, the primary sources of tension are to be found in: The unresolved nature of outstanding political issues in Sino-Soviet relations; Soviet-Japanese relations; the accompanying 20-year Soviet military build-up and modernisation of land, air and naval forces; and the use of force and intimidation by Soviet clients Vietnam and North Korea against neighbouring states.

This paper will focus on confidence building measures and tension reduction in Northeast Asia: The Korean peninsula and the North Pacific. I will leave it to others to discuss issues related to Sino-Soviet relations and relations between the Soviet Union and Japan.

The Korean peninsula

US policy toward South Korea has, over the past four decades, sought to enhance security on the peninsula, advance domestic political development, and promote economic growth. The US security commitment has contributed significantly to stability on the Korean peninsula and to the security of South Korea. At the same time, the Korean people have made South Korea a competitive force in international commerce. And, over the past year, the Korean people, the political parties and the government have engaged in a process which suggests a maturing of political development.

Yet, the political division of the peninsula remains as a legacy of the Korean war. Fundamental differences in economic, political and social systems between the Republic of Korea and the Democratic People's Republic of Korea mark the Korean peninsula as a source of continuing tension in Northeast Asia. Tensions have been heightened by the North's growing international isolation, — a result of its own activities against the accepted norms of international behaviour — by its earned reputation for volatile and unpredictable behaviour, and by the continuing military confrontation across the demilitarised zone (DMZ).

Militarily, the North, for most of the period since the Korean War, has maintained a distinct military advantage over the South — North Korea's military budget absorbs over 20 per cent of its gross national product. Today, the North still maintains quantitative leads in critical areas, such as number of troops, artillery and armour. In ground forces, the North enjoys a 250,000-man advantage in personnel (850,000:600,000), a nearly 3:1 advantage in armour (3,000:1,000) and, with 5,000 artillery tubes (as well as 2,000 multiple rocket launchers), a 1.5:1 edge in artillery. In the air, the North's quantitative lead in fighter aircraft, 680:440, is at least partially offset by the South's more technologically advanced air force. However, recent improvements in the North's air arsenal, MiG-23s, MiG-25s and surface-to-air missiles (SAMs), whittle at the South's qualitative lead and the recent appearance of Soviet supplied MiG-29s and SA-5 surface-to-air missiles are troubling developments.*

The US, in support of its commitment to the 1953 US-South Korean Mutual Defence Treaty, stations more than 40,000 army, navy and air force personnel in the South. The US army ground component accounts for approximately three-quarters of the total US presence. Given the fact that 65 per cent of the North's military strength is deployed within 40 miles of the border, that Seoul and much of the South's industry and one-third of its population is located 25 miles from the border, the threat to the South, and to stability and security on the peninsula is real. The US and South Korea have attempted to deal with this condition through realistic, practical and pragmatic proposals for tension reduction and through confidence building measures aimed at normalising the environment. The US sees such normalisation as establishing an environment in which cross-recognition can be effected, leading to a further reduction of tensions and the ultimate reunification of the peninsula.

The key to resolving South-North problems — and in reducing tensions — is to be found in Seoul and Pyongyang. A critical first step must be the resumption of the South-North dialogue. The June 3, 1988 proposal by South Korea for 'talks between high-level authorities of the South and the North' to discuss participation in the Seoul Olympics, the exchange of people, and 'ways to facilitate the resumption of the existing channels of dialogue' appears to suggest that the resumption of the dialogue is a major objective of the Roh Tae-Woo administration.

Thus far, tension reduction proposals by the North, such as calls for the withdrawal of all foreign forces, for a meeting of South-North government and non-government leaders, and its recent call for a meeting between student leaders have, in reality, been aimed less at reducing tensions than at circumventing or undercutting the authority of South Korea to manage South-North issues and at splitting the US and South Korea. A *sine qua non* for the reduction of tension on the peninsula and for the success of tension reduction measures must be acceptance by the North of the legitimacy and reality of the government of South Korea.

The US shares with South Korea policies aimed at drawing the North out of its isolation, reducing tensions, and developing relations between the South and the North. To this end, the US in March 1987 modified its diplomatic contact guidance toward North Korea. The North was informed that US officials would be prepared to discuss any topic, provided the discussions took place in neutral settings. It was also made clear that such contacts could lead to an improvement in US-North Korean relations. For reasons unclear to the US, the North — despite its repeated calls for direct contacts with the US — ignored this opportunity.

In response to the destruction by North Korean agents of KA-858, the US rescinded its modest initiative. The US continues to be interested in drawing the North out; that interest can be best served by more responsible behaviour on the part of the North. The successful, non-disrupted conduct of the Seoul Olympic Games will serve as a test of the North's stated intentions.

As for military confidence building measures, practicality and realism are the criteria by which they should be judged. Over the past 20 years, the US has advanced the following measures:

- 1967: A proposal to disarm guards in the Joint Security Area at Pammunjon.
- 1970: A six-point tension reduction proposal including disarming and separation of guards in joint security area and informal security officers' meeting.
- 1971: A three-point proposal — effective use of joint duty officers, easing of tension in DMZ and disarming DMZ.
- 1981: A four-point proposal — proper use of joint observer teams, inspection of DMZ, disarming of guards in DMZ and informal security officers' meeting.
- 1981: Proposal for mutual notification of major military exercises.
- 1982: Annual pre-notifications of, and invitations to North Korean observers to, Team Spirit exercises.

The North's proposal for troop reductions — the North has proposed a reduction of 100,000 in its armed forces by 1992 to coincide with the simultaneous withdrawal of US forces from the South — and for a nuclear free zone on the peninsula is an effort, under the guise of confidence building, to drive a wedge between the US and South Korea. By attempting to undermine the US-South Korean security relationship, the North's proposals subtract from, rather than add to, the measure of confidence on the peninsula. Similarly, proposals which fail to recognise that US forces are deployed in the South at the request of South Korea also must be seen as attempts by the North to deny the legitimacy of the government of South Korea. CBM proposals which deny reality are inherently non-starters.

Military exercises on the peninsula are a reality — on both sides of the DMZ. Because exercise enhances military effectiveness, manoeuvres are a fact of military life. However, exercises run by the North are in a north-to-south offensive direction, while those of South Korea and the US are conducted on an east-west axis. To deal with concerns arising from training activities, such as the annual US-South Korean Team Spirit exercises, the US and South Korea since 1982 have offered a CBM regime of pre-notification coupled with invitations to the North and to China to send observers. In 1989, the US and South Korea will again give pre-notification and extend invitations for observers to attend the Team Spirit exercise. We hope for a more forthcoming response from the other side of the DMZ.

The North Pacific

It is important to recognise that the US presence in the Asia-Pacific region has, over the past 20 years, enhanced political stability and security throughout the region. The US security presence has also helped to establish an environment which has nurtured the remarkable economic success story of the region. And, it should be recognised that the US military presence in the region remains there in response to the security concerns of our allies and is welcomed by them.

Today, in Northeast Asia a major source of tension is to be found in the massive Soviet military buildup over the past two decades. (Also, see appendix).

Let us look at the record:

- Soviet ground forces in the Far East consist of 57 divisions — a four-fold increase since 1985 — predominantly deployed against China. Equipment continues to be upgraded.*
- The Pacific Fleet, the largest of the four Soviet fleets, has increased to 861 — an increase of 42 ships since the end of 1984. Over the past three years, a modest reduction in ballistic missile submarines, attack submarines and principal surface combatants is attributable to the removal of obsolete units from service and their replacement by newer, more capable units, such as the Kirov class nuclear-powered, guided-missile cruiser and the Akula class nuclear-powered attack submarines.*
- It should also be noted that Soviet presence in the region has been enhanced by its access to air and naval facilities at Cam Ranh Bay, access secured at a time when the US presence in the region was contracting.*
- Over 2,300 aircraft — 353 long-range bombers and 1,955 tactical combat aircraft — are deployed by the Soviet Union in the Far East. Reorganisation and introduction of fourth-generation fighter and fighter-bomber aircraft have enhanced overall Soviet capabilities. Soviet air forces in the Far East have been reconfigured to emphasise deep-strike operations.*

Over the past decade, the US force presence in the region has remained relatively static. Today, there are approximately 160,000 US military personnel forward deployed in Japan, Korea and the Philippines — much the same number as in 1978. The number of air wings has remained constant at five; similarly, the number of army divisions at two — in Hawaii and South Korea. Of the six carrier battle-groups assigned to the Pacific only one is forward deployed, in Japan. Major improvements involved the deployment of two F-16 squadrons at Misawa, the deployment of two battleship battle-groups to the Pacific (home ported on the west coast of the US and Hawaii), the deployment of Special Forces battalion to Okinawa and the modernisation of aircraft, ships, and weapons systems.*

It is against this background — one of increasing Soviet military presence in the region, of unresolved political and territorial disputes involving the Soviet Union and its allies in the region — that proposals for confidence building measures in the region have been advanced. For analytical purposes, such proposals can be divided into three broad categories: Proposals for a Helsinki-like conference for security and disarmament, proposals to limit or deny naval operations in particular areas, and proposals for nuclear free zones.

Proposal for a Helsinki-like conference

From the 1975 Helsinki Accord through the Stockholm Conference, Europe has witnessed the evolution of a regime of confidence and security building measures. These treaty agreements have established a CBM discipline that calls for: Exchanges of annual military calendars, advance notification of military activities of specific size and composition, mandatory invitation of observers, and the right of on-site inspection to assure compliance.

However, it is essential to recognise that geographic, political and strategic factors that made for success in Europe are, by and large, lacking in the Asia-Pacific region. In Europe, both US and Soviet forces are forward-deployed on the territory of allies on opposite sides of a clearly-demarcated land division of the continent. The Asia-Pacific region is without the clear North Atlantic Treaty Organisation (NATO)-Warsaw Pact division.

In contrast to Europe, among the countries of the Asia-Pacific region there is a tendency to define security issues at the individual country rather than regional level. For example, South Korea focusses on North Korea while Thailand looks at Vietnam. Security perceptions are less clearly defined for the region as a whole and, as a result, there is a much weaker basis for multilateral co-operation. For both the US and the Soviet Union, alliance relationships are bilateral and lack the close integration of Europe. In Europe, ground forces are key components in the NATO-Warsaw Pact balance, with air and naval forces in supporting roles. In the Asia-Pacific region — with the exception of the Sino-Soviet border and the Korean Peninsula — naval and air forces dominate.

Soviet land, air and naval forces in Northeast Asia operate from Soviet territory and waters adjacent to the Soviet Union while US forces, primarily naval and air units, are forward deployed in Japan and Korea to provide for the defence of allies in the region. In addition to a regional defence role, the US naval presence serves, at a strategic level, to enhance global deterrence.

China's possession of nuclear weapons also complicates a regional approach to nuclear arms control. It is unlikely that China would participate in multilateral nuclear arms reduction talks before the US and the Soviet Union agree to drastic reductions in nuclear weaponry. Although Chinese officials have in the past indicated that 50 per cent would represent such a reduction, its position is somewhat less clear today. Former Foreign Minister Wu Xueqian told an April 6, 1988 news conference that 50 per cent does not represent a drastic reduction.

Finally, we should remember that the Helsinki Conference was called to ratify an European settlement of European political and territorial issues. In an area marked by unresolved political and territorial claims, the Helsinki model does not apply to the region at this time.

In short, the strategic equation in the Asia-Pacific region is a complex one, reflecting the nature of its security problems. The region's unique geographic, political, military and strategic factors must be taken into account in any realistic approach to confidence building and conflict reduction in the Asia-Pacific region. Geographic and force asymmetries in the Asia-Pacific region suggest that nuclear arms control measures in the region will be most effectively addressed in the context of US-Soviet global negotiations.

Proposals on naval activity

In contrast to the Soviet Union which is a self-sufficient land power, the US is a maritime nation, pursuing a coalition strategy, dependent — as are its friends and allies in the Asia-Pacific region — on seaborne commerce for economic well-being and ultimately for security. From a US perspective, the practical effects of such proposals, however well intentioned, is to restrict the mobility of US naval and air forces, limit the US ability to respond effectively to threats to the security of our allies and friends in the Asia-Pacific region, and undermine the US global deterrent strategy.

Let us look at some recent proposals for confidence building measures:

- *Proposal by the Soviet Union to freeze the number of nuclear-capable aircraft in the Soviet Asia — on the condition that the US does not introduce additional nuclear means capable of reaching the Soviet Union.*
  This proposal would constrain the deterrence of nuclear capable US forces and, because of their dual capability, also restrict US conventional defence capabilities in the area. A freeze on the deployment of Soviet aircraft would not make less threatening the capability of Soviet air power, as presently configured and based, to strike the region's capital cities, target its highly concentrated population and industrial centres, and threaten the sea lines of communications. Even if the Soviet Union were willing to freeze the growth of all its nuclear means in Asia, this capability would remain.
- *Proposal to limit the areas in which ships carrying nuclear weapons could navigate, keeping such naval platforms out of range of each other's homeland.*
  This proposal would result in major changes in US military deterrence in the region. Because nuclear systems are capable of long-range operations, the practical effect of such proposals would be either to limit naval operations crucial to deterrence or to denuclearise the navy.

  Given our wide-ranging alliance relationships in the Asia-Pacific region, restricting the area of US naval operations is not acceptable. And, given the navy's role in US global deterrence strategy, denuclearisation of the navy is not a reasonable option. Such restrictions would detract from, not enhance, regional and global security. Finally, verification of such proposals would be next to impossible.
- *Proposals for submarine free zones and for anti-submarine warfare free zones.*
  From a US perspective, such proposals, by creating safe havens for both attack and ballistic missile submarines, are aimed at offsetting the technological edge possessed by the US navy. And, the creation of anti-submarine warfare (ASW) free zones would free up Soviet ASW assets for deployment beyond their present stations. In addition, because so many air and naval platforms have ASW capabilities, definition and verification problems would again be raised.
- *Proposals to limit the scale and number of naval exercises in the region.*
  Given the strong naval/air component of our deployments throughout the region, such restrictions would fall most unevenly on the US and on exercises with our Asian allies. The complexity of co-ordinating air/naval operations with our allies requires continuing attention and exercise.

Behind the words, the real intention of such Soviet proposals is to restrict US naval activities. They also serve to deflect attention from what are the real sources of tension in the region. As such, they fall short in building real confidence. Despite the ongoing debate over particular elements of the US strategy toward the region, it is important to recognise that there are key constants which will continue to shape it:

(1) The US is a maritime nation, following a maritime strategy.
(2) Its allies in the Asia-Pacific region are located on the western littoral of the Pacific.
(3) To defend its allies, forward deployment of its naval and air assets is essential.
(4) The effectiveness of the US naval and air forces in supporting our alliance relationships as well as in contributing to regional and global deterrence will require maximal training and operational freedom.

Proposals to establish regional nuclear free zones

The US is deeply committed to bringing about a safer strategic environment involving progressively less reliance on nuclear weapons. As in the Intermediate-range Nuclear Forces (INF) agreement, the US goal in arms control talks with the Soviet Union is to reach equitable and verifiable agreements on deep reductions in nuclear arsenals that will serve to enhance global stability and reduce the risk of war throughout the world, including the Asia-Pacific region.

In pursuit of measures to enhance nuclear non-proliferation, the US has signed treaties and protocols establishing nuclear weapons free zones in Latin America and Antarctica, areas well removed from superpower rivalry. At the same time, the US has pursued an international security policy based on the concept of deterrence — a 40-year success story in preventing the recurrence of global war with nuclear weapons. In so doing, the US has accepted the hard reality that one of its major roles on nuclear weapons is to deter their use by others and to deter major conventional attacks.

Toward the Asia-Pacific region, the US has developed security policies aimed at maintaining a stable military balance, enhancing the credibility of its commitments to friends and allies, and reinforcing global deterrence. Under current circumstances, however, the growing number of proposals for regional nuclear-free zones has the potential to undermine the US policy of global deterrence. A proliferation of nuclear free zones could limit the US ability to meet security commitments worldwide. As a matter of policy, the US opposes proposals for regional zones that erode nuclear deterrence and undercut existing security arrangements.

In reaching the decision not to adhere to the Protocols of the Treaty of Rarotonga, the US was unable to isolate concern for regional views from larger global concerns and responsibilities. US practices and activities in the region are consistent with the treaty and its three protocols.

Conclusion

In its approach to confidence building measures and tension reduction proposals for the Asia-Pacific region, the US has to ask:

- Do they strengthen global and regional deterrence?
- Do they enhance, not erode, US alliance relationships?
- Do they enhance the confidence of our friends and allies in the US's continuing commitment to common security objectives?
- Do they really reduce military tensions and build confidence between the superpowers?

The US sees the fundamental source of tension in the Asia-Pacific region as arising from its unresolved political conflicts and from the 20-year Soviet military buildup in the region. A resolution of the political questions and the development of a more benign Soviet approach to the region are the single, most important steps that need to be taken to reduce tensions and to build confidence.

Elements for tension reduction and confidence building in the region do exist. There are indications that Vietnam may be moving to reassess the cost/benefit analysis of its invasion and continuing occupation of Cambodia. A resolution of the conflict in Cambodia would be a real step in the direction of building confidence in the region. Similarly, a restarting of dialogue on the Korean peninsula based on the North's acceptance of the government of South Korea as a dialogue partner would move the process of confidence building along. The opening of the Siberia and the Maritime Provinces would move the Soviet Union toward real participation in the economic life of the region.

Real confidence building requires real deeds. It means tackling the tough issues and making the hard decisions.

NOTE

* All data are from open sources.

APPENDIX

Soviet military deployments in East Asia, 1968-88

	1968	1978	1988
FAR EAST TVD			
Divisions	25	43	57
Tanks	5,150	11,900	14,900
APC/IFVs	2,600	11,340	17,500
Artillery	1,850	5,400	13,700
Tactical SSMs	70	315	400
Tactical aircraft	1,050	1,400	1,300 *
PACIFIC OCEAN FLEET			
Ships: Total	660	726	861
Carriers	0	0	2
Principal surface combatants	55	67	75
Subs (general purpose, attack, cruise missiles)	95	90	92
Submarines (ballistic missiles, SSB, SSBN)	10	30	30
Amphibious warfare ships (LPD/LST)	0	9	14
Mine warfare ships and craft	110	110	105
Auxiliaries, patrol, amphibious craft	390	420	540
Naval aviation (combat, transport, trainer)	265	365	560
Naval infantry division	1-2 regt	1	1

Note:
* Drop due to reorganisation and more modern/capable aircraft.

COMMENTS

I WANT to thank Andrew Mack for a first rate paper — one I thoroughly enjoyed — and offer a few comments.

I agree with him that arms control is a difficult process in the Asia-Pacific region. In a region where there are unresolved territorial disputes, asymmetries in alliance and force structures, and a recognition that there is not one power balance but several, there are real difficulties in applying a Helsinki-type model.

Secondly, I agree with the proposition that strategic arms control is a process best conducted at a global rather than regional level. The INF treaty is a case in point, in which a global-level negotiation has had regional impact. Similarly, I believe that the current Strategic Arms Reduction Talks (START) negotiations, aimed at deep cuts in strategic arms, will have a similar impact on the region.

The exposition on issues related to SLBMs (submarine-launched ballistic missiles) underscores the difficulty posed by the weaponry for arms control in the region. Again, the SLBM issue is one best discussed at a global level — as it is being discussed currently in the START negotiations. Whatever the outcome of the negotiations, I do not believe the US will compromise its long-standing 'neither-confirm-nor-deny' policy which is at the heart of its strategy of deterrence.

As for operational arms control, in particular issues related to notification and transparency, I would like to clarify what seems to be a misperception as to the conduct of US naval exercises in the region, namely that they are conducted without notification to the international community. It should be recognised that, on the contrary, there is at least a 48-hour advance notice of most exercises — and in some instances, even greater advance notice. In passing, I would observe that in general this 48-hour advance notification has been sufficient to attract Soviet intelligence collection ships to 'observe' our exercises on an uninvited, informal basis.

As for confidence building that could be engendered by the publication of military information and data relating to defence budgets, this so far has been a one-way street. The US does this as a matter of practice. On the other hand, the Soviet Union has yet to initiate a similar process. We wait and, of course, encourage the Soviet Union to do so.

Another point which Andy makes — and with which I agree — is the self-serving nature of the Soviet Union's naval limitation proposals. Beyond the analysis in my paper, I would like to comment on one that was offered at the conference; namely, the removal of all foreign bases from the region. It requires little imagination to understand the implications of this proposal for the US presence in the region and for its alliance relations. This proposal, if accepted, would be tantamount to the biggest steal since the Alaska purchase. If I thought it were a serious offer, I'd counter with an offer to remove all bases East of the Urals to the West coast of the Sea of Japan — and throw in Petropavlosk too.

As for the discussion of the Maritime Strategy, despite the ongoing debate over whatever are the elements of the strategy at any particular time, it should be recognised that there are certain fundamental assumptions that govern, and will continue to govern, US deployments in the Asia-Pacific region. The simple fact that our allies are dispersed throughout the region — on the far side on the Pacific ocean — requires continued forward deployment of air and naval assets. But deployment without exercise is meaningless. And to make deterrence credible and effective, exercise is essential.

Also, Andy seems to suggest that the defence of the sea lanes is less important in the Pacific than in the Atlantic. I find this hard to accept in a region that is overwhelmingly dependent in general on seaborne commerce and in particular on energy supplies from the Persian Gulf. It is a simple fact that the sea lanes can be threatened not only by submarines but also by land-based Soviet naval air power with anti-ship weapons. And the Soviet base at Cam Ranh Bay provides expanded operational capabilities against seaborne commerce.

Again, a key objective of the Maritime Strategy — which is but one part of the US overall deterrence strategy — is to complicate Soviet planning, to deny the Soviet Union the option of concentrating on a particular preferred theatre of operations. I think the Maritime Strategy does this effectively, and to the extent that it does, it enhances the US global deterrence strategy. And this gets us back to the issue of deterrence.

And here Andy and I have a philosophical disagreement. The issue is not assuming what he claims needs to be determined, that is, that unprovoked Soviet aggression is a fundamental security problem. Rather, deterrence aims at convincing any potential aggressor that the risks and costs of aggression will exceed any possible gains. Naval deployments and exercises in the Pacific are aimed at reinforcing deterrence. They serve to enhance our confidence in our capabilities and, at the same time, provide the other side with a similar picture of those capabilities. In short, as a practitioner, I come back to the fact that deterrence has worked and continues to work at this time.

One last observation: The US force presence in the region has always corresponded to the security needs of the US and its allies. If the regional security environment changes, if conflicts are resolved, and if the Soviet military presence is moderated, I would think you would see a similar accommodation in terms of the US presence.

Kampuchea: One way forward

MOHAMED NOORDIN SOPIEE
Director General, Institute of Strategic and International Studies (ISIS) Malaysia

IT should be understood beyond any doubt at the very outset that everything in this paper* represents absolutely the personal opinion of the author. It should be equally clear that it is not a diplomatic document — in both meanings of that word; and should not be treated as one. It is also not an instrument of or for negotiation. It is nothing more — and nothing less — than an attempt to see how we can get out of the Kampuchea stalemate (should we think that that is a worthwhile thing to do).

Alternative solutions

It might be suggested that the situation in the last few years already constitutes one kind of solution: the stabilised stalemate solution. It is an interim solution and not a very moral one. Nevertheless, to be absolutely callous but realistic, what has been 'achieved' with great effort on all sides has been a stabilised stalemate, one that is awesomely costly to the Kampuchean people and burdensome to the Vietnamese people, but one that limits the internal and external repercussions of conflict. Like it or not, it has been the 'best' 'under the circumstances' 'solution' that has been achievable by any of the parties. It has been possible and it has been sustained only because of the contribution and the collaboration of all the key actors. No one really likes it but all have been prepared to live with it, while striving (within the present parameters) for a more 'optimal' solution from the point of view of their perceived interests.

* The author is highly indebted to the pioneering work done by Rohana Mahmood. It was she who first worked out a framework, thus sparking off a new line of research in ISIS.

If one refers to the present stalemate as ***Solution One*** there are at least nine rough alternative solutions to the Kampuchean Question. (One apologises to the countries concerned for the gross oversimplifications. The intention is to establish value-free models, not to describe present reality or past history. Also, all the scenarios below are premised on an unpartitioned Kampuchea).

Solution Two might be called the 'Vietnamese Annexation Solution' (involving the annexation of Kampuchea and the assimilation of the Kampuchean people and the Kampuchean state within, possibly, a Vietnamese federation of Indochinese states or the state of Vietnam).

Solution Three might be called the 'Vietnamese Satellite Solution' (involving a puppet government and a Kampuchea permanently and massively garrisoned by Vietnamese troops).

Solution Four might be called the 'Laos Solution' (involving the existence of a legally sovereign and stabilised Kampuchea that takes into the very fullest account the interests and policies of Vietnam on all major issues, that unswervingly goes along with Hanoi on all the critical issues and that has a very large Vietnamese military presence on its soil).

To re-state, the 'Laos Solution' is seen to be a situation that is:

- viable and sustainable, involving the existence of a state that is:
- legally sovereign,
- less than fully politically independent,
- not neutral (but strongly allied in the regional context),
- as 'nonaligned' as some members of NAM (Non-Aligned Movement),
- largely peaceful,
- politically stable, and
- no serious or even substantial threat to Thailand (and of course Vietnam).

Solution Five might very roughly be called the 'Yugoslavia Solution' (involving the establishment of a sovereign and fully independent Kampuchea that is not antagonistic towards Thailand or China [and that has normal relations with them] but that takes Vietnam into account on many issues and that will be appreciative of Vietnam's views and policies on the core key issues). It might be involved in an Indochinese association of states, but there will be no or few Vietnamese troops in Kampuchea.

To re-state, the 'Yugoslavia Solution' as it is envisaged here is one that involves:

(1) a political settlement that is viable and sustainable and that will establish a Kampuchea that is:
(2) legally sovereign,
(3) fully independent,
(4) neutral but sensitive,
(5) non-aligned,
(6) generally peaceful (but with continuing internal threats to peace),
(7) reasonably politically stable, and
(8) unthreatening (to Thailand and Vietnam).

The official position of Asean is that there should be a political resolution of the Kampuchean Question essentially on the basis of the 'Yugoslavia Solution'.

Solution Six might be referred to as the 'Switzerland Solution' (involving the existence of a sovereign and independent Kampuchea that is thoroughly and fiercely neutral).

Solution Seven might be called the 'Austria Solution' (involving the existence of a sovereign and independent Kampuchea that is legally neutral but that tilts towards Thailand and the West).

Solution Eight might be called the 'Burma Solution' (involving the existence of a sovereign and independent Kampuchea that lives in near complete isolation).

Solution Nine might be called the 'South Korea' or pro-West Solution.

Solution Ten might be called the 'Democratic Kampuchea Solution', involving a Kampuchea that is strongly tilted towards China (without, however, the inhuman excesses of the Khmer Rouge).

It is the belief of the writer that Solutions One to Four cannot be negotiated and can only be imposed by military means (which cannot now be found or will not now be found). Even the 'Laos Solution' is out of the question. Similarly, Solutions Six to Ten are not within the realm of possibility. At least from today's perspective, they cannot be politically negotiated.

It would be extremely important to discuss this point should there be a contrary viewpoint. Should the analysis somehow be right, and should we wish to seek a political solution to the Kampuchean Conflict, it is important to seek ways by which the compromise 'Yugoslavia Solution' (or if one wishes, the 'Finland Solution') can be secured.

One framework for a viable political settlement involving the establishment of a sovereign and reasonably independent, neutral, non-aligned, peaceful, stable and unthreatening Kampuchea

Purely as a theoretical exercise, embodying absolutely the personal views of the author, this section sets out one rough 'framework':

for a possibly viable
political settlement

involving the establishment of a Kampuchea that is:

legally sovereign,
independent,
non-aligned,
neutral,
peaceful,
stable, and
unthreatening

to both Vietnam and Thailand. (It is important to emphasise that the entire process is not a legal process, not a bureaucratic process; but a supremely political process with critical military and diplomatic dimensions. What is important is not form but substance).

Some may have their justifications for not being interested even in a theoretical framework, or in a viable political settlement, or in one that ensures sovereignty and a Kampuchea that is substantially independent, neutral, non-aligned, peaceful or stable. *If we are*, it might be useful to specify to some degree of concreteness:

(1) the conditions of viability, and
(2) the process of political settlement itself.

The conditions of viability

It would be ideal of course if it were possible to achieve a settlement that everyone, including the tuna fishermen in the South Pacific, would be delighted with. To be more practical, it might be suggested that the minimal conditions of viability are few:

(1) a settlement that Vietnam can accept and live with,
(2) a settlement that China can accept and live with,
(3) a settlement that Thailand can accept and live with (in both cases, for a substantial time, anyway),
(4) a viable structure and process of internal reconciliation, peaceful coexistence, and 'co-operation' between the critical Kampuchean parties to the Kampuchean conflict. It is preferable if this involved all four parties but it would appear that only three (including at least part of the Khmer Rouge) are absolutely essential,
(5) the establishment of a reasonably viable, independent, non-aligned and neutral (in the short and medium-term at least) *government* in Phnom Penh, and last,
(6) the construction of a viable structure and process of international 'guarantee'.

Although the conditions of viability are few, any settlement should also seek to set in place a series of factors and a set of forces that are conducive to and buttressing of the settlement result. Several countries are important in this regard. Among them are the United States, the Soviet Union, the Asean states, Japan, etc.

The process of political settlement (which could secure the conditions of viability)

This section sets out:

(1) the necessary components and the extremely useful components of the process of political settlement which could secure the conditions of viability, and
(2) one political critical path, one road map out of the Kampuchea dead end.

The necessary or extremely useful components of the process of political settlement

The following appear to be necessary or extremely useful components of any settlement process that is in keeping with the design specifications set out above:

(1) the achievement of the minimum necessary level of agreement among all vetoists, key actors and important actors with regard to processes and ends,
(2) gradual Vietnamese troop withdrawals, leading to complete withdrawal,
(3) achievement of the minimum level of Khmer national reconciliation required at each stage of the settlement process,
(4) military de-escalation and military ceasefire on all sides,
(5) the securing of sufficient internal security to allow for just about all the necessary or extremely useful conditions,
(6) the securing of sufficient government in Kampuchea,
(7) the securing of substantial international buttressing for a Kampuchean political settlement,
(8) a reasonably free, fair and legitimate exercise of self-determination,
(9) the retirement of some Khmer Rouge leaders,
(10) a very substantial role for Prince Sihanouk,
(11) ensuring that Kampuchea has the comprehensive basic infrastructure to exist as a viable state, and
(12) the establishment of an association of all Southeast Asian states.

As the above list suggests, we should not be interested in a solution process *a la* Afghanistan, which is so tightly focussed on Soviet troop withdrawal and so inadequately focussed on what comes after.

One political critical path

Purely as a theoretical exercise, let me test out one political critical path (that is not ideal but that might at the opportune time prove acceptable and practical). As with all critical paths, although there is one theoretically optimal path, the permutations are very great in number. A particular journey intended to reach a specific destination can be stopped and diverted at any particular step (although there are of course generally ways to get back on course). There are no doubt countless weaknesses and as many imponderables with regard to the three-phased, 11-staged process set out below. (Those who prefer fewer stages can themselves merge or 'collapse' those stages which can quite easily be merged, until they reach the personally preferred number. *En passant* also, it might be noted that the political critical path outlined below was initially worked out five months ago and remains virtually untouched).

PHASE ONE: THE CONFIDENCE-BUILDING, CONFLICT-SOLVING, PROBLEM-SOLVING, CONSENSUS-MAKING AND AGREEMENT-REACHING PHASE

Stage One:
The tete-a-tete. This tea for two between Prince Sihanouk and Mr Hun Sen was able to proceed, with very mixed results as we all know. But without it, the peace process would not have started to move as it has. I argued in February that Stage One may not be necessary before proceeding to Stage Two. Quite clearly, Stage Two has already started to begin.

Stage Two:
Discussions and negotiations. Writing five months ago, I suggested that these discussions and negotiations could be 'formal, informal and both, hopefully drawing in the other two Khmer factions, or at the very least, the Khmer Rouge or enough of the effective Khmer Rouge'.

'This process can start off with a cocktail party or a gathering by any other name convened by Asean.' It is gratifying to see the Indonesians taking the initiative to convene the 'Jakarta Informal Meeting' (otherwise known as 'JIM') starting on July 25.

Also writing five months ago, it was suggested that 'at the start of this stage and as an act of sincerity, which is of course reversible, Vietnam should make the first of its four-phase troop withdrawal'. (Please note that what is envisaged in this 'framework' is withdrawal in four rather than three phases).

'With regard to this voluntary withdrawal of a percentage of Vietnamese troops to be determined by Vietnam, it might be useful for an International Group of Eminent Observers, including representatives from all the Asean countries, the United States, the Soviet Union, China, Japan and others, to physically witness the actual withdrawal. This group should be accompanied by an International Observer Force consisting perhaps of contingents from such countries as India, Australia, Norway, Poland and Canada, etc.'

It is gratifying to note that Vietnam has announced its intention to withdraw 50,000 troops before the end of 1988, a figure that is somewhat higher than just about anyone could have expected even a few months ago. It would now gain a great deal by proceeding to organise an observer group which could help to verify troop withdrawal. (Otherwise the more cynical would believe that yet again troops were being rotated rather than withdrawn).

In my proposal of five months ago, it was also suggested that 'as an act of sincerity, all the other Khmer factions should unilaterally declare and effect a unilateral ceasefire in the pre-determined and specified period of voluntary Vietnamese troop withdrawal'. There has been no such formal declaration of a ceasefire but even the Vietnamese have conceded that a *de facto* military de-escalation is already in effect on the ground in Kampuchea.

It was also strongly argued that 'it is not wise to proceed to Stage Three without achieving the political and psychological transformations that are necessary and that should be achieved under Stage Two'. Once consensus is reached, progress can be extremely rapid, depending of course on the quality and durability of that consensus.

Stage Three:
We are very obviously still a very long way from Stage Three. But as envisaged, Stage Three would involve:

(1) formal agreement on the political process of settlement to be immediately followed by the Khmer factions forming, say,
(2) a Council of National Reconciliation, which would monitor:
(3) the actual withdrawal of one third of all remaining Vietnamese forces,

(4) the actual and effective cessation of military hostilities on the part of the Khmer resistance, and
(5) the actual cessation of all external aid to all the four Khmer factions.

(Above all, this is the stage when all sides will have to demonstrate their sincerity and political will or lack thereof. Neither the CGDK nor the PRK need yet be dissolved. [The option to go into reverse and to opt out at some future date — the escape hatch — is thus provided for]. Prince Sihanouk should obviously be the Chairman of the Council of National Reconciliation).

Stage Four:
The immediate convening of an International Conference on Peace in Cambodia, perhaps in Geneva, perhaps in Jakarta, perhaps in Bangkok, which should be quickly convened by the Council of National Reconciliation and which should invite all the key actors, all the core actors, all the concerned actors and all those nations which will constitute and establish an International Peace-Keeping Force (IPKF). This IPKF should be tasked with the responsibility of ensuring security, law and order in Kampuchea.

Secondly, the Conference should agree on the establishment of an International Control Commission (whose task should be:

- to supervise the IPKF,
- to supervise further Vietnamese withdrawals,
- to act to ensure as far as possible no external interference, and
- to supervise the general elections that will be held later).

(This conference will work out the specific details for the introduction of an effective International Peace-Keeping Force, an effective ICC and the final international guarantee).

PHASE TWO: THE IMPLEMENTATION PHASE

Stage Five:
(1) The quick introduction of an effective IPKF,
(2) the quick introduction of an effective International Control Commission — both formally at the request of the Council of National Reconciliation,
(3) the careful preparation of the PGC (Provisional Government of Cambodia),
(4) the confining of all Khmer armed forces to barracks, and
(5) the withdrawal of the second third of the Vietnamese forces in Kampuchea (so that:

- if there are 140,000 troops now,
- if the number voluntarily withdrawn under Stage Two is 50,000,
- with the number withdrawn under Stage Three being one third [30,000],

at the end of the withdrawal of the second third, there would be only 30,000 Vietnamese troops left).

Stage Six:
At the end of the third phase of Vietnamese troop withdrawal, the establishment of

a Quadripartite Provisional Government of Cambodia. This should include all the present factions although certain leaders may be excluded (or will have retired, or will have to be retired).

At this stage, it might be useful to introduce an international aid package for the development of Kampuchea.

Stage Seven:

(1) The completion of Vietnamese military withdrawal,
(2) the disarming of all Khmer military forces, and
(3) the convening of a Southeast Asian Conference for Peace and Co-operation, to be attended by all the countries of the region.

Stage Eight:

(1) The holding of free and fair general elections,
- under the auspices of the PGC,
- under the direct supervision of the ICC,
- policed by the IPKF.

(2) The election of a constituent assembly, which will work out:
(3) a Constitution of a free and neutral Cambodia, and
(4) choose a Government of National Unity that does not violate the conditions of viability.

Stage Nine:

(1) Internally, the actual and effective establishment of a Government of National Unity,
(2) bilaterally, the signing of a treaty of non-aggression and peaceful co-existence between Kampuchea and Vietnam, to be quickly followed by,
(3) externally, the Second Meeting of the International Conference:
- to work out the modalities of phasing out the IPKF and the ICC, and
- the actualisation of international guarantees.

Stage Ten:

(1) Withdrawal of the IPKF,
(2) withdrawal of the ICC, and
(3) the actualisation of international guarantees.

PHASE THREE: THE POST-SETTLEMENT PHASE

It is the view of the author that it is important to structure a Post-Settlement Phase that will support and buttress the settlement, and that will contribute to the building of a system of peace, amity and co-operative coexistence for all of Southeast Asia.

Stage Eleven:

Firstly, the re-convening of the International Conference every year until decided otherwise. This institution will supervise and check on the effective adherence to the conditions of the peaceful political settlement and will be concerned with the international guarantees.

Secondly, the establishment of something like an Association of Southeast Asian States (ASAS) which will bring together (hopefully) all the 10 countries of Southeast Asia for the first time, in an exercise aimed at tension reduction, confidence building, peaceful resolution of conflict and the making of a community of peace and co-operative coexistence. (Among its first acts might be to jointly sign a Southeast Asian treaty of peace and amity).

It might also be useful to ponder Indonesian normalisation of relations with the PRC, Soviet concessions with regard to Soviet military deployments in central Asia and other gains for the PRC.

Needless to say, 11 stages is 10 too many. The peace march could be fatally tripped at any one step.

At the end of this laborious and tortuous process, what can be expected, if it is a success? Certainly not a brave new world for Kampuchea, for Vietnam, for Indo-china, for Asean, for Southeast Asia. There are few brave new worlds in international relations. And when they arrive, it is only after tireless effort and unlimited luck over long periods of time.

Even after the Kampuchean Settlement, Kampuchea's position may remain extremely tenuous. History or some version of history can repeat itself.

Some concluding remarks

It is the view of this author that the Asean states will not be seriously threatened by just about any foreseeable outcome of the Kampuchea Question. It is however necessary for the Asean states to be involved in a way that will help to ensure a preferred result, should another option other than the present stalemate solution be forthcoming. It is also useful not to lose sight of political opportunity costs and of longer run considerations. Real as opposed to illusory opportunities for making advances in the development of a secure, peaceful, stable and co-operative Southeast Asian future should not be squandered.

As ever there is the continuing need for caution on all sides and for all sides. It is important for those of us who are in Asean not to make mistakes. There must be no betrayal of Thailand, no enragement of China, no splitting of Asean. It is also important for Vietnam not to make mistakes of the kind which will damage the chances of us all to build a peaceful and co-operative future for this region.

Confidence building and conflict reduction in the South Pacific

RAMESH THAKUR
*Senior Lecturer,
University of Otago,
New Zealand*[1]

A particular feature of the independent states in the South Pacific has been their degree of political stability since independence. There has been no effective challenge to the democratic institutions in place at the time of constitutional transition.

Australia's Department of Foreign Affairs, 1983.[2]

...the South Pacific is one of the more peaceful regions of the world... Island nations have displayed a commitment to stable, democratic, non-ideological forms of government.

New Zealand Defence Review, February 1987.[3]

...the South Pacific is now a less stable place than it was when my Government came to office in 1983. I refer to the uncertainty over the future of New Caledonia, the unwelcome interest displayed in our region by Libya, and of course the troubling implications of the two military coups in Fiji.

Australian Prime Minister Bob Hawke on December 9, 1987.[4]

CONFLICT has been a distressingly common feature of international history. There is no reason to believe that hostility and tension with potential for violent conflict will not be a persistent feature of human relations in the foreseeable future. While conflict resolution — let alone conflict eradication — may be an ideal to be envisioned, confidence building and conflict reduction measures (CBCRMs) can reduce environmental uncertainty and ambiguity, and so reduce tension, establish a regime which inhibits potentially threatening political-military activities, and diminish the probability of violent conflict by design or miscalculation.

As the opening three quotes from official Australian and New Zealand sources indicate, the South Pacific used to be characterised by exceptional stability, but is now no longer so. In modern times, a major cause of international conflict has been frontier disputes, while superpower rivalry has been a main source of international tension in unsettled spheres of influence. As a corollary, two major factors behind South Pacific tranquillity have been the absence of land borders between countries of the region,[5] and the absence of any meaningful Soviet presence. In the late 1980s, however, troubles have spread even to the South Seas. CBCRMs must pay due regard to the distinctive regional requirements and nuances of the South Pacific. Standard measures are not necessarily all that pertinent. The region is a Western strategic lake, with the Soviet profile barely visible: so regional measures to increase crisis communication channels, negotiate mutual verification modalities, discuss mutual troop or armaments reductions, etc, between the two superpowers are irrelevant. The Soviet Union has no nuclear basing, porting or testing programme: so the potential for an accidental nuclear exchange centred on the South Pacific, requiring appropriate prophylactics, is nil.

CBCRMs are not arms control measures in the conventional sense. Rather, they are instruments intended to inhibit the use of military force for coercion or intimidation by promoting military, economic and political confidence, for example by providing information on military-related activities. That is, CBCRMs both reinforce conventional arms control agreements and provide alternative instruments if the latter cannot be successfully negotiated or sustained under pressure. As a supplementary and alternative approach to crisis prevention, conflict management and conflict resolution, CBCRMs broaden and deepen the agenda of legitimate international security concerns.

Before discussing confidence building and conflict reduction in the South Pacific, we need to be clear about three things: the region to which we are referring, the areas of present and prospective conflict in the region, and the issues on which the countries of the region face the future with less than total confidence. I will begin therefore with a sketch of the region before proceeding to a discussion of the sources of tension and seeds of conflict in the South Pacific.

The South Pacific region stretches 17,000km longitudinally from Australia and Papua New Guinea in the west to South America in the east, and 7,000km latitudinally from the equator to the Antarctic Ocean (60°S). In the distinctive marine environment of the South Pacific, the ocean is viewed by islanders as bringing vastly separated peoples together: hence the peculiar significance of the seas to the Pacific peoples. In addition to the two 'metropolitan' countries of Australia and New Zealand, there are nine states which attained full independence between 1962 and 1980. Fiji, Nauru, Papua New Guinea, the Solomon Islands, Tonga, Tuvalu, Vanuatu and Western Samoa. Another two, Niue and the Cook Islands, are self-governing in free association with New Zealand, a status which circumscribes their freedom of manoeuvre in external relations.

Somewhat simplistically, the South Pacific can be divided into three broad groupings: Melanesia in the west, Polynesia in the east, and Micronesia in the north (Fiji's location in Melanesia or Polynesia is problematic: in fact it lies at the geographical crossroads, and half its population is ethnically Indian). Prior to World War II, Japan had administered the islands of Micronesia under a League of Nations Mandate. In 1947, the United Nations Security Council created the Trust Territory of the Pacific Islands — comprising the four political entities of the Northern Mariana Islands, Palau (also known as Belau), the Federated States of Micronesia (Kosrae, Ponape, Truk and Yap), and the Marshall Islands — and formally transferred the mandate to the United States. In the 1980s, all four entities have moved separately to a Commonwealth (Northern Marianas) or Free Association relationship under Compact with the US.

While the area and population of the ministates and microstates of the South Pacific are very small, their geographical location gives them a strategic, political and economic importance transcending their size. Furthermore, despite the disparities in size and economic development, the relationship between Australia, New Zealand and the Forum Island Countries (FICs) is in a political and institutional sense a relationship of equals. The South Pacific countries have become increasingly assertive in the view that they should not only have the decisive say in issues affecting their own region, but that they should also be able to express a regional viewpoint on international issues. An important benefit conferred by the regional institutions — including the South Pacific Commission, the South Pacific Forum, the South Pacific Bureau for Economic Co-operation (SPEC), the Pacific Forum Line and the Forum Fisheries Agency — in the context of the microstatic size of FICs is the nurturing of personalised interactions among the political leaders.

I intend to examine CBCRMs under three headings: economics, politics and military. Security for South Pacific island states would be an empty concept if it did not include their economic welfare in general, and protection of their fisheries in particular. Politically, while there have been sporadic troubles elsewhere, the two principal zones of conflict are Fiji and New Caledonia. On the military dimension, the South Pacific appears to be free of any realistic threat of invasion, but would not be free of the lethal after-effects of a global nuclear war; regional countries therefore have a vested security interest in trying to avert such a calamity.

Economics

A Commonwealth study group looking at the security problems of small states argued that there was 'a direct link between economic and political instability, making the economic factor the single most important ingredient of the security of small states'.[6] Shared economic problems include the domination of export trade by one product and one market, limited resources, limited domestic market, an unfavourable international economic system, shortage of skilled labour, and gaps in infrastructural support. Western powers generally, and Australia and New Zealand in particular, have been sensitive to this fact in the South Pacific: Foreign Minister Russell Marshall of New Zealand for one talks of a broad definition of security which includes economic wellbeing.[7]

In the South Pacific, natural resources are scarce and unevenly distributed, population growth rates are high, but contact with the outside world has raised expectations higher than traditional standards of living. The Forum Island Countries are indeed still dependent upon metropolitan countries (Australia, New Zealand, Britain, France, the US and, latterly, the European Economic Community) for development assistance: Papua New Guinea receives half its budget revenue as a direct grant from Australia. (Papua New Guinea has some 80 per cent of the region's land area and 60 per cent of the population). The Commonwealth study group singled out protectionist policies of the industralised countries as a threat to the economic security of small states: The South Pacific Regional Trade and Economic Co-operation Agreement (SPARTECA) was signed at the 11th Forum meeting at Tarawa, Kiribati, in 1980 and came into operation on 1 July 1981. It grants non-reciprocal, unrestricted duty-free access to the Australian and New Zealand markets for almost all products exported by FICs on a positive list basis, that is, only those products specifically listed are excluded from access. At the same time, it is only fair to recognise that foreign aid has its drawbacks, and can actually diminish self-sufficiency.[8]

Outside countries have been forced to acknowledge the reality of South Pacific indentities and aspirations because of the move to 200-mile Exclusive Economic Zone (EEZs), the archipelagic nature of most FICs and the attractiveness of South Pacific fishing zones which have been incorporated into EEZs. Australia's Ambassador to the US, F Rawdon Dalrymple, has noted how when the concept of EEZs was becoming important in the mid-1970s in the context of the Law of the Sea discussions, he was astonished at the changed map of the South Pacific once the EEZs were drawn.[9]

> ...from a map in which the great spaces of the ocean were separated or differeniated by tiny pinpoints of land with names attached to them, you suddenly had a map where huge areas of the earth's surface were marked off as areas of claim or potential sovereign claim by political entities most of which were virtually unknown to the outside world.
>
> It was a most striking transformation. And it seemed to all of us contemplating that transformaton that this was something that was going to change not only the resources and sovereignty map of the South Pacific but was going to change its political importance and strategic importance to us.

Japanese involvement has taken the form of joint fishing ventures and fisheries development assistance in providing ships and training. Foreign Minister Tadashi Kuranari visited several South Pacific islands countries in 1987, and announced a US$2 million special fund for Pacific islands. He was keen to promote Japan's renewed interest in the region, an interest underlined by a follow-up officials' visit in April 1987 which looked at specific proposals for future Japanese development assistance to the region.[10]

Recent Soviet gains in fishing must be set in the context of special arrangements for access to New Zealand fishing zones since the late 1970s. The origins of the arrangements go back to a matching desire to link the question of meat exports to the Soviet Union to that of access to New Zealand fish resources and shore facilities. The Soviet Union had been turned down in the initial request for shore facilities in 1975. Moscow then approached Tonga and Western Samoa in mid-1976, offering them assistance in the development of fishing industries in return for shore access. (The Soviet Union also established diplomatic ties with Fiji and Western Samoa in 1976). While the approach to the island countries proved abortive, discussions were started with New Zealand in 1977. It was argued that access to satisfactory port facilities in New Zealand would obviate the need for the Soviets to look elsewhere in the South Pacific. In the late 1970s, New Zealand agreed to license Soviet fishing activity in its EEZ on a short-term basis in order to ensure a mutual trade dependence, and to provide the Soviet Union with access to shore facilities under strictly controlled conditions. The New Zealand decision drew an expression of concern from Australia, which was uneasy about the potential Soviet role in the region, and worried that the impending agreement would limit Australian-New Zealand ability to discourage other island states from granting similar shore facilities to the Soviet Union. New Zealand of course shared Australian anxiety regarding the need to maintain a careful watch on Soviet activities in the South Pacific. But it also believed that Soviet activity could be monitored more satisfactorily in New Zealand than in the island states. Moreover, New Zealand had reserved the right to withdraw shore facilities at short notice.

In 1985, it was New Zealand's turn to become apprehensive about the Soviet fishing agreement with Kiribati. The agreement, signed in August 1985, allowed Soviet boats to fish within Kiribati's 200-mile EEZ, but prohibited any Soviet ship from entering the 12-mile territorial limit, and did not grant any landing rights or shore facilities to the Soviet Union.

The US Department of Defence identified six direct strategic advantages for the Soviet Union in developing a base in Kiribati:[11]

- Proximity to US territory;
- Surveillance of US missile and Strategic Defence Initiative (SDI) research on Kwajalein;
- Operational benefits for the Soviet space and military satellite programme;
- Missile testing advantages;
- Support for Soviet strategic minerals deep seabed mining in the Pacific;
- Improved Soviet cross Pacific air traffic capabilities.

The alarmist-speculative nature of the above list is clearly shown in the fact that the fisheries agreement was not renewed in 1986 because of the Soviet insistence on a lower fee. The agreement with Vanuatu which replaced it was also allowed to lapse in January 1988 for similar reasons. The commercial component is clearly more important to Moscow than the political profile in the region stemming from fishing activity. Those who are concerned about malevolent Soviet intrusion in the South Pacific need to balance legitimate anxieties against the dangers of being seen to have cried wolf (bear?) once too often.

If Westerners have been anxious about expanding Soviet fishing presence, islanders have been agitated about predatory US tuna fishing. At one stage, President Ieremia Tabai observed that if the American Tuna Boat Association had not refused to renew a fisheries deal on terms favourable to Kiribati, he would not have needed the Soviet agreement. (Soviet fishing fees were the largest source of aid or income, being worth 15 per cent of Kiribati's budget). The 1978 South Pacific Forum meeting in Niue was divided on the question of US membership of the proposed regional fisheries agency.[12] Fiji and Papua New Guinea opposed US membership because of fears of US domination, because of the US refusal to recognise coastal state sovereignty over highly migratory species like tuna, and because of a potential conflict of interest if the US as a major distant water fishing nation was to be involved in controlling South Pacific fishing on behalf of regional nations.

The 1985 meeting of the South Pacific Forum expressed satisfaction that the Forum Fisheries Agency had been fully recognised by the major foreign fishing nations, and called for the speedy conclusion of a multilateral treaty with the US. Such a treaty was of importance to the island countries because it concerned the one substantial resource they have. The most important fish stocks in the region are the highly migratory species, principally tuna. The US does not recognise coastal state jurisdiction over tuna; the Pacific island states, along with a majority of the world's countries, recognise the right of coastal states to levy access fees and to issue licences for distant water fishing nations to catch fish in their EEZs. When the Solomon Islands confiscated the marauding *Jeanette Diana* in June 1984, the US, acting under the Magnusson Act, immediately imposed trade bans on all fisheries exports from the Solomon Islands to the US. The juridical basis of the US retaliation was itself open to dispute; its political consequences if repeated across the region would have been clearly adverse for the Western world. The US embargo threatened the entire economy of the Solomon Islands, whose government publicly suggested that the Soviet Union be permitted access to its waters for fisheries. The owners subsequently repurchased the *Jeanette Diana*, and the embargo was lifted.

The US State Deartment and the US navy at least have been sensitive to the strategic implications of the commercially motivated US policy on tuna fishing in the region. Over the last three years, their voices have been increasingly heeded in the US administration. A South Pacific multilateral fisheries treaty was signed in Port Moresby on April 2, 1987 by 12 South Pacific states, including New Zealand and the US (Niue and Vanuatu became the 13th and 14th signatories at the Forum meeting in Apia in May 1987). The product of a series of long and complicated negotiations initiated formally at the 1984 South Pacific Forum meeting in Tuvalu, the treaty allows US tuna vessels access to an extensive area of the South Pacific in return for a five-year, US$12 million per year package of fees and assistance to regional countries. The treaty thus removed a major irritant from South Pacific-US relations and should contribute to regional security from a broader economic perspective as well as from the more conventional perspective of strategic denial.[13]

Politics

The fishing issue looks like having been resolved satisfactorily, both in regard to the primacy of commercial over political motivations for the Soviet Union, and in respect of insensitive poaching by Americans. An issue just beginning to acquire international prominence, by contrast, is that of racial, ethnic and geographic divides in the region, and the associated question of the legitimacy of settler governments. Australia and New Zealand are by no means immune to assertions of ancestral rights. While this may take on more generalised forms of violence in the future, so far at least it has been contained within tolerable limits in all South Pacific countries except New Caledonia and Fiji.

Considerations of the two trouble spots together suggests that democratic institutions may be an underrated CBCRM. The concept of liberal democracy embraces both a set of political institutions (popular elections, accountable government, majoritarian decisions) and a set of principles (civil liberties, legal equality, rule of law) which the institutions embody. It is 'a way of coming to terms with the need for authority without accepting a duty to submit to whatever abuses it might bring in its train'.[14] Liberal democracy does not create social and political cleavages. It simply recognises and legitimates the struggle for power in politics, and provides constitutional means of managing it. Democratic government links power to authority, and so converts might into right. Power connotes ability to enforce particular behaviour. Authority signifies the capacity to create and enforce rights and obligations which are accepted as legitimate and binding: it entails acceptance of right by those to whom it is applied. The decisions of a democratically representative government command authority because they are the outcome of an inter-communal, national, political process of the assertion and reconciliation of sectarian interests. It is the political process which authenticates democratic decisions and converts them into authoritative prescriptions for the common good of a citizenry.

That is, acceptance of the need for adequate protective measures for indigenous claims that are judged to be just does not necessarily lead to an endorsement of the more extreme claim that half a country's population, be it Indians in Fiji or Kanaks in New Caledonia — or ethnic Fijians and *caldoches* — should be deprived of constitutional safeguards. It is difficult to see how even the ethnic Fijians could be guaranteed that concentrated and unfettered power will be used to pursue communal wellbeing and not private gain. By failing to distinguish genuine grievances from the hypocrisy of a ruling elite, we do a disservice to the cause of all disadvantaged groups.

Since Fiji's independence in 1970, it is parliamentary democratic institutions which have been accepted as possessing the power of legitimisation. The Indian community accepted this for 17 years of rule by the Fijian-dominated government of Ratu Sir Kamisese Mara. That is, even though the Indians were out of power, they accepted the authority of successive Fijian governments because of the parliamentary-democratic process which had legitimated it. Under the 1970 constitution, parliamentary politics was available to the Indian community as the route to sharing political power; it was not seen as the instrument for sectarian domination. By contrast, significant elements of the Fijian community were not prepared to accept power-sharing in practice. Faced with rule by an 'Indian-dominated' government they rejected the democratic process.

The importance of democracy as a stabilising force is particularly relevant to peaceful changes of leadership. In a recent article in the influential London *Economist*, Sir Karl Popper argued that the fundamental problem of a rational political theory is 'how is the state to be constituted so that bad rulers can be got rid of without bloodshed, without violence?'[15] A military dictatorship stands the pyramid of a political structure on its apex. This is inherently unstable — either a displacement of the apex or a movement at the base will topple the whole structure. If the proof of the pudding be in the eating, then the 1970-87 years of remarkable Fijian stability under democratic rule stand in marked contrast to the troubles and uncertainties in Fiji since the overthrow of democracy in May 1987.

New Caledonia

Similarly, any hope of stability in New Caledonia too must rest on a genuine power-sharing formula between the settlers and the Kanaks; only democratic institutions, either of the Westminster type or of a consociational type, will command the loyalty and obedience of major communities, and so be conducive to a peaceful and stable political order. Annexed by Napoleon III of France in 1853, New Caledonia has been the scene of periodic violent rebellion against French rule, for example in 1878 and 1917 (as a result of which land was alienated from the indegenes and reallocated to the settlers), and more recently in 1984. There have also been violent clashes in 1988 between the Kanak Socialist National Liberation Front (*Front de Liberation Nationale Kanake et Socialiste*, or FLNKS), led by Jean-Marie Tjibaou, and French security forces, in an escalating cycle of attacks and reprisals that has seen mass killings, hostage abductions and armed raids to release kidnapped gendarmes. Kanaks constitute about 43 per cent of the territory's 150,000 population, French settlers (*caldoches*) comprise 37 per cent, and largely pro-French Polynesians (13 per cent), Indonesians (4 per cent) and Vietnamese (2 per cent) make up the balance. (Demographic trends suggest that the Kanaks could constitute a majority by the turn of the century). Migrants are resented by the Kanaks because they help to perpetuate the Kanak's minority status and impede an independent New Caledonia under Kanak control.

The control of French Melanesia-Polynesia is important to France because of its global strategic vision and its programme of nuclear testing in the South Pacific (discussed below). French military presence in the region has been strengthened in recent years. New Caledonia itself is viewed as an important site for projecting French power as a balancing and stabilising element in a region becoming increasingly more volatile, as well as a critical link between the Indian and Pacific ocean interests of France. The substantial *caldoche* population with its single-minded determination to remain French and the minority status of pro-independence Kanaks add racial and democratic reinforcements to the French justifications for remaining in New Caledonia. Upheavals in Fiji (1987-88) and riots in Vanuatu (1988) stemming from a power struggle between Prime Minister Walter Lini and sacked cabinet colleague Bark Tamé Sopé, who was also General Secretary of the ruling Vanuatu Party, are viewed as vindications of French policy.

In the perception of the South Pacific's pre-colonial peoples, New Caledonia is culturally, ethnically and geographically part of the Melanesian region. The Forum countries' concern that it should take full part in the region's economic and political affairs and institutions is perfectly understandable. Their broad goal is that an independent New Caledonia should emerge as a stable Melanesian state with values, aspirations and a regional-international worldview in harmony with prevailing ones. The Forum has consistently emphasised that its approach to the New Caledonian issue is not dictated by anti-French feelings, and that a France which is sensitive to Pacific peoples will always be welcomed in the region for its cultural and economic contributions.

The Melanesian countries have been at the cutting edge of the Forum's involvement in the issue of New Caledonia, driven in particular by memories of Vanuatu's difficult birth. French tardiness in the granting of independence to the New Hebrides allowed nationalist leaders to import communist liberationist ideology from Cuba, and served to legitimise an indigenous socialist ideology with an international posture of nonalignment.[16] The transition to independence on July 30, 1980 was marked by a rebellion on the island of Espiritu Santo, which had French settler involvement and was suspected of having had the tacit support of the French government. Franco-British troops in the New Hebrides were sent to the island on July 24, but in fact the rebellion was put down with the help of Papua New Guinea forces which landed on August 18 and ended the secession by the end of the month. (New Zealand made a cash grant of NZ$50,000 to Papua New Guinea in December 1980 to help defray its expenses for the operation).[17] Certainly those with memories of French decolonisation in Indochina and Algeria have no cause to be sanguine about the course of events in New Caledonia.[18]

The South Pacific Forum first addressed the question of the future status of French territories in the Pacific in 1979, on the eve of Vanuatu's independence. Reaffirming the principle of self-determination and independence for all Pacific islanders, the Forum called on the metropolitan powers to work with their Pacific wards to this end. The 1981 Forum meeting decided to send a delegation to Paris, led by Fiji's Prime Minster Ratu Sir Kamisese Mara, to hold discussions with the French President. The delegation reported to the 1982 Forum that satisfactory changes had been made in French policy towards New Caledonia designed to meet the aspirations of the indigenous Kanak people. The 1983 Forum requested a precise timetable for independence and suggested that France invite a Forum observer mission to New Caledonia to assess progress on decolonisation. France responded to this indirectly, issuing individual invitations to Forum countries to visit New Caledonia. The 1983 meeting also considered for the first time the desirability of reinscribing New

Caledonia on the United Nations List of Non-Self-Governing Territories (NSGT), to which reporting and other requirements of Chapter IX of the UN Charter apply.

The 1985 Forum meeting had been prepared to endorse the socialist French government's independence-in-association formula for New Caledonia. The statute proposed by the successor Chirac government would not have accorded New Caledonia the same degree of anutonomy as that enjoyed by French Polynesia; nor would the powers accorded to the regions be as wide as those under the Laurent Fabius-Edgard Pisani statute of the previous socialist government. At the 1986 Forum meeting in Suva, fuelled by apprehensions that the Chirac government was moving away from the old formula towards the status of a more autonomous territory, there was an unanimous decision to seek a reinscription of New Caledonia on the UN List of NSGT, while pursuing dialogue with all parties involved in the New Caledonia question, including France. The reinscription move received the support of the Nonaligned Summit conference in Harare in September, and the relevant resolution was adopted by the General Assembly on December 2, despite strong French opposition, by a vote of 89-24-34: Asian-Pacific countries voted virtually unanimously in the affirmative (Resolution 41/41 A).[19]

Forum representatives met in Auckland on March 3, 1987 to discuss the planned referendum in New Caledonia, and requested France to delay the referendum until certain UN principles and practices on decolonisation, regarded by Forum countries as fundamental to a free and genuine act of self-determination, could be guaranteed. The subsequent Forum meeting held in Apia in May adopted the conclusions of the March ministerial meeting, and again urged France to abandon the referendum scheduled for September, while reaffirming its commitment to a dialogue with France. The Forum favoured an act of UN-supervised self-determination offering 'free, honest and genuine choice' between maintenance of the status quo, integration with France, internal self-government, associated independence, or unqualified independence; inclusion in the franchise 'of only those who can demonstrate long-term residence in and commitment to New Caledonia'; and an information campaign which educated the people on the options.[20]

The referendum was held on September 13, but did nothing to calm the tense atmosphere in New Caledonia. It failed to establish legitimacy in regional eyes because co-operation with the UN was refused; because people with three years' residence in New Caledonia were permitted to vote; and because it did not include a political education programme regarding the options, and in fact restricted the options to the dichotomous choice of remaining with France or being cast adrift. (Some Kanak leaders would be happy with a compact of free association which left France to look after strategic interests while transferring control on internal matters to the region). The FLNKS call for a boycott was heeded by 83 per cent of the Kanaks. Not surprisingly, of the 60 per cent who did vote, 98 per cent opted to remain a part of France — a result that was gladly accepted by Overseas Territories Minister Bernard Pons. Yet the result also showed the geographical split along racial lines: Noumea and the west coast are European and loyalist, the east coast and islands are Melanesian and pro-independence. The climate of mistrust between the Kanaks and the French settlers was exacerbated by the continuing high military presence (about 6,000 troops in 1986-87), and by the acquittal in October 1987 of seven men charged with the murder of 10 pro-independence Kanaks in an ambush on December 5, 1984 (the Hienghene massacre).

The new government named by French President Francois Mitterrand after his re-election on May 8, 1988 moved swiftly to defuse the situation in New Caledonia. Prime Minister Michel Rocard organised two-week long talks between Kanak leader Jean-Marie Tjibaou and settlers' leader Jacques Lafleur in Paris. The new peace plan announced on June 26 proposed a division of the colony into three provinces after a year of central rule from Paris, one for the white settlers and two for the Kanaks, with substantial internal autonomy. France is to boost economic and social development throughout the islands during the year of transition. A referendum on the agreement is to be held in France on November 6, 1988, with an independence referendum for New Caledonia envisaged in 10 years' time. Electoral rolls will be revised in the colony three times, in 1989, 1992 and 1993. The agreement seems to have been met with general relief and praise in France, New Caledonia and the South Pacific.[21]

Australian Foreign Minister Bill Hayden endorsed the socialist government's stand and rejected Kanak independence or Kanak control of New Caledonia, arguing instead for an act of self-determination that leads to a multiracial society acceptable to all.[22] An editorial in the *Australian* argued that the Australian government, pursuing 'a woolly policy on New Caledonia,' has never clarified what would constitute an acceptable franchise. Allowing permanent residents to vote is an acceptable practice in several democratic countries. The September 1987 ballot in New Caledonia 'was a fair and democratic ballot' by 'all reasonable standards,' and therefore Australian opposition to it is 'a policy that brings no honour to Australia and does nothing to promote democratic values in the Pacific'.[23] The newspaper's comment serves to highlight the difficulty and delicacy of efforts to strike the correct balance between the competing principles of democracy and inter-confessional justice. For example, Kanaks objected to the three-year residential qualification in the 1987 referendum. Yet three years' residence is sufficient in New Zealand not just to get on the electoral roll, but to become eligible for full citizenship.

Fiji

The failure to defend democratic values in the region effectively was much more evident during the crisis in Fiji. Only five members of the South Pacific Forum — Australia, New Zealand, Tonga, Papua New Guinea and Fiji — have standing defence forces. Regrettably, the army in one of these turned against its own elected government in 1987. Leading a coup in two instalments, Colonel Sitiveni Rabuka overthrew 17 years of parliamentary democracy because Fiji-Indians were 'dominant' in the government elected in April 1987.

The issue in Fiji was quite straightforward and had two elements. First, lawful government had been overthrown by brute force. As long as legally elected prime minister and cabinet were not returned to office, constitutional democracy could not be said to have been restored in Fiji. Second, racism had reappeared in the South

Pacific. But the racists this time were not white Europeans. The 1970 constitution of Fiji was already a significant compromise with democratic principles in its deference to indigenous rights. Fijians were disproportionately represented in the lower house of parliament, and in dominant control in the upper house. Indians on their own could not have formed the government; the government of Dr Timoci Bavadra was elected by many Fijians voting for the coalition of the race-based, mainly Indian national Federation Party and the class-based Labour Party. Fijian rights were doubly entrenched in the constitution. They were protected from legislative encroachments except by overwhelming Fijian consent, and the means of changing the amendment procedure were similarly entrenched. Indians enjoyed no such constitutional guarantees exclusively for their community. The coup was thus a refusal by some Fijians to *share* power with Indians — indeed with fellow-Fijians, since race-based explanations of the coup are less persuasive than interpretations which see it as a desperate measure by a defeated regionalised power elite to reverse a loss of office after enjoying the trappings of power for 17 years[24] — on the basis of some parity within a modified but still recognisable form of parliamentary democracy which was race-sensitive but not racist. I have discussed the coup elsewhere.[25] Here I wish to address some issues thrown up by the crisis in Fiji which are relevant to building confidence and reducing conflict in the region.

Constitutional issues. The manner in which both Australia and New Zealand appeared to support the Governor-General as the sole constitutional authority in Fiji after the May coup was perturbing. If the elected government was overthrown at the point of the gun by Lt Col Rabuka, then the constitutional trigger was in fact pulled by the Governor-General. Of course the Governor-General was faced by a genuine crisis, and had to react under the doctrine of necessity of state. If he had acted so as to pardon the treason committed by the coup leader and return the government to Bavadra — or even form a government of national unity with party positions in cabinet reflecting party strengths in Parliament — then that would have been an act of statesmanship and compromise, and constitutional niceties would not have mattered much. But in fact he acted, not as Governor-General of all Fijians, but as high chief of Melanesian Fijians and in furtherance of the interests of the defeated power elite from the eastern Tovata confederacy. Regrettably, Australia, Britain and New Zealand continued to support, *and therefore implicitly to endorse*, such actions by the Governor-General as pardon of the coup leader, promotion in rank of the coup leader, ouster of elected government, ouster of the two senior army chiefs, entrustment of the command of the army to coup leader, and entrustment of home affairs portfolio to coup leader. His acceptance of the post of President of the Republic of Fiji merely completed the cycle of using the authority of the chief executive to further the objectives of the coup. Recognising reality is a perfectly reasonable and understandable line to take — but only so long as there are no important damaging consequences to one's own system of government. If we consider the signals that Australia and New Zealand sent to their own army officers and Governors-General in the way that they handled the Fiji crisis, then the implicatons are truly appalling. All that the coup leader needed in Fiji was 10 soldiers to take over the country.

In sum, what I am saying is that the need to accept the reality of the coup in Fiji was less pressing than, and therefore should have been subordinated to, the need to preserve the fundamental conventions of the Westminster systems of government in regard to the relationship between elected government, Governor-General and armed forces. In a related vein, there is insufficient heed paid to the really long-term consequences of the coup. Half the community of Fiji is not going to accept a permanent status of second class citizenship. Attempts to impose such a status will therefore merely create yet another time-bomb in the region, with all the potential for meddling by outside mischief-makers as well. Sometimes it is more difficult to recognise the 'soft' reality of a longer timeframe than the 'hard' reality of the moment but it is true that no group of people has accepted oppression in perpetuity.

The other respect in which Australia and New Zealand failed to recognise repercussions of the coup in Fiji for their own governments was the implicit delegitimisation of democratically elected settler regimes by indigenous groups in the numerical minority. The ultimate obscenity of indigenous rights was of course Hitler's Nazi Germany. Even short of that, liberal consciences would be stirred should a Western country, say Britain, were to enact discrimination against non-whites into law on the grounds that they were aliens, that is, non-indigenes. Liberal consciences are less easily agitated if the racists are non-whites. Yet the fact remains that if Fiji-Indians, the majority of whom are third- or fourth-generation natives of Fiji, can be denied roughly equal rights in Fiji, and such denial is accepted by Australians and New Zealanders, then no *principled* defence is left against the claims to sovereign paramountcy by Aborigines and Maoris regardless of their fewer numbers. Indeed the latter have greater equivalent justice on their side, if we consider the example of land rights. In Fiji, four-fifths of the land was owned by ethnic Fijians, and only 1.7 per cent by Indians: and the balance could not have been altered within the 1970 constitution without the overwhelming consent of the Fijian community. But in terms of the subject of this paper, if rights to land and politial power are going to turn on claims of indigenous status, then the world is in for the most destabilising period known to human history.

All this is in addition to the damaging economic implications of the events of Fiji for the country as a whole. The cumulative effect will be to perpetuate conflict, insecurity and instability in the region.

Diplomacy of pressure. The last comment highlights a major shortcoming in present day international relations in regard to conflict reduction mechanisms. The international community, if it is to establish a peaceful world order, must ensure that the order is based upon justice and equity. Violent challenges to such an international order must be discouraged and defeated. Equally, however, channels must be provided for the articulation of legitimate grievances. This necessarily implies the creation of institutional means for effecting change which is regarded as just and desirable by the international community. Since the world community has no such effectively functioning mechanisms, regional agencies could initiate developments for possible emulation by international organisations in the future. The South Pacific, with an absence of frontier disputes and the tradition of consensual decisions, might be a particularly suitable region for collective innovations in cross-national conflict reduction measures, such as the problem-solving approach developed by the British-based Centre for the Analysis of Conflict.[26]

Not everything in Western civilisation is automatically bad; not every attempt to assert tradition and reject Western values is necessarily laudable. Democratic government, racial-religious equality, human and minority rights: these are some of the major contributions of Western civilisation to humanity. The Commonwealth study group had concluded that an effective parliamentary system seen to be operating fairly in the interests of all sections of the people was an important counter to the development of subversive movements, and a helpful element in obtaining the sympathetic involvement of other Commonwealth countries in an emergency.[27] Unfortunately, the preservation of such values, and of institutions which embody and give practical meaning to such values, can never be taken for granted. As the events in Fiji show, there will be times when Australia and New Zealand will be challenged on the subject even within the South Pacific region. Of course they cannot impose their values indefinitely on everyone else. Nor can they always send in the equivalent of the cavalry or the marines. But, as the French showed in relation to the *Rainbow Warrior* affair, it is possible to secure national objectives by a concrete and judicious application of diplomatic and economic pressure short of military intervention.[28]

Problems are not solved by running away from them; sometimes they can only be eliminated through confrontation. Yet Australia and New Zealand seem to feel uncomfortable with the idea of being assertive in their relations with South Pacific countries. It seems to me that the whole subject of the values in the defence of which we are prepared to apply sustained, graduated pressures; the resources and means available for the application of such pressures; and the relationship between military and diplomatic-economic means, especially the *threat* of use of force (since the actual use quickly becomes a wasting asset) needs to be studied in depth and without too many distracting scruples. (Scruples might well become relevant at the time that the decision has to be made as to whether or not to apply pressure; but they should not be allowed to override *a priori* a study of the feasibility and modalities of applying pressure). I say this because I am not convinced that Australia and New Zealand were as publicly emphatic in their defence of the Bavadra government as perhaps they might have been, or that they mobilised their considerable resources for shaping and influencing events within their own region. Had they been firmer in their reactions after the coup in May 1987, events in Fiji might conceivably have taken a less unsatisfactory course. (The distinctions between intervention and assertiveness are evident in the Kampuchean conflict. Vietnam intervened by force; the Association of Southeast Nations [Asean] countries have been assertive — rightly and successfully — in denying legitimacy to the Vietnam-backed government of the People's Republic of Kampuchea).

In short, the world is still striving for the correct balance between the principle of national sovereignty, with its corollary of non-interference in affairs essentially within the domestic jurisdiction of states, and the doctrine of legitimate international concern, with a right to involvement in certain classes of issues even within national frontiers. Racial discrimination on a legalised and systematic scale in South Africa is one such area: Is it the only one? In September 1988, deposed Prime Minister Dr Timoci Bavadra was reported as calling on the United Nations to impose punitive sanctions on the interim Fiji government because of 'an unprecedented scale of racial discrimination and oppression'. Racism, he said in a seven-page submission, had become systematically and progressively institutionalised since the coup of May 1987.[29] Efforts by the international community to dismantle apartheid in South Africa can only be progressively delegitimised if they condone it elsewhere in their midst.

Military

The events of 1987-88 in Fiji suggest too a strong case for all the South Pacific countries to examine the feasibility and wisdom of *regional peacekeeping forces*. The 1984 Commonwealth study group had recommended the establishment of a Commonwealth Defence Force on the reasoning that 'no small country could defend itself on its own, and no international organisation currently existed which was capable of reacting quickly enough to protect the security of a small state in an emergency situation'.[30] The force was to be regionally organised, with members having the right of non-participation in actions with which they disagreed, but not the power to veto collective action.

The nature and requirements of peacekeeping operations are qualitatively different from those of combat troops or municipal police forces; the nature of violent conflict since World War II has often placed a premium upon international peacekeeping troops. Australian, New Zealand, and more recently Fijian, policy has tended towards responding to overseas requests on an ad hoc basis. The Scandinavian countries are prime examples of countries having relatively clear policies on peacekeeping thought out well in advance, and underwritten with the maintenance of units specifically trained for international peacekeeping duties. Even the Scandinavian countries, however, face no real prospect of peacekeeping contingencies arising within their own region.

Such a contingency cannot be ruled out for the South Pacific region. The absence of land borders between South Pacific nations means that there are no border disputes requiring mediation and peacekeeping by the regional organisation. Nevertheless, if in fact the South Pacific is required to deal with instability in the region, then a peacekeeping operation may well prove to be an appropriate response. Therefore, I believe it is important that the South Pacific countries should address the possibility in advance, and come up with broadly agreed upon guidelines. This would be a major advantage in avoiding the danger of having to react to crises under the pressure of time, inadequate information and conditions of emergency. There is much to be said for tackling regional problems through efforts within the region in the first instance, and taking them to international fora only if they prove incapable of resolution by local means. Opposition to the creation of peacekeeping forces often rests on a failure to understand their consensual basis. A peacekeeping force, in terms of the standard UN model, could not be introduced into Fiji, nor maintained there subsequently, without the consent of that country's government; the host government even has the power of veto over who contributes troops to the peacekeeping operation.[31] The most appropriate authorising agencies would be the South Pacific Forum, the Commonwealth and/or the United Nations, with the proviso that even the last two could not mount a peacekeeping operation against the opposition of the South Pacific Forum. I would expect the creation and maintenance of regional peacekeeping units to be as important and useful, if not more so, than the more dramatic 'Ready Reaction Forces' to launch 'rescue' operations on the Grenada model. The prior existence of peacekeeping forces may not in the end have solved the Fijian crisis satisfactorily; but at least they would have provided an additional option to Forum countries in working out their response.

The pursuit of *regional security* requires an assessment of possible, plausible and probable threats, the institution of policies to alleviate such threats, and the development of military capability to counter them. The range of threats that might have an adverse impact upon South Pacific security include:

(a) Invasion of the South Pacific by an unfriendly external power. This seems most unlikely.
(b) Externally sourced subversion or destabilisation of island governments.
(c) Internally sourced civil disorder/war resulting from secessionist movements, communal clashes, colonial bunglings, etc.
(d) A major expansion of military presence by potentially hostile powers, including the acquisition of bases, onshore or porting facilities, or significant political or economic influence.
(e) Intimidation of South Pacific countries through interference with trade routes, mining of harbours, etc.
(f) The spillover of international terrorism into the South Pacific, including street bombings, sea piracy and aircraft hijacking.
(g) Illegal incursions into territorial space or EEZs by drug traffickers, smugglers, illegal immigrants or fish poachers.

The two 'major powers' of the region are Australia and New Zealand. Because both include the South Pacific within their area of direct strategic interest, and because their assessments of the threats to regional security are likely to be the most sophisticated in this context, it is useful to look at these evaluations. Fortunately, we can do this relatively simply by examining the defence white paper issued by the two governments in 1987.[32]

Australia's geographic location and the lack of land borders are said to give it an enviably benign security environment. No country in Australia's neighbourhood has the capability to mount a large-scale conventional attack on Australia. But a prudent defence policy guards against even the less probable lower level threats to security interests. Remote settlements in northern Australia, offshore territories and resources, and sea lines of communication (SLOCs) could be targets of mobile guerrilla attacks and trade interdiction. Australian forces are to develop the capability to detect and respond to such threats through a mix of offensive and defensive strategies. The reorganisation, development and re-equipment of the Australian forces is to be guided by these considerations to produce a force structure characterised by range, endurance, logistic support and mobility. They should also be capable of expansion if necessary to meet higher levels of threat, although it is expected that Australia would have a lead time of a decade to identify the emergence of threats on the basis of military programmes or rising tensions.

Pacific-region threats include the New People's Army insurgency in the Philippines and a margin of uncertainty about the US bases at Subic Bay and Clark Field; the unresolved situation in Kampuchea; and the continued air and naval presence in Vietnam. On the last point, nevertheless, the Australian White Paper recognised that while the military concentration in Vietnam is a Soviet asset in peacetime for purposes of surveillance, intelligence and intimidation, it would be highly vulnerable to allied attack in the event of actual fighting.

The South Pacific straddles important SLOCs for Australia. Island countries of the region lack human, economic and material resources to protect their interests, and bilateral Australian defence co-operation has been directed particularly at regional concerns over sovereignty protection and economic vulnerability. Soviet fishing activity in the region is of potential worry to Australia, and there is some unease at the prospect of Libyan meddling.[33] The Australian response includes the development of interrelated surveillance systems, a Pacific Patrol Boat (PPB) project to the island nations, and increased ship visits to them as visible demonstration of Australian goodwill and credibility.[34] Australia has built four PBBs, at a cost of A$3 million each, for Papua New Guinea, Vanuatu and Western Samoa, with eight more on order for other island countries. The Royal Australian Air Force (RAAF) operates 10 surveillance flights a year, with each mission lasting seven to 10 days, across the entire region. (Royal New Zealand Air Force [RNZAF] Orions fly 15 surveillance missions a year, concentrating on the eastern part of the South Pacific). On December 9, 1987, Australia and Papua New Guinea also issued a Joint Declaration on Principles Guiding Relations between them, including a commitment (Article 12d) — to consultation and action to repel external armed attack — in language similar to that contained in the ANZUS (Australia-New Zealand-US) treaty.[35] A shift from isolationism towards a regional security policy was noticeable in Defence Minister Kim Beazley's statement to Parliament on February 23, 1988.[36] The Forum Fisheries Agency and the Australian and New Zealand defence departments organised a five-day meeting in Port Vila, Vanuatu, in March 1988 to discuss increased integrated surveillance of the region.[37] While an operational Australian-New Zealand surveillance system provides reassurance to the island nations against predatory distant water fishing fleets,[38] it also provides a flow of information helpful in mapping the region's security environment.

The ***New Zealand*** paper too foresaw no threat of invasion or armed attack in the next decade, although it prudently recommended being prepared for lower-level threats and the possibility of a rapid change in the country's security environment for the worse. Only the superpowers were said to possess the logistic capability to launch an invasion against New Zealand, but not the intention to do so. More credible threat would be an air or sea raid, perhaps with the goal of coercing trade or political concessions; harassment of New Zealand's sea and air lanes of communication and trade; terrorism and hijacking; EEZ infringements; and natural disasters.

Superpower rivalry

The most important motivating factor in efforts at constructing confidence building measures is to reduce the prospect of a war between the superpowers. Such an eventuality is more likely in regions of rivalry between the two. Conversely, it is less probable in areas where one side enjoys unchallenged supremacy over the other. The seizure during World War II and the transfer after it of administration of the Micronesian islands from Japan to the US brought new Pacific responsibilities to the US. Nearly all the islands north of the equator from the Philippines to the West coast of the US were, for the first time, under US control. Even the South Pacific has long been regarded as a Western lake, and owes a substantial part of its history of freedom from cold war types of tension and crises to this fact. Western ascendancy has been achieved alongside a low-profile US military presence, with no US ships, aircraft or forces being based in the South Pacific. Military technological advances have also rendered the island stepping stones strategy of World War II obsolete in modern times. Washington has been happy to accept broader Western security interests in the South Pacific coming under Australian-New Zealand jurisdiction with correspondingly diminished political costs for FICs. Nor has Washington been required to assume an internal security role outside its own territorial responsibilities.

Threats to regional stability will therefore arise from attempts by the Soviet Union to challenge Western ascendancy, or from policy initiatives by the US which provoke Soviet retaliation. The most important security goal for Australia and New Zealand in the South Pacific has been the strategic denial of the region to the Soviet Union.[39] The absence of a Soviet military presence in the region has precluded a direct security threat from this quarter. But increased power projection capability has meant an indirect threat since the 1970s. Derivative security interests include maintaining secure lines of communication between the ANZUS partners as a fallback should the South China Sea, the Indonesian archipelagic and Malacca straits lines be interdicted, and a denial of the same fallback lines to Soviet communication by a mix of successful sea assertion north of the equator and effective interdictory capability in the South Pacific. The United States has also entered into Treaties of Friendship with Kiribati, Tuvalu and the Cook Islands which preclude bases from being provided to third countries without prior American consultations, and require consultations should threats be perceived to the islands' security. According to a State Department official, the object of the treaties — negotiated under the Carter administration but ratified in 1983 under Reagan — was to renounce weak and obsolete US territorial claims more than to enter into fresh military relationships.[40]

Denial of South Seas SLOCs to the Soviet Union has been underscored by lack of political influence among the FICs. The South Pacific is not generally receptive to Marxist ideology: firstly because the absence of an industrial base and an impoverished mass of landless peaseantry have precluded the development of politically significant class conflict; and secondly, because of the persistence of traditional values, a belief in Christianity, and the positive record of most European powers. The variety of Soviet interests in the South Pacific include, in addition to regional and global military objectives, fishing, commerce, oceanographic research and transport. Nevertheless, the Soviet Union does not have a major military presence in the South Pacific; it has also failed to secure a resident diplomatic presence[41] or develop a significant aid presence. (Moscow has non-resident accreditation with Fiji, Papua New Guinea, Tonga, Vanuatu and Western Samoa). A good illustration of regional suspicions of Soviet motives comes from 1980. In October that year, membership (via the Bangkok-based Economic and Social Commission for Asia and the Pacific [ESCAP]) in a technical advisory group enabled the Soviet Union to attend a meeting of the Committee for Co-ordination of Joint Prospecting for Mineral Resources in South Pacific Offshore areas (CCOP/SOPAC) in Kiribati. Acceptance by officials at the meeting of a Soviet proposal for a five-year study of tectonic plate movement was subsequently rescinded by governments — and a more limited study under Australian-New Zealand-US financing substituted. Fishing contact with the Soviet Union and its generally more favourable international image under Mikhail Gorbachev have begun to attenuate island suspicions of the Soviet bear.

Much has been made in recent years of the significant expansion of the Soviet navy in the Pacific and its enhanced power projection capabilities as a result of developments in Danang and Cam Ranh Bay in Vietnam. While the situation clearly merits constant monitoring, it is no cause for alarm. The combat capability of the Soviet navy in the Pacific is limited by several factors. The open-ocean effectiveness of Soviet naval forces is adversely affected by geographic constraints on their operations. The Western alliance is still regarded as having a favourable overall balance of maritime power in the Pacific, with advantages in such areas as amphibious assault forces, anti-submarine warfare and sound quieting and detection capabilities. When to this are added the irrelevance of the Soviet economic model for the countries of the South Pacific, and the strong suspicions in the region of Soviet motives, it becomes clear that the Soviet Union lacks the ability, at least at present, to translate global military power into political and economic influence in the South Pacific. Australian Foreign Minister Bill Hayden noted at a press conference in Manila that according to Western intelligence estimates, Soviet naval activity in the Pacific had been halved over the past year. Moreover, the Soviet Union had also been 'punctilious' in restricting its South Pacific activities to commercial operations. Therefore, while not losing 'a sense of vigilance,' Australia had failed to see 'any evidence of any surge let alone threat of Soviet activity'.[42] Recently, Australia's immediate neighbour started sending students to the Soviet Union in response to Australia's 'closed door' policy: six Papua New Guinea nationals had taken up Soviet scholarships by March 1988, and many others were involved in sporting, youth and cultural exchanges.[43]

China's presence in the South Pacific, motivated perhaps by opposition to the Soviet Union and Taiwan, has not been perceived as threatening by the countries of the region: China has embassies in Fiji, Papua New Guinea and Western Samoa.

Nuclear issues

The pursuit of nuclear non-proliferation has been a major international concern of our times. While attempts to bring about arms control regimes and disarmament seek to tackle the level of armaments directly, efforts to establish zones free of nuclear weapons are confidence building measures undertaken by those who do not possess nuclear weapons. The Antarctic Treaty of 1959 is of great historical significance for having created the world's first nuclear-free zone. The Treaty of Tlatelolco of 1977 established the first internationally recognised nuclear-weapons-free-zone (NWFZ) in a populated region of the world, namely Latin America. The Non-Proliferation Treaty (NPT) of 1978 was an attempt to bring in a global regime to prevent the acquisition of nuclear weapons by non-nuclear-weapon states (NNWS). States in the latter category can adhere to the NPT while accepting the stationing of nuclear weapons on their territories, as long as they do not exercise jurisdiction and control over the weapons. West Germany is an obvious example of such a country. A NWFZ, however, prohibits such stationing of nuclear weapons. The three essential characteristics of a NWFZ are non-possession, non-deployment and non-use of nuclear weapons. NWFZs can help to strengthen and promote non-proliferation by providing a means of extending and reinforcing the PNT.

South Pacific Nuclear Free Zone. The second NWFZ in an inhabited region was established at the 16th South Pacific Forum meeting held in Rarotonga, Cook Islands, when Forum countries adopted the South Pacific Nuclear Free Zone (SPNFZ) Treaty on August 6, 1985 (Hiroshima Day).[44] It is probably the most significant confidence building measure in the history of the South Pacific, and arguably one of the most important CBMs worldwide in the 1980s. The preamble to the treaty expresses the commitment to world peace, a grave concern at the continuing nuclear arms race, the conviction that every country bears an obligation to strive for the elimination of nuclear weapons, a belief in the efficacy of regional arms control measures, and a reaffirmation of the NPT for halting nuclear proliferation. The core obligations are contained in Articles 3-7. Each party agrees not to manufacture or otherwise acquire, possess or have control over — or seek to do so — any nuclear device; not to assist or encourage others to make or acquire nuclear weapons; to prevent the stationing or testing of nuclear weapons on its territory; not to dump radioactive wastes at sea anywhere in the zone, and to prevent such dumping by others in its territorial sea. The boundaries of the SPNFZ Treaty generally follow the territorial limits of the South Pacific Forum members, and are based on the so-called 'picture frame' (rather than an 'incomplete patchwork') approach. When we examine the zone alongside the adjoining Latin American and Antarctic ones, then the combined area covers some two-fifths of the earth's surface.

The Treaty of Rarotonga goes beyond the minimalist definition of NWFZs. Firstly, the title itself is of some significance. A NWFZ suggests an arms control objective. Indications that the Japanese intended to dump low-level radioactive waste in the North Pacific in the 1970s sensitised the peoples of the Pacific to the issue of toxic waste disposal; the SPNFZ prohibits the dumping of any nuclear waste in the zone (Article 7). In this respect the Rarotonga Treaty is an advance upon that of Tlatelolco, and more closely resembles the Antarctic Treaty. The Treaty also called for parties to support the conclusion of a global convention on the matter. After four years of negotiations, a convention for the protection and development of the region's natural resources and environment, the South Pacific Regional Environmental Programme (SPREP), was adopted at a plenipotentiary conference of the South Pacific Commission member governments in Noumea on November 25, 1986. The convention area comprises the EEZs of all Pacific island countries and territories, and also those areas of high seas which are enclosed from all sides by Pacific EEZs. The Convention is concerned with the protection of the marine environment against pollution from land-based sources, seabed activities, and storage of toxic and hazardous wastes; the prohibition on dumping radioactive waste applies irrespective of whether or not such dumping causes pollution. The Convention obliges parties to 'prevent, reduce and control' pollution from any source; sets up a 'blacklist' of substances that cannot be put into the ocean under any circumstances, eg mercury, oil and certain plastics; and requires special permission for dumping some other substances, eg arsenic, lead and nickel. While nuclear testing is not prohibited, parties are committed to sound environmental management in regard to the consequences of nuclear testing. The prohibition of any future dumping constituted a significant concession by France and the US, both of which signed the convention of November 25. The SPREP thus constitutes a significant international regime for the protection of the marine environment of the region.

The Treaty of Rarotonga is an improvement upon Tlatelolco also in its arms control objective: 'peaceful nuclear explosions' are prohibited in the South Pacific, but — arguably — permitted in Latin America. Rarotonga is an improvement upon Tlatelolco in its entry into force provisions. The Treaty of Rarotonga is considerably simpler — and therefore stronger — for having gone into force as soon as any eight parties ratified it; it goes into force for subsequent adherents upon their individual dates of ratification. The zone came into effect on December 11, 1986, when Australia became the eighth country to deposit its instruments of ratification with SPEC. The seven countries which had already ratified were Fiji (October 4, 1985), the Cook Islands (October 28, 1985), Tuvalu (January 16, 1986), Niue (May 12, 1986), Western Samoa (October 20, 1986), Kiribati (October 28, 1986) and New Zealand (November 13, 1986). Nauru has ratified since then, while Papua New Guinea and the Solomon Islands had signed but not ratified as of November 1987; the two remaining non-signatories are Tonga and Vanuatu. Rarotonga is an improvement upon Tlatelolco, finally, in introducing a longer delay before the regime can be dismantled. The Treaty of Tlatelolco imposes a three-month period of denunciation (Article 30); Rarotonga requires a 12-month notice of withdrawal (Article 13).

For all these improvements, the SPNFZ has not escaped criticism. There is a slight apprehension among the conservative tendencies in the region that the zone might be a 'Trojan horse' which will eventually undermine Western security networks. The more substantial attack comes from anti-nuclear groups. Activities of most concern to such groups — port calls, transit facilities for nuclear-capable aircraft, command, control and intelligence (C^3I) facilities in Australia and New Zealand, movement of nuclear-capable warships in the South Pacific waterways — remain untouched by the treaty.[45] Not only does the treaty carefully avoid impinging upon the substantial US nuclear involvement in the region; its geographical limits specifically exclude US Micronesian territories. US nuclear testing in Micronesia ceased in 1962. Nevertheless, Kwajalein Atoll in the Marshall Islands has a permanent US Missile Range (testing) facility; Guam has a nuclear stockpiling site and a strategic bomber base at Andersen airfield; both have C^3I facilities; and the US has plans for establishing nuclear naval and air bases in Palau and the Mariana Islands.

The Compact of Free Association between the US and the three entities of the Marshall Islands, Palau and the Federated States of Micronesia (FSM), because it has no exact precedent in international practice, has generated some confusion about US motives and Micronesian independence of US strategic calculations. The Compact provides that; the US will defend the three states as it would the US for a minimum period of 15 years in the cases of the Marshall Islands and the FSM, and 50 years in the case of Palau; the US has the right to preclude the military use of the territory of any of the three states by any third party; in the case of Palau, the US has the further right, under a Military Use and Operating Rights Agreement, to use various areas under certain contingencies and after consultation with the government of Palau;[46] and continued peacetime use of the Kwajalein Missile Range facility for 30 years.

Palau, which was placed under the supervision of the UN Security Council in 1947 (rather than the usual General Assembly supervision) by being designated a strategic trust, presented problems. The complicating element in its case came from the constitutional requirement of a 75 per cent majority in a referendum on a compact. Such majority having proven non-obtainable before (and the island's Supreme Court having upheld the constitutional ban against presidential attempts to circumvent it with the help of simple majority referendums), on August 4, 1987 a referendum amended the constitution to enable a compact to be approved by a simple rather than a three-quarter majority; then on August 21, 1987 a UN-observed plebiscite approved acceptance of the Compact of Free Association by a 73 per cent majority. Nevertheless, a three-quarter majority is still required to approve the use, testing, storage or disposal of harmful substances, including nuclear weapons and waste. Under the Compact, the US may not engage in such proscribed activity but has the right to operate nuclear-capable and nuclear-propelled ships and aircraft within its global 'neither confirm nor deny' policy. Suspicions remained that the US was able to bribe its way out of a constitutional difficulty with a US$1 billion aid package for 50 years — or US$1,230 per capita in Palau. In any event, in late August 1988 the country's Supreme Court again invalidated the two plebiscites of August 1987 and thereby frustrated the government's attempt to circumvent the anti-nuclear constitution.[47]

In the light of these 'loopholes' for the entry of nuclear weapons into the South Pacific, the SPNFZ has been described as a 'sham' by various opponents, and has failed to lessen French cynicism about the goals and worth of the zone. One peace activist concluded that the SPNFZ 'seems more a cosmetic measure aimed at containing and defusing growing popular pressure for regional denuclearisation than a serious move towards regional disarmament'.[48] Furthermore, because the loopholes are largely in the categories of growing regional nuclearisation; while the achievements lie in the marginal categories in the South Pacific, there is suspicion that the SPNFZ may represent a net liability in serving to demobilise regional efforts at genuine denuclearisation. As one critic put it, the SPNFZ 'permits and implicitly legitimises the worst aspect of the nuclear arms race and superpower rivalry in the region'.[49] For these reasons, the Treaty of Rarotonga has been ridiculed as an agreement by non-nuclear states to stay non-nuclear, akin to a 'smoke-free zone' which applies only to non-smokers.

The last comment in particular highlights the unfairness of the criticisms. A 'smoke-free zone' is fully effective when smokers refrain from lighting up within the zone; they are not required to quit smoking permanently, nor even to hand over all cigarettes and matches to guardians of the zone at its gates. Similarly, a NWFZ will have achieved its objective if nuclear-weapon states (NWS) refrain from lighting up their nuclear arsenals within the zone. Attempts to ban transit of nuclear-armed ships through zonal high seas, by being legally impermissible and practically unenforceable, would merely generate international scepticism towards the zone as a whole. The framers of the treaty were guided by the principle of 'stretching the fabric of the Treaty to its widest possible extent'.[50] Some of the attacks on the SPNFZ arise from a confusion between an arms control and a confidence building measure. The SPNFZ is defective if viewed as an arms control agreement. Yet it remains valuable as a CBM which enlarges and deepens the area of peace. It does not eliminate the possibility of nuclear weapons use in the South Pacific; it does promote security and raise the threshold of nuclear initiation in the region by reducing instabilities, and diminishing uncertainties about military arrangements by facilitating exchanges of information on nuclear-related military activity. The SPNFZ is primarily a means of influencing the nature of peacetime relations between the NWS in the South Pacific.

The most serious gap in the SPNFZ regime remains the lack of endorsement by the NWS. The Treay of Rarotonga adopts the simple expedient, following Tlatelolco, of containing additional protocols for integrating NWS into the SPNFZ. Protocol 1 is addressed to France, Britain and the US, and invites them to apply NFZ prohibitions on manufacture, stationing and testing, to their territories within the zone. (The British territory involved is Pitcairns Island; the French territories are New Caledonia, French Polynesia and Wallis and Futuna; and those of the US are American Samoa and [uninhabited] Jarvis Island). Protocol 2 is addressed to the five NWS and contains the negative security guarantees. In it, each NWS party agrees not to violate the NFZ treaty, and not to use or threaten to use nuclear weapons against any treaty party, or in the territory of any party to the treaty or to Protocol 1. Protocol 3, which does not have a counterpart in Tlatelolco, prohibits the testing of any nuclear device anywhere in the region. The 1985 Forum meeting had adopted the protocols in draft form. Subsequently, a representative delegation visited all five NWS capitals between January 28 and February 14, 1986, and then revised the protocols to give each party the right to withdraw from each protocol, upon a three month notice, 'if it decides that extraordinary events, related to the subject matter of the Protocol, have jeopardised its supreme interest'. The 17th Forum meeting in Suva finalised the protocols on August 8, 1986, and decided to open them for signature on December 1, 1986.

The ***Soviet Union***, which has been a longstanding advocate of NWFZs, became the first NWS to sign the relevant SPNFZ Protocols (2 and 3) on December 15, 1986. But its signature of the protocols was qualified: it declared its compliance with Protocol 2 to be conditional on party states not committing an act of aggression in alliance with another NWS or, during such aggression, permitting transit or visiting rights to air or sea vessels of a NWS. (This was similar to the Soviet position on the Tlatelolco regime). While the Soviet signature in 1986 was qualified, its ratification in 1988 was not. It did not take ***China*** long in 1985 to indicate support for the Treaty of Rarotonga; the Chinese ambassador to Fiji signed Protocols 2 and 3 in Siva on February 10, 1987.

The ***US*** and France were expected to be the two problematical nuclear powers. In September 1985, Prime Minister Hawke had approached the US to exert pressure on France to cease nuclear testing in the Pacific. The Reagan administration however confirmed the primacy of the North Atlantic over the South Pacific in its strategic worldview. The State Department described French nuclear tests as 'essential to the modernisation of the French nuclear deterrent'; in any case, the US regarded 'these matters as French decisions'.[51] While the people who have to live in the South Pacific can understand US concerns about the intricacies of an alliance which has been central to the defence of Europe, they also believe that such concerns belong to Europe. It is gratuitously offensive to subordinate Pacific sensitivities to European and global strategic calculations. The Australian Ambassador used justifiably forceful language in an address to the Asia Society in Washington, DC on September 24, 1985:

> 'If you want the South Pacific to become an area where the Soviet Union, Cuba and others of that stripe can find fertile ground for anti-United States, anti-West propaganda and activity and in which they can develop activities directly prejudicial to our interest — then continue with a policy of indifference to what the French are doing there'.[52]

The Americans have been less than enthusiastic supporters of a SPNFZ. With nuclear proliferation not being an issue in the region, and with the Soviet profile barely visible, Washington did not see any of its major security goals being served by the Treaty of Rarotonga. It was reported in April 1986 that the US had adopted a tough uncompromising stand towards the treaty. Washington was reported to have concluded that the Australian initiative had been meant as a sop to party activists rather than as a serious commitment to regional nuclear arms control; that the SPNFZ would directly benefit Soviet global objectives to the detriment of US interests; and that the SPNFZ could create a serious precedent for the establishment of interlocking

NWFZs which would impede the free movement of US forces around the world.[53] The formal US decision not to sign the Rarotonga protocols was announced on February 4, 1987.

Nevertheless, the US does not in fact conduct nuclear tests, base or store nuclear weapons, or dump nuclear waste in the South Pacific — or intend to do so. But the US does have distinctive security relationships with Micronesian states, as was noted above. The fact that the Marshall Islands and the Federated States of Micronesia are now members of the South Pacific Forum means that they have become eligible to join the SPNFZ. Membership in the Forum and in SPEC would bring mutual advantages to other Micronesian territories upon the termination of UN trusteeship: Micronesia would be reinvigorated with fresh ideas and the experience of non-ideological regional decision-making processes; the region would benefit from increased strength of numbers and enhanced economies of scale in the sorts of activities performed by SPEC. Yet Micronesian membership of the South Pacific Forum cannot but complicate the issue of inclusion of Micronesia within the zonal boundaries of the Treaty of Rarotonga, and the implications of this for US accession to the protocols.

French testing. As Australian Defence Minister Kim Beazly conceded subsequently, the SPNFZ treaty was aimed primarily at France.[54] The subject of French nuclear testing in turn is tied inseparably to what many South Pacific residents perceive as Gallic visions of grandeur as a world power, in the sense that Moruroa is irrelevant to French regional military strategy; it can be explained only at the level of global military strategy. In combination with a colonial mind-set, this means that the South Pacific becomes a mere appendage to the metropolis, and the aspirations of the South Pacific peoples are made subservient to the interests of the state of France.

Not only can France be said to be a Pacific power; it is in fact the most substantial power in the South Pacific. It has three groups of island territories — 'Confetti of the Empire' — in the region: New Caledonia, comprising the main island and six outlying island groups; the Wallis and Futuna islands to the northeast of Fiji (occupied in 1886); and French Polynesia comprising five groups of islands administered from Papeete (Tahiti having been occupied in 1842). Successive French governments have reaffirmed the commitment to the security of all French overseas territories. In addition, French policy since World War II has been characterised by a continuity of conviction that France is a global power which must maintain the capability to project its military forces to any part of the world. The final consideration with a bearing on France's attitude towards its overseas possessions is the EEZ-based potential for commercial exploitation.

France has traditionally been an 'activist' in its foreign policy, prepared to assert claims, and willing to act in defence of such claims. It is neither reticent in articulating its rights against external opposition, nor reluctant to commit troops as needed to protect or advance its self-proclaimed rights. Its rapid deployment force is structured, trained and configured primarily for a swift response to national emergencies; but it can also, as a secondary objective, be deployed in response to overseas contingencies.

The legendary Foreign Legion provides garrison forces for such overseas territories as Tahiti.

Thus France has the will and the ability to deploy forces in the Pacific. Furthermore, overseas territories in the South Pacific give France ready bases for deploying forces in the region. The two French overseas military commands in the Pacific are centred on New Caledonia and French Polynesia.[55] Given the tranquillity of the region until very recently, French military forces, based at Papeete and Hao Island, have concentrated on the tasks of civil aid projects, training, EEZ maritime surveillance and infrastructural support for nuclear tests. The naval repair facility in Tahiti is virtually self-sufficient in providing the necessary maintenance for the entire French Pacific fleet.[56]

France can therefore be described as having the political will, the military muscle and the infrastructural support facilities to project its intrusive power into the South Pacific. The policies of the government, it may be noted, are underpinned by a seven-strand ideological consensus of the French people:

- The South Pacific is a vacuum, to be used as the French wish.
- France cannot afford to cop out of the dynamic Pacific as the new centre of the world.
- France cannot discard its duty to resist growing Soviet encroachments in the South Pacific.
- France must persevere in the final, Pacific manifestation of the historic rivalry between the Gauls and *les Anglais*.[57]
- The commercial (fishing and deep seabed mining) and technologial (space and communications high-technology laboratory) attractions are too good to ignore.
- The cultural (Gauguin) and leisure (Club Med) images of the South Pacific exercise a magnetic pull upon the French consciousness.
- France is the champion of the indigenous peoples' rights against Anglo domination by big brothers Australia and New Zealand.

A French analyst notes that the 'seven obsessions' are internally inconsistent (for instance, the power vacuum versus the new centre of the world image).[58] In part this reflects the fact that some French public support comes from the left of the ideological spectrum, some from the right; some apply to the North Pacific, some to the South Pacific, and some to the Pacific rim. But they all relate to the Pacific, and they all exclude the wishes of the Pacific inhabitants from any significant input into French policymaking.

These general comments on French policy in the Pacific acquire particular cogency with regard to nuclear testing. France tests nuclear weapons in the South Pacific as a consequence of having decided to protect its status as a world power and to pursue the option of an independent nuclear deterrent. The decision on the independent deterrent was taken in the mid-1950s, with the Sahara being chosen as the initial testing site (1960-63). France was compelled to relocate the testing site in 1963 after newly-independent Algeria objected to such activities in the Sahara. It was then shifted to the South Pacific. The tests embrace the variety of weapons systems constituting France's independent *force de frappe* (strike force): the world's third largest nuclear arsenal. The French attitude seems to be that the bomb is French, the testing is done by France, so the choice of testing site is solely a French decision. In September 1985, a spokesman for the French president took this argument a step farther by declaring, while in Moruroa, that no country could take decisions in France's place with regard to its Pacific interests unless it wanted to be seen as an adversary.[59]

Countries of the South Pacific have been united, vocal and persistent in their opposition to French nuclear testing. The opposition has been expressed by national leaders, through regional agencies and in international forums. Nor is the opposition always confined to nice diplomatic langauge. For example, Senator Gareth Evans, representing the Minister for Foreign Affairs, was quite blunt in his statement in the Australian Parliament on September 12, 1985:

> 'It is the government's position that if France is as genuine as it claims to be in its assertions that no damage in terms of radioactive pollution will follow from the carrying out of those tests, it ought to put its money where its mouth is and conduct those tests on metropolitan French soil'.

The regional position is very simple and very clear. If the tests are harmful, then they should be terminated. If they cause no harm, then they should be conducted on metropolitan Fench soil.

The political fallout from the sinking of the *Rainbow Warrior* in 1985 focussed sustained international attention on French nuclear testing in the region. The fact that the French testing brought the first act of international terrorism to New Zealand also strengthened regional opposition to French nuclear activities. Even after the international embarrassment of the *Rainbow Warrior* affair, France refused to budge on the issue of nuclear testing at Moruroa. Indeed President Francois Mitterrand flew to Moruroa in mid-September 1985 to emphasise French determination on the subject, an act that was interpreted — and probably intended — as a calculated rebuff to pressure from the South Pacific countries to cease testing in the region.

Mitterrand's trip to Moruroa was chided as 'an extremely provocative act' by Australian Foreign Minister Bill Hayden in Parliament on September 11. (This was still not as provocative as the returning of the two convicted agents to France in 1988, contrary to the explicit terms of the UN Secretary-General's arbitration). Hayden described French motive as being 'to evidence a tough determination to proceed with nuclear testing in the South Pacific'. Subsequently, in a news release on October 25, Hayden repeated that if 'France insisted on conducting these tests it should do so on its home territory, especially if the tests were as harmless as France claimed'. He took issue with French claims that the report by scientists from Australia, New Zealand and Papua New Guinea who visited Moruroa in 1983 established that the nuclear tests were completely harmless. The group had not cleared the test in respect of long-term environmental consequences. And the South Pacific countries, unlike France, had no option but to be in the region for the long term. Therefore, Hayden concluded, 'the presence of French political leaders at Moruroa Atoll could not legitimise France's nuclear testing programme there'.[60]

More recently, a report tabled by the European Parliament's committee on the environment, public health and consumer protection also noted 'serious flaws' in the work and findings of the team of scientists from Australia, New Zealand and Papua New Guinea which travelled to Tahiti and Moruroa atoll in October 1983, headed by New Zealand National Radiation Laboratory Director Hugh Atkinson.[61] The Atkinson mission lacked medically qualified staff. It was barred from an independent choice of sampling sites on Moruroa and was not permitted to collect sediment from the lagoon. The committee, citing the number of studies which document the health effects of US atmospheric nuclear tests in the Marshall Islands, called for the EEC to pay for an independent team of scientists to investigate the health and environmental effects of French nuclear testing in the region; the mission to have unrestricted freedom of investigation from French and Tahitian authorities; and the World Heath Organisaton to receive complete statistics on mortality rates and causes.

There was a time-lag of nine years between the first atmospheric and underground test at Moruroa in 1966 and 1975 respectively. The site was originally chosen because its isolation allegedly made it particularly suitable for atmospheric tèsts. The infrastructure built up after 1966 made Moruroa a convenient but not an essential site for underground testing; conversely, the economic and political costs of relocating could prove to be a substantial deterrent. (Bill Hayden has pointed out that a technical report by Australia's own Office of National Assessments had concluded that France could safely carry out nuclear testing on the Massif Central of mainland France and in Corsica).[62] Nor is the strategic justification for the programme of nuclear testing self-evident. The case for a Comprehensive Test Ban (CTB) has not been disproven even worldwide. For France, *sufficiency* rather than over-ambitious parity seems adequate to its posture of deterrence. Sufficiency is quite compatible with maintenance of existing sophistication of nuclear weaponry and cessation of further testing. These two comments are in addition to possible safety and environmental apprehensions, as well as harmful social, cultural and political consequences in the region.

French opposition to the SPNFZ is expressed on three counts: The major part of the zone comprises international sea space free of any constraints; risks of horizontal proliferation are minimal in the South Pacific; the five NWS have already given negative security guarantees at an international level.[63] Given such an attitude on the part of the French government, it would appear unrealistic to expect a modification of their nuclear activity in the foreseeable future. In February 1987, France formally informed the South Pacific Forum that it would not adhere to any of the SPNFZ protocols. Its testing programme at Moruroa continues unabated. The South Pacific countries simply lack the power of military might, diplomatic sanction or economic resources to compel France to terminate its testing programme. Such a conclusion is unlikely to stop regional countries from trying to change French policy, since in the long term the basis of opposition to French testing is more durable. As an Assistant Secretary in the New Zealand Ministry of Foreign Affairs noted, 'No one pretends for a moment that (the SPNFZ) will stop France testing, but it will serve further to isolate the French if they persist with this activity in face of the region's concern'.[64]

Britain followed the French example by stating, on March 21, 1987, that signing the SPNFZ protocls would not serve its national interests, although it would not in practice act contrary to their requirements, and would keep its formal position under review.[65] The deciding factor with Britain was undoubtedly its relations with its two NATO allies — France and the US. The net result, therefore, is that the communist countries have signed, and the Western powers have not. The political repercussions of this alignment may be felt in due course.

The goals behind the establishment of the SPNFZ — which has already attracted Southeast Asian attention for possible emulation by Asean[66] — were thus the need to prevent the region from becoming a theatre of superpower rivalry, the need to preserve in perpetuity the existing peace and security of the region, and the wish to protect the natural resources on which the wellbeing and livelihood of the South Pacific depend. Regional disarmament can at best supplement universal disarmament. Efforts towards the first are spurred by lack of visible progress in the latter. Because the effects of nuclear war would be global and species-threatening, all countries have both the right and the responsibility to make efforts towards halting and then reversing the nuclear arms race. The hope is that each step forward such as a NWFZ will lessen the suspicion and distrust that underlies the arms race. While comprehensive disarmament remains a long-range goal of the international community, the conviction has grown that immediate and partial measures which would increase confidence and create a more favourable atmosphere for overall disarmament should be pursued. Arms control efforts look too much to the past, and are reactive and curative. For a region which seeks to perpetuate the status quo of isolation from nuclear weapons strategy and deployment, the greater need is for measures that are anticipatory and preventive. The SPNFZ can be commended for being prophylactic rather than abortive or therapeutic. This therefore gives it a military significance additional to its political importance as a means of raising the threshold of nuclear initiation and as a confidence building measure.

Alliance stability and unilateral antinuclearism

The years since 1984 have seen a divergence between Australia and New Zealand on the most appropriate strategy of reducing the conflict potential and enhancing the security environment of their nations and region.

Australia is firm in its belief that it is part of the Western community of nations and that an effective strategic balance under US leadership is therefore in its national security interests. Conversely, a redistribution of power in favour of the Soviet Union globally, or an extension of Soviet influence regionally, would have an adverse impact upon Australian security interests and a destabilising effect in the South Pacific region. Describing Australia as 'a respected and self-respecting member of the Western community,' the White Paper on defence set the goal of defence self-reliance 'firmly within the framework of our alliances and regional associations. The support they give us makes self-reliance achievable'.[67] The Australian paper specifically mentioned port visits by US warships as an example of the opportunities provided to the Australian forces for combined exercises with advanced technology vessels, as well as providing rest and recreation facilities for US naval deployments in the region. Australia's collective defence arrangements were viewed as enhancing self-reliance by improving technological capabilities, providing training opportunities for the armed forces, and facilitating access to vital military and political intelligence on both global and regional developments. Australia's access to the highest level of technology was explicitly described as 'one of the most important benefits of our alliance with the United States'.[68] As a practical example, the paper pointed out that the Jindalee OTHR (over the horizon radar) system was produced by Australian scientists building on access to US technology. In return, the US gains information from Australian surveillance and intelligence gathering activities.

A fundamental threat to Australian security would activate the ANZUS security guarantee. The ANZUS security guarantee also complicates the planning environment of a potential aggressor by making him contemplate the prospect of an allied response to an attack on Australia. But it is prudent for Australian defence planners to assume that the threshold of US intervention could be quite high, and therefore to pursue policies of enhanced self-reliance to cope independently with a range of lower-level but more probable threats.

The Australian White Paper accepted that Australian security, like that of all other countries, is ultimately dependent upon a stable relationship between the two superpowers and the avoidance of nuclear war between them. Australia therefore believed that it is important to maintain a stable strategic balance to support mutual deterrence. As part of that process, Australia hosts joint defence facilities: the Northwest Cape Naval Communication Station in Western Australia, Pine Gap and Nurrungar. The government of Australia accepts that the basing of joint facilities carries an attendant risk of Australia itself being a target in the event of nuclear conflict, but believes that the net damage to Australian security would be greater if the international strategic environment was to deteriorate because of their dismantling.

New Zealand has rocked the Western alliance boat rather vigorously in the last few years.[69] The anti-ANZUS constituency, presently in ascendance, blames ANZUS for making New Zealand a nuclear target, compromising New Zealand's sovereignty, linking New Zealand to objectionable US foreign policies, failing to guarantee New Zealand's security, and hindering the development of an indigenous threat-definition and intelligence-gathering capability. Major threats to New Zealand are difficult to discern, and the value of ANZUS is questionable against the more probable low-level threats. While some do see value in ANZUS, they are not prepared to stay in the alliance at the cost of abandoning the anti-nuclear ships policy. The White Paper reiterated the commitment to ANZUS obligations, but 'in conventional terms' only.[70]

There are several reasons for the strength of New Zealand's anti-nuclear conviction. Most New Zealanders believe that the nuclear arms race has gone out of control and that the US is as culpable as the Soviet Union. Second, many more people have begun to appreciate the dangers of the paradox of nuclear deterrence. If the West seeks to deter the Soviet Union with nuclear weapons, then it must convince the Soviets that in certain circumstances these weapons will be used. But if in fact nuclear weapons are used and produce a like response, then even the West is worse off than if it had not relied upon nuclear weapons in the first place. Third, the fact that New Zealand too would be devastated in the aftermath of a nuclear war between the superpowers is seen to give it both the right and the responsibility to speak out on the dangers of nuclearism. Fourth, New Zealand's geopolitical environment means that the most realistic, and the most serious, threat to its national security is posed by the prospect of a global nuclear war. Efforts to lessen the chances of such an outbreak are therefore a direct pursuit of national security interests, not just based in idealism divorced from the nation's real needs. Fifth, the fact that the South Pacific is the only region where nuclear testing is carried out by an extra-regional nuclear power,[71] namely France, gives particular cogency to anti-nuclear sentiments. Finally, the history of the relationship of nuclear weapons use (in 1945) and testing with the Pacific area has sensitised Pacific peoples to the nuclear evil perhaps rather more deeply than others.

The rationale for New Zealand's anti-nuclear posture is not to be found in the White Paper on Defence. But it was eloquently expressed by Prime Minister David Lange in an address to the Dunedin branch of the New Zealand Institute of International Affairs on April 30, 1987:

> ...nuclear weapons are themselves the greatest threat which exists to our future... far from adding to our security, they only put us more at risk...
>
> New Zealand cannot be defended by nuclear weapons and does not wish to be defended by nuclear weapons. We have disengaged ourselves from any nuclear strategy for the defence of New Zealand.

There would probably be general support for the claim made in a submission to defence inquiry in 1986 that 'The effects of New Zealand's nuclear warship ban is more significant than anything this country has ever done to try to promote international peace'.[72] (This is not necessarily a creditable reflection on New Zealand's efforts in the field of international disarmament; gesture diplomacy cannot adequately substitute for a substantive record). New Zealand does believe that deterrence is divisible, and indeed that it is irrelevant to the security of New Zealand and the South Pacific region. As Lange explained in his address in Dunedin on April 30, 1987:

> When I think of the world's nuclear arsenals I know that what New Zealand has done as a measure of arms control [excluding nuclear warships from its ports] is a small step indeed. I also know that if we cannot take that step in New Zealand we cannot take it anywhere. If we cannot start in New Zealand we cannot start anywhere.

In short, while Australia supports ANZUS and hosts joint facilities by pointing to their conflict dampening role, New Zealand has distanced itself from aspects of the alliance because of perceptions of their conflict generating potential. Yet it is possible to construct an argument that the presence of US nuclear ships in New Zealand waters is a guarantee against the outbreak of nuclear war, and that therefore the resumption of such ship visits could be an important confidence building measure. Logically, there are only three scenarios in which a US warship on rest and recreation in a New Zealand port could be the object of an enemy attack:

(a) The Soviet Union launches a surprise first strike against the US.
(b) The US attacks the Soviet Union first, and the latter retaliates against all US military targets.
(c) The US and the Soviet Union end up at war after a steady build-up of tension.

The first scenario can be ruled out reasonably confidently: there is not much credibility in the suggestion that the Soviet Union has a sufficient margin of nuclear superiority to launch a surprise suicidal attack upon the US.

One of the major advantages that the Americans have over the Soviets in their nuclear force configuration is that the US weapons are better distributed. With about half its strategic armoury being sea-based, the US can more easily conceal its nuclear weapons through dispersing its ships globally on and under the seas. By contrast, warships sitting idle in ports are soft targets because they are at a known, fixed and static location. If the US was planning a nuclear strike on the Soviet Union, it would not leave nuclear warships in ports as 'sitting ducks' for enemy retaliation.

A similar argument holds for the final scenario as well. If war breaks out as a result of a steady increase in tension, then US warships are not likely to come steaming down to New Zealand for rest and recreation. Instead they will head for the wide blue oceans to hide on and under the seas in readiness for battle.

In short, a Soviet first strike is not credible, and a US first strike or a nuclear exchange resulting from escalating tensions will see US nuclear ships leaving from New Zealand ports before the point of nuclear war is reached. Therefore, if it is nuclear war that New Zealand wants to avoid, then it should perhaps welcome the presence of US nuclear-armed warships with open ports. For as long as there are American warships in New Zealand waters, they provide reassurance against the imminent onset of a nuclear war.[73]

On the other hand, it is only fair to record that any attempt to bring a US warship into a New Zealand port in the present socio-political environment would seriously split the country and lead to major confrontations on the streets. Given the marginal contribution of ship visits to the country's security, this would be a somewhat peculiar policy of national defence. It should be noted too that the New Zealand anti-ships policy *has* served to strengthen the worldwide process of delegitimising nuclear weapons. Australia supports efforts to maintain a stable strategic balance, and accepts the need for current levels of arsenals by the West 'as a basis for substantive arms control and disarmament negotiations'.[74] For Australia, the path to diminished international tension lies through verifiable arms control agreements in both nuclear and conventional fields. Australia and New Zealand are united nevertheless in their support of a CTB, which was endorsed by a record 143 nations in a United Nations General Assembly vote in December 1987, and are prepared to participate in the development and management of a global seismic monitoring network to verify compliance with a CTB. The two countries, which participate actively in the work of the Group of Scientific Experts, signed a seismic monitoring agreement on April 30, 1987. (The GSE also designated Australia as one of four international data centres for the major network trial planned for 1988-89. In September 1986 the Australian government opened the Australian Seismological Centre in Canberra drawing together information from seismic stations and arrays in Australia and Antarctica. In June 1987 the government dedicated a new seismic array processor, capable of detecting and identifying nuclear explosions at the main Chinese, French, Soviet and US test sites, which will provide enhanced analysis of seismic data). There is a rough consensus in the South Pacific that the Treaty of Rarotonga is a practical confidence building measure. There is a clear consensus that French nuclear testing in the region should cease and that no radioactive waste should be dumped in the South Pacific.

I have also suggested that a regional peacekeeping force could act as a confidence building measure in advance, and a conflict management mechanism in the midst, of a crisis. Australia and New Zealand join Fiji and New Caledonia as areas of potential problems involving a clash between races, and/or between the dominant group and an indigenous group with a sense of historical grievance. Finally, I have argued that conflict can be reduced and the sense of confidence in a secure future enhanced by policies of economic development based on relationships of equality and expanded trade opportunities. Western political interests in the South Pacific are susceptible to damage more by insensitivity and neglect than as a result of periodic Soviet probing through windows of opportunity.

The three major problem areas of long standing in the South Pacific have been New Caledonia, nuclear issues and concern about fishing stocks. And in these three matters, the two problem states have been France and the US. Virtually all the countries in the South Pacific region are conservative, pro-Western and anti-Soviet. It is American policy on fishing, and French policy on nuclear testing and decolonisation, rather than Soviet capabilities *per se*, that have offered tempting targets of political and economic penetration and, in addition to communal problems, could produce serious political dislocation.

NOTES

1. I would like to thank Trevor Findlay, John Groom and Richard Kennaway for helpful comments upon earlier drafts.
2. *Australian Foreign Affairs Record* (AFAR) 54 (August 1983), p 380.
3. *Defence of New Zealand: Review of Defence Policy 1987* (Wellington: Government Printer, February 1987), p 12.
4. *AFAR* 58 (November/December 1987), pp 609-610.
5. The one significant exception to this is the Irian Jaya region on the border between Indonesia and Papua New Guinea, with spillover implications for Australia. This is ignored in the present paper firstly because it begins to extrude into the Asean region and secondly because its salience as a potential zone of conflict seems to have receded. Indeed former Indonesian Foreign Minister Dr Mochtar Kusumaatmadja believes that the manner in which the issue has been removed from the agenda of regional security concerns with the construction of adequate tension defusing machinery could serve as a model of conflict resolution in general. Personal interview, Kuala Lumpur, July 4, 1988.
6. John Henderson, rapporteur, 'The Security of Small States: Report of a Study Group of the Commonwealth Parliamentary Association,' *The Parliamentarian* 55 (October 1984), p 258.

7. Russell Marshall, 'Comprehensive Security,' in *International Conflict Resolution*, edited by Ramesh Thakur (Boulder and Dunedin: Westview and University of Otago Press, 1988).

8. Harle Freeman-Grenne, 'Aid in the South Pacific: Is It Doing the Job It Should Be?' *NZ Foreign Affairs Review* 37 (April-June 1987).

9. 'Partners, Friends and Allies: Australia and the Pacific,' *AFAR* 56 (September 1985), p 820.

10. For an European perspective on this development, see Peter Odrich, 'Japan's Interest in South Pacific,' *Otago Daily Times* (Dunedin), April 3,1987; this is an abridged version of an article which was published in the *Frankfurter Allgemeine Zeitung*.

11. Richard A Herr, 'The Soviet Union in the South Pacific,' (Canberra: Australian Development Studies Network, *Briefing Paper*, October 1986), p 4.

12. Gregory E Fry, 'Regionalism and International Politics of the South Pacific,' *Pacific Affairs* 54 (Fall 1981), pp 471-472.

13. The Japanese however did not seem to regard the treaty as having provided a just solution to an unjust situation; see Robert Keith-Reed, 'Treaty Turbulence,' *Far Eastern Economic Review*, July 23, 1987, pp 16-17.

14. S I Benn and R S Peters, *Social Principles and the Democratic State* (London: Allen & Unwin, 1959), p 355.

15. 'The Open Society and its Enemies Revisited,' *The Economist*, April 23, 1988, p 24.

16. Cf Bill Hayden in a speech to the Foreign Correspondents Association of Australia in Sydney on April 30, 1987: 'In the view of the Australian Government, the decolonisation experiences of Vanuatu and New Caledonia are directly responsible for the Libyans arriving to stir the South Pacific pot,' *AFAR* 58 (April 1987), p 178.

17. Prime Minister Robert Muldoon described the deployment of the Papua New Guinea defence force in Vanuatu as a historic event of great importance to the region: 'Two Melanesian nations showed that by a calm and determined approach they could jointly counter an insurrection which was being fuelled by mischievous external elements.' *NZ Foreign Affairs Review* 30 (July-September 1980), pp 48-49.

18. Cf an Australian journalist: 'France seems at present determined to create a mini-Algeria in New Caledonia'; P P McGuinness, 'French Brutality Incites Sympathy,' *National Business Review* (Wellington), Sept 11, 1987, p 22; reproduced from the *Australian Financial Review*.

19. *UN Chronicle* 24 (1), February 1987, p 131.

20. Text of *communique* in *AFAR* 58 (June 1987). One quarter of the territory's population is overseas-born; John Connell, 'New Caledonia: A Crisis of Decolonisation in the South Pacific,' *Round Table* 305 (January 1988), p 54. Thus, if the franchise was limited to those born in New Caledonia, then the Melanesians would constitute a majority. (75 per cent of 150,000 is 112,500 New Caledonians by birth; 43 per cent of 150,000 is 64,500 Melanesians in total; 64,500 out of 112,500 is 57 per cent).

21. See Daniel Carton, 'New Caledonia Marathon Ends in Agreement,' *Le Monde* section of the *Canadian Weekly*, Aug 28, 1988, p 13.

22. *Otago Daily Times*, May 21, 1988.

23. 'Slogans Over Substance,' *The Weekend Australian*, May 21-22, 1988.

24. Thus the spokesman for deposed Prime Minister Bavadra: 'Race was used as a vehicle to return to power a group of people for whom power had become an unbreakable habit'; Richard Naidu, 'The Rise and Fall of Fijian Democracy,' *The Dominion* (Wellington), Jan 26, 1988.

25. Ramesh Thakur and Antony Wood, 'Crisis in Fiji,' *The World Today* 43 (December 1987).

26. See A J R Groom, 'Problem-Solving in International Relations,' in *International Conflict Resolution*, edited by E Azar and J W Burton (Brighton: Wheatsheaf, 1986).

27. Henderson, 'Security of Small States,' pp 255-256.

28. See Ramesh Thakur, 'A Dispute of Many Colours: France, New Zealand and the *Rainbow Warrior* Affair,' *The World Today* 42 (December 1986).

29. *Otago Daily Times*, Sept 15, 1988.

30. Henderson, 'Security of Small States,' p 262.

31. See 'International Peacekeeping,' in *International Conflict Resolution*, edited by R Thakur (Boulder, London and Dunedin: Westview and University of Otago Press, 1988).

32. See *The Defence of Australia* (Canberra: Australian Government Publishing Service, March 1987); and *Defence of New Zealand: Review of Defence Policy* 1987 (Wellington: Government Printer, February 1987). For a comparison of the two papers, as well as the Canadian, see Ramesh Thakur, 'God Defend the Queen: Three Commonwealth White Papers on Defence,' *Journal of Defence & Diplomacy* 6 (February 1988).

33. A recent report in the *Australian* identified Malaysia as the base of Libyan operations in the South Pacific; Bruce London, 'Gaddafi's Outpost in Malaysia,' *Dominion Sunday Times* (Wellington), June 19, 1988.

34. On Australia's defence initiatives in the South Pacific, see, for example, Defence Minister Kim Beazley's statement to Parliament on Feb 20, 1987.

35. For an elaboration of the ANZUS treaty and alliance, see Ramesh Thakur, *In Defence of New Zealand: Foreign Policy Choices in the Nuclear Age* (Boulder: Westview, 1986), Chapter 3.

36. For the parliamentary debate on the statement, see Commonwealth of Australia, Parliamentary Debates, *House of Representatives Weekly Harvard*, No 2, 1988, pp 499-509 and 524-33.

37. See Terry O'Connor, 'South Pacific Security Watch,' an Australian Associated Press dispatch in the *Otago Daily Times*, March 30, 1988.

38. Thus a RNZAF Orion sighted and photographed purse-seiners in Kiribati and Tuvalu EEZs in 1987, leading to the arrest of an American tuna boat by Kiribati; *Otago Daily Times*, May 6, 1987.

39. See Richard A Herr, 'The Soviet Union in the South Pacific,' in *The Soviet Union as an Asian Pacific Power: Implications of Gorbachev's 1986 Vladivostok Initiative*, edited by Ramesh Thakur and Carlyle A Thayer (Boulder and Melbourne: Westview and Macmillan, 1987).

40. John C Dorrance, 'United States Security Interests in the Pacific Islands,' *Asia-Pacific Defence Forum* (Special Supplement Winter 1985-86), p 8.

41. Although the new government of Prime Minister Rabbie Namaliu is reported to have decided to allow Moscow to open an embassy in Papua New Guinea, amidst some controversy; see Ian Vallance, 'Soviet Mission Questioned,' *Otago Daily Times*, Sept 1, 1988 (an AAP report).

42. Text of press conference supplied to author by the Australian High Commission in Wellington; a Reuter report was published in brief in the *Otago Daily Times*, April 15, 1988.

43. *Times Higher Education Supplement*, March 25, 1988, p 10.

44. For a discussion of SPNFZ, see Ramesh Thakur, 'The Treaty of Rarotonga,' in *Nuclear Free Zones*, edited by David Pitt and Gordon Thompson (London: Croom Helm, 1987).

45. In a written reply in Parliament on Sept 15, 1987, the Australian Defence Minister confirmed that British, French, Soviet and US nuclear-propelled and nuclear-capable warships had operated in the SPNFZ area since August 1986.

46. The 50-year agreement provides for contingency access to anchorage rights in Palau's main harbour and use of 40 acres of nearby land for support facilities; contingency joint use of the two main airfields; contingency use of 2,000 acres of land for logistics installations; and periodic access to Babelthuap Island for training exercises.

47. *Otago Daily Times*, Sept 1, 1988.

48. Michael Hamel-Green, 'South Pacific: A Not-So-Nuclear-Free Zone,' *Peace Studies* (October 1985), p 6.

49. *Ibid*, (November/December 1985), p 42. The article was published in two parts.

50. David Sadleir, 'Rarotonga: In the Footsteps of Tlatelolco,' *AFAR* 58 (September/October 1987), p 492. Sadleir was Chairman of the Working Group of Officials on SPNFZ appointed by the South Pacific Forum in 1984.

51. Quoted by Denis Reinhardt, 'Soviet Pledge on Nuclear-Free Zone Hits US Diplomacy,' *The Bulletin* (Sydney), April 1, 1986, p 85.

52. Dalrymple, 'Partners, Friends and Allies,' p 823.

53. Geoff Kitney, 'US Gets Tough with Australia over Nuclear-Free Zone,' *National Times*, April 25, 1986, p 5.

54. *NZ Times*, Sept 1, 1985.

55. See *The Military Balance* 1987-88 (London: International Institute for Strategic Studies, 1987), pp 63-64.

56. For a description of French forces in the South Pacific, see P Lewis Young, 'France Still a Power, though Far From Home,' *Pacific Defence Reporter*, March 1986.

57. A New Zealand historian believes that the French presence in the South Pacific lacks legitimacy in New Zealand because of 'a feeling which is rooted in last century's Anglo-French rivalry in the Pacific'; Malcolm McKinnon, 'The End of the Alliance?' *NZ International Review* 13 (May/June 1988), p 17. To the extent that the French perceive Australian-New Zealand led opposition to their presence in the region as being the product of the same historical legacy, they in turn accord no legitimacy to regional opposition. Yet the fact is that a programme of American or British testing in the South Pacific would generate equally intense resentment from the peoples of the region in the 1980s.

58. Jean Chesneaux, 'France in the Pacific,' *Peace Studies*, April/May 1986, p 20.

59. Senator Gareth Evans in the Australian Parliament on Sept 16, 1985; *AFAR* 56 (September 1985) p 872.

60. *Ibid* (October 1985), pp 1046-1047.

61. See David Robie, 'Pressure Mounts for French Test Probe,' *Dominion Sunday Times* (Wellington), June 19, 1988.

62. *AFAR* 56 (September 1985), pp 865-866.

63. 'South Pacific Nuclear-Free Zone', *France: Facts and Figures* (Wellington: Embassy of France, June 1985).

64. Graham Fortune, 'The South Pacific and New Zealand,' *Perspectives of New Zealand's Foreign Policy* (Wellington: MFA Information Bulletin No 18, 1986), pp 29-30.

65. *Canberra Times*, March 22, 1987.

66. But for a slightly sceptical analysis of the notion, see Muthiah Alagappa, 'A Nuclear Weapons-Free Zone in Southeast Asia: Problems and Prospects,' *Australian Outlook* 41 (December 1987).

67. *Defence of Australia*, p vii.

68. *Ibid*, p x.

69. For a fuller discussion of the NZ-US dispute, see Ramesh Thakur, *In Defence of New Zealand: Foreign Policy Choices in the Nuclear Age* (Boulder: Westview, 1986), especially Chapter 8.

70. *Defence of New Zealand*, p 31.

71. Britain of course carries out tests at American sites. But because this is a bilateral arrangement, it does not invalidate the assertion made here of the uniqueness of French testing in an external region.

72. *Defence and Security: What New Zealanders Want - Report of the Defence Committee of Enquiry, July 1986* (Wellington: Government Printer, 1986), p 45.

73. This argument is clever rather than substantial and is intended to make a point. In point of fact I believe that the presence in or absence from New Zealand ports of allied nuclear warships is irrelevant to is security.

74. *Defence of Australia*, p 10.

List of participating individuals*

Dato' Abdullah Hj Ahmad Badawi
Former Minister of Defence, Malaysia

Dr Muthiah Alagappa
Senior Fellow, ISIS Malaysia

Dr Roderick Alley
Senior Lecturer, School of Political Science and Public Administration, Victoria University, New Zealand

Mr Luis R Baltazar
Deputy National Security Director, National Security Council, the Philippines

Ambassador Philippe Baude
Ambassador at Large, First Delegate of France to the South Pacific Commission

Dr James A Boutilier
Professor, Department of History and Political Economy, Royal Roads Military College, Canada

Mr Bui Xuan Ninh
Head of Information and Documentation, Institute for International Relations, Ministry of Foreign Affairs, Hanoi, Vietnam

Dr Leszek Buszynski
Australian National University, Australia

Dr Chan Heng Chee
Director, Institute of Policy Studies, Department of Political Science, National University of Singapore, Singapore

Mr Charivat Santaputra
Royal Thai Embassy, Thailand

Ambassador Dr Chawan Chawanid
Ambassador of Thailand to Malaysia

Dr Chin Kin Wah
Senior Lecturer, Department of Political Science, National University of Singapore, Singapore

Professor Choi Sang-Yong
Department of Political Science, Korea University, Republic of Korea

Professor Harold Crouch
Senior Fellow, Department of Political and Social Change, Research School of Pacific Studies, Australian National University, Australia

Dr Gennady I Chufrin
Head of Department, Institute of Oriental Studies, Academy of Science, Soviet Union

Dr Chun In-Young
Associate Professor of Political Science and Research Director, Institute of Social Sciences, Seoul National University, Republic of Korea

Ambassador Buyantyn Dashtseren
Ambassador of Mongolia to Japan

Mr Djunaedi Sutisnawinata
Head, Pusat Penelitian & Pengembangan, Ekonomi Sosial Budaya, Badan Litbang, Ministry of Foreign Affairs, Indonesia

Dato' Dr A Fadzil Che Wan
Deputy Minister for Foreign Affairs, Malaysia

Mr Trevor Findlay
Senior Research Fellow, Peace Research Centre, Australian National University, Australia

Mr Gao E
Deputy Director-General, Centre for International Studies, People's Republic of China

Mr Gulam Hussein Gulam Haniff
Deputy Secretary-General, Ministry of Foreign Affairs, Malaysia

Professor Ha Young-Sun
Chairman, Department of International Relations, College of Social Sciences, Seoul National University, Republic of Korea

Dr Hamzah Ahmad
Senior Fellow, ISIS Malaysia

Ms Linda Laurel Hazou
Political Affairs Officer, Office of the Special Representative of the Secretary-General for Humanitarian Affairs in Southeast Asia, United Nations

Professor Carolina Hernandez
Professor of Political Science and Director, Centre for Integrative and Development Studies, University of Philippines

Mr Hiam Phommachanh
Vice President, Lao Committee for Peace, Solidarity and Friendship, Laos

Mr Ho Sok Chol
Senior Researcher, Institute of International Affairs, Democratic People's Republic of Korea

Dr John Stephen Hoadley
Associate Professor of Political Science, University of Auckland, New Zealand

High Commissioner Cavan Hogue
High Commissioner of Australia to Malaysia

Tun Hussein Onn
Former Prime Minister of Malaysia and Chairman, ISIS Malaysia

Pengiran Haji Ismail bin Pengiran Haji Hassan
Desk Officer, Ministry of Foreign Affairs, Negara Brunei Darussalam

High Commissioner Pengiran Dato Paduka Hj Jaludin bin Pengiran Mohd Limbang
High Commissioner of Negara Brunei Darussalam to Malaysia

High Commissioner R L Jermyn
High Commissioner of New Zealand to Malaysia

Professor Chandran Jeshurun
Institute of Southeast Asian Studies, Singapore

Mr Ji Guoxing
Director, Asian Affairs Department, Shanghai Institute for International Studies, China

Mr Junizar Jacub
Embassy of the Republic of Indonesia, Malaysia

Mr Jusuf Wanandi
Executive Director, Centre for Strategic and International Studies, Indonesia

Dr Miles Kahler
Professor, Graduate School of International Relations and Pacific Studies, University of California, San Diego, United States

Professor Joyce Kallgren
Director, China Centre, Institute of East Asian Studies, University of California, Berkeley, United States

Mr Bilahari Kausikan
Deputy Director (Southeast Asia), Ministry of Foreign Affairs, Singapore

Dr Richard Kennaway
Senior Lecturer in Political Science, University of Canterbury, New Zealand

Mr Anthony Charles Kevin
Assistant Secretary, Policy Planning Branch, Department of Foreign Affairs and Trade, Australia

Professor Yoneji Kuroyanagi
Professor, Toyo Eiwa Junior College and Visiting Research Fellow, Japan Institute of International Affairs, Japan

Dr Kusuma Snitwongse
Faculty of Political Science, Chulalongkorn University, Thailand

Professor Dr Mochtar Kusumaatmadja
Professor of Law, Padjajaran University and former Minister for Foreign Affairs, Indonesia

Mr Kwa Chong Guan
Vice President, Singapore Institute for International Affairs, Singapore

Dr Michael Leifer
Department of International Relations, London School of Economics and Political Science, London

Ambassador Li Song Gi
Ambassador of the Democratic People's Republic of Korea to Malaysia

Mr Ly Southavilay
Chief, Department of Southeast Asia, Ministry of Foreign Affairs, Laos

Mr Andrew Mack
Head, Peace Research Centre, Research School of Pacific Studies, Australian National University, Australia

Mr V V Malygin
Department of Policy Planning, Ministry of Foreign Affairs, Soviet Union

Mr Mohamad bin Mohd Yassin
Prime Minister's Department (Research), Malaysia

Dato' Mohamed Sopiee
Board Member, ISIS Malaysia

Mr Mohd Fadil Ali
Ministry of Foreign Affairs, Malaysia

Dato Haji Mohd Yunos bin Haji Hussein
Officer with Special Duties, Ministry of Foreign Affairs, Negara Brunei Darussalam

Ambassador John C Monjo
Ambassador of the United States of America to Malaysia

High Commissioner S R Nathan
High Commissioner of Singapore to Malaysia

Mr Ng Bak Hai
Ministry of Foreign Affairs, Malaysia

Dr Haing Samnang Ngor
Los Angeles, California

Mr Nguyen Can
Director of the Department of Asia III, Ministry of Foreign Affairs, Vietnam

Dr Noordin Sopiee
Director-General, ISIS Malaysia

SAC Tuan Haji Nordin Omar
Director of E4, Royal Malaysian Police, Malaysia

Tun Dato' Omar Yoke Lin Ong
Board Member, ISIS Malaysia

Ambassador Phan Wannamethee
Director, International Studies Centre, Institute of Foreign Affairs, Ministry of Foreign Affairs, Thailand

Mr Douglas Pike
Director, Indochina Studies Project, University of California, Berkeley, United States

Ambassador F I Potapenko
Ambassador of the Union of Soviet Socialist Republics to Malaysia

Assoc Prof Prasert Chittiwatanapong
Assistant to the Rector for Research Affairs, Faculty of Political Science, Thammasat University, Bangkok

Dr James J Przystup
Deputy Director, Policy Planning Staff, Department of State, Washington DC, United States

Maj Gen Raja Dato Rashid bin Raja Badiozaman
Ketua Staf Perisikan Pertahanan, Bahagian Staf Perisikan Pertahanan, Kementerian Pertahanan, Kuala Lumpur

Professor Rhee Sang-Woo
Director, Institute for East Asian Studies and Dean, Graduate School of Public Policy, Sogang University, Republic of Korea

Mr Michael Richardson
Editor for Asia, International Herald Tribune, Singapore

Mr Jose del Rosario
Minister Counsellor, Embassy of the Republic of the Philippines, Malaysia

Professor Leo E Rose
Professor of Political Science, Department of Political Science, University of California, Berkeley, United States

General (Retd) Saiyud Kerdphol
Bangkok, Thailand

Professor K S Sandhu
Director, Institute of Southeast Asian Studies, Singapore

Mr M Santhananaban
Principal Assistant Secretary, Ministry of Foreign Affairs, Malaysia

Senator Tan Sri C Selvarajah
Board Member, ISIS Malaysia

Professor Robert A Scalapino
Robson Research Professor of Government and Director, Institute of East Asian Studies, University of California, Berkeley, United States

Dr A V Sergiev
Senior Advisor, Policy Planning Department, Ministry of Foreign Affairs, Soviet Union

Dr Soedjati Djiwandono
Member, Board of Directors, Centre for Strategic and International Studies, Indonesia

Ambassador Dr Sohn Jang Nai
Ambassador of the Republic of Korea to Malaysia

High Commissioner JNT Spreckley
High Commissioner of Britain to Malaysia

Ambassador Pablo R Suarez
Ambassador of the Philippines to Malaysia

Colonel Subagyo DMA
National Defence Institute, Ministry of Defence, Indonesia

M R Sukhumbhand Paribatra
Director, Institute of Security and International Studies and Associate Professor of Political Science, Chulalongkorn University, Thailand

Dr Kazuo Takahashi
Programme Director, Sasakawa Peace Foundation, Japan

Mr Kazunori Tamaki
Lecturer, Kokushikan University, Japan

Dr Ramesh Thakur
Senior Lecturer, Department of Political Studies, Otago University, New Zealand

Professor Seki Tomoda
Department of International Studies, Sanyoegakuen Junior College, Japan

Ambassador Tran Le Duc
Ambassador of Vietnam to Malaysia

Professor Henry Trofimenko
Professor of History and Diplomacy and Head, Foreign Policy Department, Institute of US and Canadian Studies, Academy of Sciences, Soviet Union

High Commissioner Manfred G von Nostitz
High Commissioner of Canada to Malaysia

Mr Wan A Hamid
Board Member, ISIS Malaysia

Mr John Wiebe
Senior Vice President, Asia Pacific Foundation of Canada, Canada

Mr Rene Wilson
Deputy Director, South Pacific Bureau for Economic Co-operation, Suva, Fiji

Ambassador Yahya Baba
Director-General, Southeast Asia/Australia/New Zealand/Pacific Division, Ministry of Foreign Affairs, Malaysia

Mr Yun Jong Gyu
Researcher, Institute of International Affairs, Democratic People's Republic of Korea

Mr Zainal Abidin Jamaluddin
Prime Minister's Department (Research), Malaysia

Tan Sri Zainal Abdidin Sulong
Distinguished ISIS Fellow, ISIS Malaysia

Mr Zhu Jingcheng
Research Fellow, Institute for the Study of the Soviet Union and East Europe, People's Republic of China

Observers

Awang Haris bin Hj Abdul Manan
Acting Assistant Director of Politics and Organisation, Ministry of Defence, Negara Brunei Darussalam

Mr Terry Baker
Deputy High Commissioner, New Zealand High Commission, Malaysia

Mr Thomas Hubbard
Deputy Chief of Mission, Embassy of the United States of America, Malaysia

Mr Glenn R Sheppy
Counsellor, Canadian High Commission, Malaysia

Dr Lee Poh Ping
Associate Professor, Faculty of Economics and Administration, University of Malaya, Malaysia

Dr Stephen Leong
Department of History, University of Malaya, Malaysia

Dr Mohamad Hear Awang
Department of History, University of Malaya, Malaysia

Dr K S Nathan
Department of History, University Malaya, Malaysia

Dr Maximus J Ongkili
Director, Political Science Department, Institute for Development Studies, Sabah, Malaysia

Dr K Pathmanathan
Faculty of Economics and Administration, University of Malaya, Malaysia

Mr M Rachmat Ardibrata
Embassy of the Republic of Indonesia, Malaysia

Mr Razak Baginda
Head of Strategic Studies and International Relations, Malaysian Armed Forces Defence College, Ministry of Defence, Malaysia

* Designations and affiliations as at July 1988

Programme

FRIDAY, JULY 1, 1988

Arrival and registration of international participants

2000 Welcoming dinner hosted by YABhg Tun Hussein Onn, Chairman of ISIS Malaysia, at The Paddock, Kuala Lumpur Hilton

SATURDAY, JULY 2, 1988

(All sessions will be held in the Conference Room at ISIS Malaysia)

0800 - 0835 Registration of participants

0845 - 0915 Keynote address by YB Dato' Abu Hassan Omar, Minister for Foreign Affairs, Malaysia (This address is to be delivered by YB Dato' Dr A Fadzil Che Wan, Deputy Minister for Foreign Affairs, Malaysia)

0930 - 1220 ***SESSION I***
CONFIDENCE BUILDING AND CONFLICT REDUCTION IN SOUTHEAST ASIA

Chairman
Mr Luis R Baltazar
Deputy National Security Director, National Security Council, The Philippines

Paper presenter
Mr Jusuf Wanandi
Executive Director, Center for Strategic and International Studies, Jakarta, Indonesia

Discussants
Mr Hiam Phommachianh, Vice President, Lao Committee for Peace, Solidarity and Friendship/ Mr Ly Southavilay, Ministry of Foreign Affairs, Laos

Dr K S Sandhu
Director, Institute of Southeast Asian Studies, Singapore

1020 - 1035 Coffee break

1220 - 1230 Group photograph

1230 - 1330 Lunch

1330 - 1630 ***SESSION II***
COLLOQUIUM ON KAMPUCHEA

Chairman
Dr Kazuo Takahashi
Programme Director, Sasakawa Peace Foundation, Tokyo, Japan

Paper presenter
Dr Noordin Sopiee
Director-General, ISIS Malaysia

1500 - 1515 Coffee break

2000 Dinner hosted by Dr Noordin Sopiee, Director-General of ISIS Malaysia at the Kuala Lumpur Hilton

SUNDAY, JULY 3, 1988

0845 - 1115 ***SESSION III***
RELEVANCE OF THE EUROPEAN EXPERIENCES FOR THE PACIFIC REGION

Chairman
Dr G I Chufrin
Head of Department, Institute of Oriental Studies, Academy of Sciences, Moscow, Soviet Union

Paper presenter
Mr Trevor Findlay
Senior Research Fellow, Peace Research Centre, Australian National University, Canberra, Australia

Discussants
Mr David Peel
Director-General, International Security and Arms Control, Department of External Affairs, Ottawa, Canada

Prof Seki Tomoda
Professor of International Studies, Sanyoegakuen Junior College, Kyoto, Japan

1115 - 1130 Coffee break

1130 - 1530 ***SESSION IV***
CONFIDENCE BUILDING AND CONFLICT REDUCTION IN NORTHEAST ASIA

Chairman
Ambassador Phan Wannamethee
Director, International Studies Center, Institute of Foreign Affairs, Ministry of Foreign Affairs, Thailand

Paper presenters
Dr James J Przystup
Deputy Director, Policy Planning Staff, Department of State, Washington D C, United States

Dr A V Sergiev
Senior Advisor, Policy Planning Department, Ministry of Foreign Affairs, Soviet Union

Discussants
Mr Ho Sok Chol
Senior Researcher, Institute of International Affairs, Pyongyang, Democratic People's Republic of Korea

Prof Rhee Sang-Woo
Department of Political Science, Sogang University, Seoul, Republic of Korea

1300 - 1400 Lunch

1400 - 1530 Continuation of discussion for Session IV

1530 - 1545 Coffee break

1545 - 1815 ***SESSION V***
THE PROSPECTS FOR BIG POWER RAPPROCHEMENT IN THE PACIFIC

Chairman
Prof Robert A Scalapino
Director, Institute of East Asian Studies, University of California, Berkeley, United States

Paper presenter
Dr James A Boutilier
Head, Department of History, Royal Roads Military College, Victoria, Canada

Discussants
Prof Ji Guoxing
Director, Department of Asian Studies, Shanghai Institute of International Studies, People's Republic of China

Mr Nguyen Can
Director, Department of Asia III, Ministry of Foreign Affairs, Socialist Republic of Vietnam

MONDAY, JULY 4, 1988

0800 - 1015 ***SESSION VI***
THE DYNAMICS OF THE ARMS BUILD-UP AND THE PROSPECTS FOR ARMS CONTROL IN THE PACIFIC

Chairman
Mr Ji Guoxing
Director, Department of Asian Studies, Shanghai Institute of International Studies, People's Republic of China

Paper presenter
Mr Andrew Mack
Head, Peace Research Centre, Australian National University, Canberra, Australia

Discussants
Dr James J Przystup
Deputy Director, Policy Planning Staff, Department of State, Washington D C, United States

Dr G A Trofimenko
Head of Department, Insitute of USA and Canada, Academy of Sciences, Moscow, Soviet Union

1015 - 1030 Coffee break

1030 - 1245 ***SESSION VII***
CONFIDENCE BUILDING AND CONFLICT REDUCTION IN THE SOUTH PACIFIC

Chairman
Prof (Dr) Mochtar Kusumaatmadja
Former Minister of Foreign Affairs, Indonesia

Paper presenter
Dr Ramesh Thakur
Senior Lecturer, Otago University, New Zealand

Discussants
Mr Anthony Kevin
Assistant Secretary, Policy Planning Branch, Department of Foreign Affairs, Canberra, Australia

Mr Philippe Baude
Ambassador, First Delegate to South Pacific Commission, France

1245 - 1330 ***WRAP-UP SESSION***

Chairman
Dr Noordin Sopiee
Director-General, ISIS Malaysia

1330 - 1430 Lunch